Lesbian Epiphanies
Women Coming Out in Later Life

HAWORTH Gay & Lesbian Studies
John P. De Cecco, PhD
Editor in Chief

The Bear Book: Readings in the History and Evolution of a Gay Male Subculture edited by Les Wright

Youths Living with HIV: Self-Evident Truths by G. Cajetan Luna

Growth and Intimacy for Gay Men: A Workbook by Christopher J. Alexander

Our Families, Our Values: Snapshots of Queer Kinship edited by Robert E. Goss and Amy Adams Squire Strongheart

Gay/Lesbian/Bisexual/Transgender Public Policy Issues: A Citizen's and Administrator's Guide to the New Cultural Struggle edited by Wallace Swan

Rough News, Daring Views: 1950s' Pioneer Gay Press Journalism by Jim Kepner

Family Secrets: Gay Sons—A Mother's Story by Jean M. Baker

Twenty Million New Customers: Understanding Gay Men's Consumer Behavior by Steven M. Kates

The Empress Is a Man: Stories from the Life of José Sarria by Michael R. Gorman

Acts of Disclosure: The Coming-Out Process of Contemporary Gay Men by Marc E. Vargo

Queer Kids: The Challenges and Promise for Lesbian, Gay, and Bisexual Youth by Robert E. Owens

Looking Queer: Body Image and Identity in Lesbian, Gay, Bisexual, and Transgender Communities edited by Dawn Atkins

Love and Anger: Essays on AIDS, Activism, and Politics by Peter F. Cohen

Dry Bones Breathe: Gay Men Creating Post-AIDS Identities and Cultures by Eric Rofes

Lila's House: Male Prostitution in Latin America by Jacobo Schifter

A Consumer's Guide to Male Hustlers by Joseph Itiel

Trailblazers: Profiles of America's Gay and Lesbian Elected Officials by Kenneth E. Yeager

Rarely Pure and Never Simple: Selected Essays by Scott O'Hara

Navigating Differences: Friendships Between Gay and Straight Men by Jammie Price

In the Pink: The Making of Successful Gay- and Lesbian-Owned Businesses by Sue Levin

Behold the Man: The Hype and Selling of Male Beauty in Media and Culture by Edisol Wayne Dotson

Untold Millions: Secret Truths About Marketing to Gay and Lesbian Consumers by Grant Lukenbill

It's a Queer World: Deviant Adventures in Pop Culture by Mark Simpson

In Your Face: Stories from the Lives of Queer Youth by Mary L. Gray

Military Trade by Steven Zeeland

Longtime Companions: Autobiographies of Gay Male Fidelity by Alfred Lees and Ronald Nelson

From Toads to Queens: Transvestism in a Latin American Setting by Jacobo Schifter

The Construction of Attitudes Toward Lesbians and Gay Men edited by Lynn Pardie and Tracy Luchetta

Lesbian Epiphanies: Women Coming Out in Later Life by Karol L. Jensen

Smearing the Queer: Medical Bias in the Health Care of Gay Men by Michael Scarce

Macho Love: Sex Behind Bars in Central America by Jacobo Schifter

When It's Time to Leave Your Lover: A Guide for Gay Men by Neil Kaminsky

Strategic Sex: Why They Won't Keep It in the Bedroom by D. Travers Scott

One of the Boys: Masculinity, Homophobia, and Modern Manhood by David Plummer

Homosexual Rites of Passage: A Road to Visibility and Validation by Marie Mohler

Lesbian Epiphanies
Women Coming Out in Later Life

Karol L. Jensen, MPH, PhD

Routledge
Taylor & Francis Group
New York London

Routledge is an imprint of the
Taylor & Francis Group, an informa business

Routledge
Taylor & Francis Group
270 Madison Avenue
New York, NY 10016

Published in Great Britain by
Routledge
Taylor & Francis Group
2 Park Square
Milton Park, Abingdon
Oxon OX14 4RN

© 1999 by Taylor & Francis Group, LLC
Routledge is an imprint of Taylor & Francis Group

Printed in the United States of America on acid-free paper
International Standard Book Number-13: 978-1-56023-964-2 (Softcover)
Cover Design by Jennifer M. Gaska

Library of Congress Cataloging-in-Publication Data

Jensen, Karol L..
    Lesbian epiphanies : women coming out in later life / Karol L. Jensen.
p. cm.
Includes bibliographical references and index.
ISBN 1-56023-963-8 Pbk. ISBN 1-56023-964-6 Hbk. (alk. paper)
1. Middle aged lesbians—Middle West. 2. Coming out (Sexual orientation). I. Title.
HQ75.6.U52M555 1999
305.244—dc21   99-13599

Visit the Taylor & Francis Web site at
http://www.taylorandfrancis.com

and the Routledge Web site at
http://www.routledge.com

CONTENTS

ABOUT THE AUTHOR

Karol Jensen, MPH, PhD, is a psychotherapist in private practice in Minneapolis, Minnesota, where she has practiced for the last fourteen years. Formerly married, with two children, she lived the transition from mother and wife to lesbian and partner that she studies and writes about in this book. Interested in many aspects of gender and sexuality, she plans further research with black and Hispanic women who have experienced this transition. Dr. Jensen has spoken in her community about formerly married lesbians and conducts therapy/support groups for this population. Dr. Jensen is a member of the Harry Benjamin International Gender Dysphoria Association and the Society for the Scientific Study of Sexuality. She earned her PhD in psychology from the Union Institute Graduate School in Cincinnati, Ohio, and she now resides in Minneapolis with her partner, Karen.

Foreword

The second millennium is ending and the third is beginning. The Stonewall Riots happened thirty years ago. The lesbian and gay civil rights movement, originally the bulwark of the sexual liberation movement in the struggle against a heterosexist establishment, is now seen by some as a new oppressor in a monosexist society. Bisexuality, once a threat to lesbian and gay politics, is now considered more radical than vanilla lesbianism and gayness. Queerness is the new frontier, and sex between lesbians and gay men (considered heterosex when I came of age during the heyday of lesbian feminism) is queerer than sex between two women or two men. Funding for HIV research is available, the first children of the lesbian baby boom are finishing elementary school in the suburbs, gay male characters are the new post-Ellen fad in network TV sitcoms, progress has been made—and unmade—toward same-sex marital rights, and support groups for queer teenagers exist—and are challenged—in high schools.

Surely, today every young person knows that lesbians and gay men—if not bisexuals and transgenderists—exist. Surely, every young person who feels attracted to members of his or her own sex or gender has a name for their feelings and positive role models for a healthy lesbian, gay, or bisexual identity. Certainly, the days when we denied our feelings and married heterosexually to cure ourselves or because we knew no other options are over. Certainly, research done by social scientists in the 1980s on "married gays" captured a historically specific event, experienced by the generation that married before or shortly after Stonewall and then came out in the 1980s during lesbian and gay liberation. Those closets must be empty by now. Coming out in midlife is an outdated topic; those 1980s publications included several books and articles written on gay men who came out in midlife in the context of a heterosexual marriage, and surely someone—although the author's name slips my mind at the moment—must have written a book on lesbians who came out in midlife.

Not quite. The closets are not empty, and not everyone who emerges from them has already been studied. As is the case with many topics, research on married people with same-sex attractions focused heavily on men. Very little research has been done on married women with same-sex attractions. Karol L. Jensen's book is long overdue, and it is of considerable contemporary relevance. Jensen interviewed twenty-five women who married men and later came out as lesbian or bisexual. Her in-depth interviews of these women form the basis of a thorough exploration of the process by which these women grew up in a heterosexist and misogynist culture, were married, became aware of or acknowledged their attractions toward other women, changed their conceptions of themselves, and made changes in their lives in response to their changed self-understandings.

In some ways, *Lesbian Epiphanies* incorporates current theoretical insights pertaining to sexual orientation—or, as Jensen prefers to call it, gender orientation—and in other ways it purposefully ignores contemporary thinking. For example, Jensen analyzes the social constructive processes by which heterosexuality, including heterosexual marriage, is prescribed for women. In great detail, she explores the ways in which females are socialized into ignoring their own experiences of self, particularly their own sexual desires, in favor of socially encouraged concepts of womanhood. However, she purposefully does not embark on a constructionist analysis of the experiences that eventually lead these women to reconstruct themselves as lesbians and bisexual women. For example, she does not call into question the experience of an essential self that is attracted to other women, and she does not allow herself to become entangled in a debate over whether her subjects' midlife transitions reflect a realization that they were always lesbian or bisexual versus a transition to being lesbian or bisexual. Instead, she seeks to convey the lived experiences of these women, complete with essentialist and non-essentialist self-understandings. Through a critical application of concepts drawn from the work of Erik Erikson, James Marcia, Ruthellen Josselson, Paula C. Rust, Lawrence Green, and others, Jensen organizes her subjects' experiences, but never allows theory to compromise her primary goal of providing the reader with a phenomenological understanding of the experiences of women who come out as lesbian or bisexual later in life.

Also in recognition of contemporary sexological thinking, Jensen treats bisexual identity as valid on a par with lesbian identity by noting that the women she interviewed self-identify as either lesbian or bisexual. She does not subsume bisexual identity within lesbian identity nor does she apply her own labels that might be contrary to her subjects' identities, for example, by referring to her subjects collectively as "lesbians"; however, neither does she focus attention on the distinction between bisexual and lesbian identities. Her focus is not on the specific identities her subjects adopt but rather on the process by which they adopt these identities. In this way, Jensen transcends contemporary identity politics, including the focus of most "coming out" research on the attainment of a specific sexual identity as a goal. Jensen herself writes, "The idea of identity as a goal rather than a process does not fit with the apparently fluid and dynamic nature of women's sexuality as found in this research."

Throughout her analysis, Jensen situates her subjects' experiences within their social contexts. Progressing through the women's experiences in chronological order, she analyzes the effects of cultural denial of both women's sexuality and same-gender sexual attractions, the expectation of marriage and concepts of adulthood based on heterosexuality, cultural images of lesbianism, the (un)availability of lesbian or bisexual role models, the attitudes of friends and family, and the accessibility of a lesbian community as they affect a woman's ability to recognize, acknowledge, validate, and act on her attractions to other women. The text circles among the women, visiting each woman several times in each phase of her life, creating a tapestry of lives connected to each other by the similar experience of living in a culture that denied them knowledge of their own sexualities. Because the experiences of several individual women are examined in depth at each step of her analysis, with lengthy quotes from her interviews with the women, Jensen's analysis itself progresses slowly and carefully. However, Jensen's ability to bring the reader into the minds of her subjects, from where the reader can look out through the subjects' eyes to see what they see—including their confusion and half-perceived experiences—is more than adequate to the task of keeping the reader's attention as Jensen paves the paths her subjects took toward their current self-conceptions. Jensen's quotable analogies—for example, her likening of the cultural expectation that women will marry to "the default program on a computer"—also help convey her subjects' experiences and produce a very readable text.

In *Researching Sexual Behavior,* a Kinsey Institute book summarizing the current state of sexological research, Diane DiMauro pointed out that much research on sexology has been motivated by social controversies and geared toward social problems such as HIV infection. The result is a glut of ungeneralizable knowledge about specific populations and a dearth of knowledge about the development and expression of healthy adult sexuality. DiMauro wrote, "What is conspicuously missing in the research agenda is a developmental focus on sexuality that acknowledges the primacy of society and culture. . . . [needed research] would incorporate a view of human sexuality throughout the life cycle, starting with infancy and early childhood and extending beyond the reproductive years. This needed approach would seek to understand exactly how societal and cultural forces 'structure' sexuality by examining how sexual socialization occurs in families, schools, the media, and peer groups, determining the impact and significance of this process for the individual within his or her social network" (1997:4-5). *Lesbian Epiphanies* helps fill this gap. By researching an understudied population of mature women and conducting a qualitative study of the influence of social and cultural factors on their lifetime experiences and sexual self-conceptions for the pure purpose of understanding, Dr. Jensen has made an important contribution to contemporary sexological research.

Paula C. Rust, PhD

Di Mauro, Diane. 1997. Sexuality research in the United States. In John Bancroft (Ed.), *Researching Sexual Behavior: Methodological Issues.* Indiana University Press: Bloomington, 3-8.

Introduction

Identity is the stable, consistent, and reliable sense of who one is and what one stands for as a functioning, contributing member of society. Identity really consists of two, perhaps three, parts: the attributes, identifications, and desires of a personal self; gender identity (what sex do I feel like I am?); and gender orientation (to what sex am I sexually attracted?). According to Falco, what is referred to as sexual identity consists of the internal development of structures that define the self, along with the external development of behaviors and attitudes that are more or less congruent with the internal identity (Falco, 1991). Formerly, identity was believed to be the goal reached by mature adults that, once attained, remained stationary. Theorists now believe that all aspects of identity formation constitute an ongoing process, not an end result. A healthy personality changes, grows, and deepens as it struggles to integrate old and new identifications, attributes, and desires into a coherent self. The ongoing resolution of this struggle for integration is a sense of identity—a sense of continuity and consistency of self over time. The purpose of this study is to examine the evolution of this identity formation for women who reach clarity about their lesbian or bisexual identity after having assumed a heterosexual identity, being married to men, and then realizing that the identity of a married, heterosexual woman did not fit them.

I am a woman who became aware of my lesbian identity after heterosexual marriages. As I grew through adolescence and into adulthood, I had the first indications that I felt different from other girls. When my girlfriends talked about boys, I felt bored. I wanted to date to be like the others, and I wanted to be friends with boys, but I felt little attraction to or sexual interest in them. I know now that I wondered then why I wasn't interested, but at the time, the question was not at a conscious level. Of course, adolescence brings many questions without answers. These unconscious wonderings,

"Why don't I feel sexually interested in boys?" and, further, "What would it feel like to be sexually interested?" were only added to the list.

However, these unanswered questions made feeling comfortable with myself very difficult. The ongoing adult resolution and integration of all aspects of identity requires complete information; all the puzzle pieces must be available, even if they don't immediately fit together. For me, this ongoing identity resolution continued without complete information because I didn't have all the pieces for my particular life puzzle. An other-than-heterosexual identity never occurred to me. I had a sense of confusion about my identity or role—a lack of certainty about who I was, or about the part I was to play in the scheme of life, but I didn't connect it to my sexual self at all. Until I became consciously aware of my same-gender attractions (at the age of forty), I experienced a subtle cognitive dissonance between my feelings and the expectations of others. I felt no consistency of self over time, and so I looked for the answers outside myself. I tried marriages. I tried careers. For awhile, I drank too much. The internal unrest was at times overwhelming, at other times, niggling, but it was always present.

A woman's general identity and her sense of the gender to which she is sexually attracted are intersecting factors. One is not easily formed without the other being clarified. However, they are also separate and can develop somewhat independently of each other. Therefore, a woman can develop a certain level of confidence that she is a woman, worker, citizen, daughter, mother, and friend without a clear sense of the gender to which she is sexually attracted. I know this can be true because it was my experience. My life through those confusing years was satisfying in some ways. I had marriages and relationships with good men. I had two great kids. I had loving and powerful friendships with women that took a large share of my energy. However, when I turned forty years old, I reached the critical, cumulative level of experiences that told me I was lesbian and that I wanted my primary life partner to be a woman. At that point, I had been in heterosexual marriages for a combined twenty-plus years. This new information about myself constituted a personal paradigm shift, but, paradoxically, it also brought great relief. The puzzle pieces fell into place, and I experienced a sense of coherency and completeness for the first time.

Why did it take me so long to know this? Why didn't I know this from the start? What kept me from being aware of my gender orientation before I made promises and plans I couldn't keep, before husbands were hurt, before children were hurt, before the entanglements became so complicated? Since my self-discovery, I have pondered these questions looking for answers.

Coincident with my new self-awareness, I completed a master's degree in psychology and began working toward my PhD. I also started a private practice in psychotherapy. Many women in my therapy practice presented with these same questions about their sexuality, about their relationships. I found little in the literature to clarify the process. I decided then that I wanted to research this issue and this population. I wanted answers to the question "What is the psychological, erotic, social process of women who come out as lesbian or bisexual after a heterosexual marriage?"

As I reviewed the psychological literature for information on identity development, I found a small, but lively and burgeoning, collection on female development. This body of literature is relatively small because until the last ten years, female development was ignored, treated as an afterthought, or forced into parallel lines of reasoning with male development. Women's experience did not conform along these parallel lines and was therefore considered abnormal, or not considered at all. I did find studies that address awareness and development of sexual identity—gender identity and orientation—in females. There is ample literature that discusses marriage to a man as the life path for a woman. However, I found little that discussed the intersection of female identity and female gender orientation, and almost nothing that considered the impact of discovering this intersection as a married adult woman. It was clear that a theoretical perspective to explain this process was/is needed.

A literature search revealed two articles that address this issue directly. The two articles are by the same author and do not make essentially different points: the 1990 article expands on the content of the 1985 article. One major point of the two articles (Coleman, 1990, 1985) is that the family structure that includes a lesbian woman is rarely described in the literature. The author notes that this is in sharp contrast to the extensive research on homosexual men who have been married. He points out further that what is known about lesbian women in marriage comes from the large-scale studies of homosexuality conducted by Saghir and Robins (1973), Bell and Weinberg (1978), and Masters and Johnson (1979). The other sources of information about lesbians and marriage are the studies on lesbian motherhood (e.g., Kirkpatrick, Smith and Roy, 1976; Green, 1978; Rand, Graham, and Rawlings, 1982); also see, more recently, Patterson, 1995). Coleman (1990) points out that a consistent pattern in the large-scale studies is that homosexual women are equally as likely or more likely to have been married than their male counterparts. However, lesbian women in marriage have not been formally studied.

Coleman (1985) initiated a research study on lesbian and bisexual women who were or had been married. He found that these women described their decisions to get married as desired and deliberate decisions, not coerced or forced. However, it was pointed out that women have traditionally married by the average age of twenty-one, which may be too early to be clear about psychosexual identity development. Coleman hypothesized further that early marriage may be a designator of adulthood. He presumed that females have difficulty separating from their parents and parents' values. He suggests in his article that the process of identity formation may be interfered with in lesbian women who avoid confrontation of their own feelings and behavior because their socialized desire for relatedness is threatened. (It should be noted that a number of authors and researchers are now saying that the desire for relatedness in women is not only socialized but probably innate as well [Jordan, 1991; Brown and Gilligan, 1992].)

Coleman (1990) was able to put together a picture of these marriages from studies of lesbian mothers and the women in his study. He found that these marriages were not more conflicted than heterosexual marriages that ended and that lesbians blamed loss of intimacy rather than conflict for the failure of the marriage. He states that few lesbian women reported antipathy toward men. By contrast, the research showed that heterosexual women were more bitter than the homosexual women about the failure of their marriages and that they reported more abuse by, and more anger at, men. Further study revealed that there is no information at all about husbands of lesbian women, whereas there are studies of wives of bisexual men. Coleman compares this lack to the paucity of knowledge about the male spouse of the female alcoholic, compared to the abundant data available about the female spouse of the male alcoholic. He reports that there is no evidence that the lesbian mother's sexual orientation has damaging consequences to her child's development and that the main trauma for children of homosexual parents is that their parents' marriage ended. Finally, the article points out that a decision by the lesbian/bisexual married woman to adopt her new identity is prompted less often by general same-sex attraction and more often by an emotional relationship with another woman.

Although a growing literature concerns itself with lesbian psychological issues and study, no further formal research directly addresses the issue of lesbians out of marriage. However, I did find an informal study, one journal article, and one book that have been published since 1991. Each addresses the issue of formerly married lesbian/bisexual women directly.

In 1991, Charbonneau and Lander contributed to an anthology on lesbians at midlife with an essay titled "Redefining Sexuality: Women Becoming Lesbian in Midlife." From surveys collected from thirty women who identified as lesbian, their essay covers many of the issues in my research, but the authors do not directly address causes for the delay in awareness of the attraction for women. They state specifically that their informants were "not those who considered themselves lesbian or bisexual and married to hide their sexual preference (sic)" (p. 36). Their population consists of women who became aware of their same-gender attraction after a marriage. Therefore, their research population is similar to mine. However, I question the discussion of women having a sexual "preference" or "becoming" lesbians at midlife. I believe this presentation is misleading in that it suggests gender orientation is based completely on choice. It is my position that women either have the predilection or capacity for sexual attraction to their same gender or they do not have it. They may choose to act on it or not, but they do not "become" lesbian, as if all women may be equally likely to choose this path. The women in this study found that their attraction to women had deep roots that had been present but not acted upon until the feelings rose to full awareness. (In Chapter 3 on identity formation, I do discuss "political" lesbians, that is, women who decide to pursue same-gender relationships for reasons other than attraction.)

Bridges and Croteau (1994) outline counseling issues related to working with lesbians who have been married. Their article briefly summarizes identity development and touches on those issues of which a counselor needs to be aware (e.g., grief and loss of home and dream, internalized homophobia, loss of heterosexual privilege, etc.) to work with this population. Although the article does not cover the subject in great depth, it is valuable because it highlights the population as underserved and points out some of its unique issues.

Deborah Abbott and Ellen Farmer compiled a series of writings in a book (1995) that address life changes of women who come out as lesbian or bisexual after marriage. Through essays, photos, book chapters, interviews, and poetry, the experiences of forty women are highlighted. These writings are of broad interest and do address causes for the delayed awareness as they arise in the narratives. However, because the writings are very personal and casual, they do not enumerate barriers to awareness of lesbian feelings, nor do they attempt to outline the process of becoming aware of these feelings, except incidentally.

In 1980, Adrienne Rich wrote an essay titled "Compulsory Heterosexuality and Lesbian Existence." This powerful, groundbreaking essay delineates male power and the denial of woman identification and women's relationships with each other as an incalculable loss to the power resources of all women. I include this essay as a part of the literature search for my topic because it systematically lays out many of the issues that prevent women from knowing about their orientation toward women. Because heterosexuality has reigned as the only normative primary relationship throughout the twentieth century, many adolescents and women have been led to believe they were heterosexual when indeed they may not have been. A heterosexual identity assumed by late adolescence—despite cues that it may not fit—is difficult to change once it is "set" (Ross, 1997), and so the women in this study failed to learn about the range of relationships that would have allowed them to know what was possible.

My research took the form of in-depth interviews with twenty-four women who came out to themselves after a heterosexual marriage. Through an analysis of these interviews, I have identified five domains or themes under which the process of becoming aware of a woman's same-gender attraction is either hindered or encouraged. In the first chapter, I discuss the inadequacy of sex education and information in the United States and how that inadequacy limits women's general awareness of themselves, their bodies, and their life options. In Chapter 2, I outline the role of marriage in American culture and how it presents itself to women as a nonchoice that tends to limit their awareness of themselves. Chapter 3 considers the challenges women experience in establishing personal identity and an other-than-heterosexual orientation in a heterosexist society. Chapter 4 presents evidence for the ways in which women's awareness, women's "knowing," is generally limited and controlled in this culture. In Chapter 5, the scarcity of lesbian role models is presented, along with the paradox of lesbians as, on the one hand, invisible and, on the other hand, revolting and repulsive. Finally, Chapter 6 presents a variety of new issues that arise for women as they begin to cultivate awareness of their same-gender attractions. The critical accumulation of pieces of awareness is outlined, and moments of life-changing internal shift are described.

Very often, authors and researchers (including many whom I quote extensively in this work, e.g., Rust [1992, 1993] and Weston [1992]) use the phrase sexual identity to encompass the orientation people feel sexually toward their own (homosexual) or the opposite (heterosexual) gender. I tend not to use this phrase in that way. When I use this phrase, I am almost always quoting another author or referring to her or his work; my preference is "gender identity," that is, the gender I feel that I am. Since "the gender I feel that I am" is not a central issue in this study, I do not use the phrase sexual identity often. When I am referring to the concept of sexual attraction between people, I use "gender orientation" or "the gender to which I am sexually attracted."

Although I have chosen to use the phrase gender orientation rather than sexual orientation, current writers and researchers use both. Issues of gender versus sex are being hotly debated in the current literature, but it is not my intention to make a statement by advocating strongly for one side or the other. It just seems clearer to me that gender orientation, or the gender to which I am sexually attracted, is most germane here. The issue is not gender identity, that is, what gender am I, or what gender do I feel that I am? The issue is to what gender am I attracted. Murray Davis expresses it well, as quoted in Bornstein (1994):

> [We] do not need a sophisticated methodology or technology to confirm that the gender component of identity is the most important one articulated during sex. Nearly everyone (except for bisexuals, perhaps) regards it as the prime criterion for choosing a sex partner. (p. 32)

Another phrase that may require clarification is *coming out*. This phrase originally described gays and lesbians telling the people in their lives about their same-gender orientation by "coming out of the closet" where they had been hiding the secret. More recently, the phrase has been used in the popular media to describe gays and lesbians, but also now may refer to other persons revealing important secrets, such as "he came out as a cross-dresser," or "she came out as a former two-pack-a-day smoker."

This study clarifies the process of women who come out as lesbian or bisexual through and after marriage by delineating five barriers to women's awareness of their orientation and relationship choices. The sociological and psychological barriers to their knowing about their orientation and their ability to act on it are addressed. This study adds to a scant psychological literature and begins to create a common path, expanding psychology's effectiveness in helping women to find, forge, or reveal their identity as lesbian or bisexual women.

METHOD

To research the process of women who marry and later come out as lesbian or bisexual, I conducted interviews with twenty-five women who now identify as lesbian or bisexual and who had been married to men. One interview tape proved to be inaudible and couldn't be transcribed, so the number of interviews analyzed was twenty-four. By design, all of these women were Caucasian because it was decided that the model for this process should be developed first with one racial or ethnic group. The hope is that the process will be replicated subsequently with women from African-American, Latin American, and Asian-American groups to clarify the differences among ethnic groups. Twenty-two of the women were born and raised in the midwestern United States; the other two had lived in midwestern states for many years.

The interviews providing the basis for analysis were conducted primarily in the Twin Cities of Minneapolis and St. Paul, Minnesota, with four occurring in Eau Claire, Wisconsin, in the summer of 1996. Although I follow tradition by using numbers and changing names throughout the study, it seems important to note that none of the participants asked me to be particularly careful of their anonymity. On the contrary, participants for the study were easy to find and eager to participate. I had names and numbers for at least ten more interviews with appropriate participants and information about many more that I didn't use.

Respondents for the interviews were gathered from two sources: fifteen women came to the study as a result of personal contacts, friendship pyramiding, and snowball sampling, all of which resulted from having lived in Minneapolis for many years. Ten more responded to an advertisement in a local women's newspaper. The sample is not random in the usual sense. However, random sampling is clearly an impossibility for a population that is not only partially hidden or "closeted" but one that also lacks consensus as to the criteria for membership (Morin, 1977). Kath Weston, author of *Families We Choose* (1992), says that advertisements tend to weight a sample for "joiners," that is, the highly educated with an overtly political agenda (p. 10). I did not find this to be true, as among those who responded to the newspaper advertisement were several with the least educational experience. Among the women interviewed, eighteen of them were college graduates, including seven with graduate degrees. Seven did not have college degrees. It is unclear how the high education levels of this group affect its generalizability. One limitation of the study may be that only women who are pleased and satisfied with their gender orientation are represented. Women who are experiencing regret and conflict regarding this identity tended not to respond. In any case, it is important to emphasize that this study represents the experience of white, midwestern lesbian or bisexual women.

Five interviews were conducted in the women's homes, four in a small-town Wisconsin motel room rented for the purpose, and the remaining sixteen were conducted in my psychotherapy office.

The twenty-four women ranged in age from twenty-eight to fifty-eight. Eleven women were in their fifties, six in their forties, six in their thirties, and two in their twenties. They had been married an average of thirteen years, with a range from one to twenty-five years. One woman is presently married. Five had no children, two had lost a child through death, two had four children, one had three, thirteen had two, and three had one child. One woman was pregnant with her second child at the time of the interview and in a committed relationship with a man.

The women I interviewed knew that I was self-identified as lesbian and that I had come out after heterosexual marriage. They knew I had two adult children. It seemed important to them to know that we shared a common experience. They were all very interested in the results of the study and asked specifically if they could receive a copy of it when I was finished. The interviews flowed smoothly for the most part—like conversations—although I was careful to use the same general structure and open-ended questions for each interview.

The interviews were structured around three open-ended questions:

1. Can you give me an overview of your life that covers significant events, transition points, and critical issues—as you look back?
2. Will you describe for me your development as a sexual person?
3. Was there a moment when you knew something in your life had to change? Tell me about that moment.

If the interviews did not spontaneously produce information about their knowledge of lesbians before they came out, and about the social support they felt as they went through this process, I asked about these two issues.

The interviews lasted from one and a half to two hours and were transcribed verbatim. Data were analyzed using the grounded theory approach of Glaser and Straus (1967). That is, emergent issues were grouped into categories or themes concerning the process in question, with new themes added until no novel responses were encountered (Glaser and Straus, 1967).

The purpose of a qualitative analysis of this kind is to elucidate the essence of experience of a phenomenon for an individual or group (Patton, 1990). According to Patton, the qualitative analyst's effort at uncovering patterns, themes, and categories is a creative process that requires making carefully considered judgments about what is really significant and meaningful in the data. Through these interviews, my intention has been to clarify the process through which women construct a heterosexual identity, live through a series of life events and transitions that develop into a critical level of information and awareness, a critical cascade, that leads to a *deconstruction* of their identities as heterosexual (predisposing factors, marriage as social fantasy, invalidation of that first relationship, pressures to leave, pressures to stay, responses of family and community, etc.), and come to reconstruct new identities as lesbian or bisexual women (enabling factors, role models, defining moments, finding a community, social support, etc.).

The analysis of these interviews revealed a process of experience falling roughly into six domains or themes: sexual information, marriage, establishing identity, allowing oneself personal awareness, role models, and taking steps to change. Each of these themes offers ideas and insights regarding the broad question of this study: Why did it take her so long to know who she really is?

The themes are covered individually in each chapter of this book. In developing each of these themes, I have followed a phenomenological perspective, that is, a perspective that considers each woman's definition of herself as of essential importance. The result is a heuristic model describing a combined process of self-discovery and learning to know—a sense of personal authority. Why do I call this study a heuristic inquiry process? I will answer that question with a quote from Michael Patton: "heuristic research epitomizes the phenomenological emphasis on meanings and knowing through personal experience; it exemplifies and places at the fore the way in which the researcher is the primary instrument in qualitative inquiry; and it challenges in the extreme traditional scientific concerns about researcher objectivity and detachment" (Patton, 1990, p. 27). Since the process of a lesbian coming out of marriage is my process, total detachment has been unlikely or impossible. However, I made an effort to distill and describe the varied experiences I heard with as much objectivity as possible.

A woman will process experience and information through cognitive (i.e., thinking), affective (i.e., emotional), and behavioral domains as she goes through this identity reconstruction process. These cognitive, affective, and behavioral awarenesses or paths all play a role in the stages of a woman's accumulating, growing knowledge that she is lesbian or bisexual. Socialization and expectations of women in this society affect their range of choices, their process of coping, their pace of self-discovery, and their resulting identity development. In addition to each of these factors, the identity reconstruction process is affected by generalized homophobia, as well as by the narrow lens of what is sexually acceptable or normative in the United States in the late twentieth century.

Chapter 1

Sex Education and Information: In the United States, She Must Find Her Way in the Dark

Women who marry and later realize they have major attractions to women as primary partners have been out of touch with major aspects of themselves. This was the first outstanding theme that emerged from the interview data. Most of the women talked of having little or no formal sex education and no space at all where it was safe to learn indirectly by exploring their sexuality. They described a subtle family and societal denigration of themselves and their own judgment as sources of knowing, in general and specifically, about sex. There was a guilt/sin/danger attitude about sex coupled with the implication that sexual experience and feelings were for men, not for them. Therefore, sex remained, for many of these women, a mystery that they wondered about and about which most felt ashamed.

Basic to the knowledge of a girl's emerging selfhood is an understanding of the anatomy of her body and its functions, as well as a "manual" for the owner to acquaint her with the range of experiences she might observe as her body grows, changes, reacts, and responds. However, in the United States, rather than being encouraged to learn all she can about herself, the young girl is discouraged from learning about her sexual self. For example, research reveals that parents do an inadequate job of teaching their children about sexuality (Reinisch, 1990). Without a working knowledge of the systems underpinning her sexuality, the girl/young woman remains ignorant of the range of outcomes she might experience in her sexual life.

Self-knowing for girls is discouraged generally, and in the sexual area, this knowing is made immensely complicated by societal conflicts about sexual learning. Girls are discouraged from speaking their own truths so often that they tend to deny or ignore them and set them aside. Thus, the girl cannot attend even to what she is able to know about herself and her body. The result is that girls' evolution of identity often stays in the limited states of what Belenky and colleagues (1986) call "silence" or "received knowledge." In these two developmental states, a woman or girl tends not to engage in original thinking or response. Instead, she tends to say and think either very little or only what she has been told. Sexual self-awareness may evolve as she moves into adulthood, but only if opportunities exist for reflection, talking, and reading about sexuality. In the United States, serious conversation or exchange about sexuality is nearly nonexistent, even among adults. As Belenky and colleagues state regarding general self-knowledge, without interchange, "individuals remain isolated from others and without tools for representing their experiences, people also remain isolated from the self" (Belenky et al., 1986, p. 26). Without permission to move naturally into deeper stages of self-knowing, women may remain ignorant of the range and facets of their gender orientation, and sexuality in general, for all or most of their lives.

It is true that girls remain ignorant, but the absence of safe space for exploring sexuality affects both girls and boys. Michelle Fine describes sex education as typically constructed around superficial notions of male heterosexuality, that is, erection and then ejaculation. That which is ejaculated *into* receives little attention, and totally missing is what Fine calls "the discourse of desire" (Fine, 1988, p. 30). That is, sex is not taught as one part of a relationship, as a means of expressing love. Sex is taught only as a mechanical process, not an emotional or relational one (Fine, 1988).

This kind of sexuality discourse miseducates adolescent women about a process "based on the male in search of desire and the female in search of protection" (Fine, 1993, p. 87). In other words, girls are taught that their sexuality is significant only as the goal boys seek, and they are told they are potential victims of this pursuit. This gives the young woman complete responsibility for either allowing or stopping sexual activity and does nothing to address questions of whether *she* wants to be sexual or not, whether *she* wants to participate in certain activities, that is, whether *she* feels desire. This emphasis reinforces traditional notions of what it means to be a woman and does little to empower women and enhance a sense of entitlement and self-valuing. The young woman remains subordinate, dependent, self-sacrificing, compliant, and ready to marry and/or bear children early (Fine, 1988, p. 98).

The limits placed on girls' knowing in general—as well as their sexual knowing—must occur in the midst of the popular discourse that places sexuality within a Judeo-Christian perspective, attributing blame and inducing guilt about sexual behavior, naming it sinful and dangerous outside of a strict set of boundaries (Ross and Ryan, 1995). The shame/guilt/sin/danger meaning of sexuality has been socially constructed through the interaction of individual and cultural beliefs and values, one reflecting back to the other the dominant, prevalent meanings of human sexuality. Within broad cultural social constructions, the individual family is but a small unit. In seeking her identity as an individual, sexual and otherwise, the young woman is obviously limited—perhaps even bound—by the contradictions and social expectations of her culture and those of her family. Her knowing about gender orientation must evolve as she proceeds through this miasma.

The family provides the earliest instruction on what sexual and other behaviors are acceptable for young women within given contexts. In families that encourage exploration of new ideas and autonomy, girls are free to consider a range of options and take their own viewpoints seriously. Families that are secure will allow girls to take their own feelings seriously as well. Conversely, if the family provides a strict set of values that must be rigidly adhered to, new or incongruous information creates anxiety. As a survival strategy, anxiety-producing thought is excluded. "Given little tolerance for differences, autonomy is much harder to achieve" (Kahn, 1991, p. 50). The independent thought of individuals (particularly individual girls) is not tolerated because it poses a threat to the rigidly held attitudes of the family (Kahn, 1991).

A girls' sexual learning and exploration is part of her search for identity. A girl who is secure and comfortable with her body, including her genitals, will have higher self-esteem than a child who is confused or frightened and will also be less vulnerable to manipulation and victimization (Pogrebin, 1983). Greven claims that parents who are punitive toward a child's sexuality are also likely to be harsh and unaccepting in general. These attitudes could result in a fearful, insecure girl/woman, as well as one who is sexually disabled (Greven, 1991). With regard to the issue of harsh parenting, it appears that among the twenty-four respondents in this research—women who experienced harsh parenting as well as those who felt acceptance from their parents—all felt limitations placed on their ability to acquire their own sexual learning.

A sense of personal authority, allowing deeper levels of knowing, will be engendered by a family that is secure, tolerant, and respectful of difference. With a sense of personal authority (i.e., "I know myself—what I need, what I want, think, feel"), a girl will be able to listen to herself, form her own opinions, and choose whether to express them regardless of social pressures (Kahn, 1991). She will then have access to what Weille calls the dialectical "oscillation," the fundamental, endlessly creative source of personal and interpersonal experiences that drive the process of development (Weille, 1993).

Clearly, the boundaries and limitations of behavior, attitudes, and values dictated by the family and culture play a crucial role in guiding and limiting the young woman as she seeks knowledge about her own sexual journey. Further, if strict limits are set on the sharing of personal realities in this early setting, girls do not become accustomed or encouraged to consult with "the self" as a valid resource and as one guide for behavior, sexual or otherwise. In addition, if low value is placed on "what she thinks" or "what she feels," the young woman is not prepared to reveal internal conflicts or to acknowledge the confusion that accompanies growth. With regard to this issue, eighteen of the twenty-four respondents said their families did not teach them to consider their own feelings and responses as important and valid knowledge when making life decisions.

This research reflects the difficulties inherent in this learning process of self-discovery. The life experience of most respondents was similar to that of respondent #3, age fifty-eight, married twenty years: "In our family, feelings were not so much repressed as they were ignored." Within such limits, failing to account for the richness of emotional response, the unique journey of each family and family member is not valued. On the contrary, experiences varying from the acceptable template are a profound secret that must be hidden from public view.

The experience of respondent #5, age forty-one, married fifteen years, generally reflects the family attitude of about one-half of the twenty-four respondents:

> My mom has such a hard time telling anybody what is going on. The more she thought about it, the more shame she felt over it, thinking about telling her friends or her siblings, and I think it just freaked her. . . . I'm sure there is a lot of shame about my stuff. She's having a hard time accepting the changes in my life, or anything that looks like she doesn't have a perfect family. She says, "I thought I had the perfect family. I guess I don't." What she means is, "The most terrible painful stuff is OK as long as nobody knows about it." Yeah. That's the thing. Nobody can know about it.

Many respondents described a family experience that prepares members to ignore or deny personal experience, for example, respondent #23, age forty-seven, married twenty-three years:

> My parents and I have a good but distant relationship. They've been encouraging over the years to try new things and so forth, so they are in general fairly liberal people . . . but they have also been, in my family, unwilling to deal with any sort of negative stuff that's happened to me and my family and in my brother's family over the years, and so its like they are right there when things are going well, and if things are not going very well, they vanish.

It is within this crucible of denial and silence that the girl and young woman must educate herself and find her sexual identity. School sex education in the United States should aid this process, but instead it remains an issue fraught with disagreement that seriously affects the psychosocial sexual development of girls. Although polls consistently show that a majority of citizens want comprehensive sex education in the schools, the minority opposition to such education is very vocal. Most school administrators are simply afraid of provoking controversy from this vocal minority (Yarber, 1992).

Those who oppose sex education in the schools say that it should happen at home, that parents should teach it so that sex is presented within the appropriate context of the values of the family. However, when adolescents and adults are asked where they gained information about sexuality, they state they learned little from parents, citing peers as their primary source (Sorenson, 1972; Rozema, 1986; Reinisch, 1990). Peers appear to be a major source of information about sex for adolescents, but what Peacock has shown seems predictable. As an information source, peers reflect culturewide misinformation and are a source of myths, such as "You can't get pregnant the first time," or "Once a penis gets hard, you have to let him come, or it will hurt his body" (Peacock, 1982).

William Yarber, a specialist in sexuality education, suggests that as a society, we are "standing by" while our children are learning to cope with the powerful force of their sexuality, and we are doing nothing to make them safe (Yarber, 1992). The message that sexuality is not something to be talked about results in young women feeling the most isolated from information and support at a time when they need it most. Parents are clearly ambivalent about their children's developing sexual nature. They may even feel ambivalent about their daughters' growing up and moving away from them (Maddock, 1983). Perhaps because of their own ambivalence about sexuality, parents may appear to become distant at this point. That is, as they recognize the pubertal signs of development in their daughters, some become reluctant to continue showing physical affection they bestowed easily at an earlier time. The result of parental distancing may be that the young woman feels rejected and isolated, ill at ease with her emerging adulthood. She may believe that her parents are withdrawing because they are not pleased with her and her developing body. If her parents are not their usual responsive selves or appear uncomfortable, she may feel that she has done something wrong (Francoeur, 1991). This perception reinforces the double binds of female sexuality and the nearly universal shame and guilt that surround it.

Parents are often fearful that their daughters will become sexually active if they have "too much" information (Yarber, 1992). However, there is evidence to counter that fear. Fisher, Byrne, and White found that children who are taught that sex is wrong do not avoid sexual activity. However, they also found that these sex-negative attitudes do discourage responsible use of contraception. That is, teens who believe that sexual involvement is wrong tend to ignore contraception because contraceptive use would legitimize "bad" behavior (Fisher, Byrne, and White, 1983).

Brock and Jennings recently did a qualitative study of women in their thirties (mostly Caucasian, 13 percent black, 1 percent Hispanic) who lived with their birth mothers during childhood and adolescence. Most of the women remembered the sexuality education they received from their mothers as extremely limited, with the strong presence of negative, nonverbal messages and the frequent use of warnings and rules. They said there was no comfortable open communication, discussion of feelings, or discussion of choices. Many women in the study expressed the wish that their mothers had talked to them about how they were free to make choices about how they would conduct their sexual lives (Brock and Jennings, 1993).

Despite the fact that parents tend not to teach their children about sexuality, the dominant source of sex education and information for girls is their parents. Girls observe their parents' behavior. They learn how and when feelings and affection are expressed, or not, and by whom. They learn whether a broad definition of sexuality is acceptable or whether a rigid boundary surrounds it. All of this is done without words (Bandura and Walters, 1969). Roberts suggests that the silence surrounding sexuality in most families, and in most communities, carries its own important messages. It communicates that it is bad to think or talk about any dimension of sexuality, that it must be kept secret (Roberts, 1980).

Although psychotherapists should be a source of sexual information and affirmation to their clients, the respondents in this research did not find that to be true in every case. Hopefully, psychotherapists are learning more about the normal reality of gender orientation, body boundaries, and personal rights, but two of our respondents were hindered in their sexual learning by psychotherapists, for example, respondent #5, age forty-one:

I had an eating disorder for two years when I finished school. [I went into a therapy group] . . . she did intakes with every-body and asked about these issues. When I said I couldn't remember . . . I didn't think . . . I wasn't sure if there was penetration or not with my brother. And she said, "Well then it's not abuse so that isn't relevant." It never got dealt with.

[What did you think about that?]

Well, I just thought it wasn't abuse. It was curiosity. It was not affecting where I was right now. . . . They weren't delving back . . . during the group a woman talked about how her brother was gay, and the therapist said, "Well that just shows you the problems in your family system." So there was no safe place here to deal with my sexuality. Or no place for me to deal with the abuse. Basically, those two issues got put in a box. And back to my life . . .

William Yarber has written extensively on the importance of giving sex information to young people. He describes adolescent sexuality in our culture as an oxymoron:

Some believe that adolescents are sexual beings and deserve information and education to aid them in achieving a healthy sexuality. Others feel that adolescents do not have sexual needs, that sexual information leads to immoral behavior, pregnancy and sexually transmitted disease, and that the sole acceptable sexual expression is marital coitus. One result is that the culture sends conflicting messages about sexuality to our youth. . . . Media scream ". . . always say yes" . . . many adults admonish "just say no" but the majority just say . . . nothing. It's no wonder that young people have difficulty accepting their sexu-ality and developing a healthy and responsible sexual code of behavior. And it's no wonder that many teenagers express their sexuality inappropriately, resulting in psychological damage, unwanted pregnancy and STDs. (Yarber, 1992, p. 326)

Some sex educators and counselors say that giving a child no sexual information is damaging. According to Raphling, the child who is isolated from the sexual dimension of life is a child who has been sexually abused. It is now acknowledged that a child who has been exploited to perform sexual favors for a parent or another adult grows up to believe that sex is something unsavory or dangerous. However, it is also true that a child who has been forced to deny sexuality to please her or his parents grows up to avoid discussion and participation in sexuality. For all these children, sex becomes too frightening a prospect to consider, and the child and the adult she or he becomes are, therefore, handicapped (Raphling, 1991).

Sixteen of the twenty-four respondents interviewed in our study said there was no information and no discussion of sexual issues in their household while they were growing up. Seven respondents said they were hungry for information but received no preparation for their body changes or information about what to expect regarding their own sexual feelings, so they sought information on their own, feeling ashamed and guilty as they did so. Nine of the women said they felt ashamed of their interest in sex and that the "atmosphere" would change when they asked questions. Four believed that they really hadn't known or thought about sex throughout their childhoods because "parents seemed oblivious to sex" (respondent #4, age thirty-three), or "I knew good girls don't do such and such, and I made a decision to be a top-class person and so I wasn't interested in sex" (respondent #3, age fifty-eight). Consider the comments of respondent #25, age fifty-three, who said she grew up in "a totally Catholic home":

> Well, you know, people have a hard time believing this, and I've suppressed it—it's embarrassing—but I never felt sexual about anything when I was growing up. And I never masturbated and I had no interest. I was absolutely asexual.

Respondent #12, age fifty-three, describes the desire for more information and the discomfort and confusion involved in seeking it:

> At my high school reunion, a couple of months or so ago, a fellow who if you danced with him at a high school dance, you could feel his erection . . .

[How did you feel about that?]

I minded in high school; yeah, I didn't like that particular fact. At first I wasn't even sure what this [the boy's erection] was. I was not knowledgeable, let me tell you. . . . Sex was not discussed at our house. Not a word. My brother [became a physician and] delivered his first baby, and my mother said to her friends, "I didn't know he knew where babies came from." And I said, "He didn't learn it at our house, I can tell you that!" One of my aunts was always pushing Mother to tell us. At a very early age, my friend Joanie and I pored over her church's youth group book called *Love in Life for Teenagers.* It didn't tell you a darned thing. If you didn't already know, it didn't tell you. I finally learned about it by reading some books my brother had up in the attic. I think my mother was scared to death. I mean she just didn't know how, so when she bought me Kotex for my first period, she just suddenly bought it. . . . Ducked in the store when we were walking down the street, and that night she said, "You know what that's for don't you?" And I said, "Yes, I'd learned at camp last summer." But never, never a book, never anything. They didn't do sex at our house.

Eight respondents either had some sex education at school or were informed by sisters, other female relatives, or friends. Two women talked about observing dogs mating as a disturbing early sex education experience. Four of the women were given some semiformal sex education by their parents.

One respondent, #10, age fifty-one, said that by the time her parents presented some sex education, she was past the age when she needed it, and as a result, it felt shameful and even invasive to think her parents would, on the one hand, suggest that she needed to know things and, on the other hand, believe she didn't know things already. According to Zani, the ambivalence in this type of situation arises from the adolescent needing reassurance and recognition of her growing adult identity, while at the same time being reluctant to shatter the image her parents have of her as a child. To talk about sex is to risk discovering that everyone is, in fact, quite unprepared for this change (Zani, 1991).

Two respondents believed they learned important things from parents, but wanted more ongoing dialogue and the permission to talk freely and ask questions as issues arose. Many women said that they didn't know what questions to ask, but they did know that "good girls" don't want to know the answers.

One way children seek answers to their sexual questions and curiosity is through early sex play with one another. By as early as the age of three, it is common for little girls to show some affection for or sexual interest in one another. By age four and a half, a girl has excellent motor control and can be quite sexually capable (Haas and Haas, 1993). About half of all adults can remember such childhood erotic play based on a combination of curiosity and pleasure (Kinsey, Pomeroy, and Martin, 1948, 1953; Roberts, 1980). Much of this play is the result of simple curiosity. Many parents punish this behavior, calling it "nasty." Pogrebin suggests that children are acting as "students" rather than "voyeurs" when they undertake such exploration. It is important for children to know what the bodies of others look like to feel comfortable about their own bodies (Pogrebin, 1983). In our study, ten of the twenty-four respondents experimented sexually with other children before age ten.

Respondent #1, age thirty-six, married fourteen years, tells how this avenue of sexual information was closed off for her:

> . . . through my teen years I really didn't experiment sexually with different people or, for that matter, with myself. A lot of people I talk to masturbate, and I was afraid. I didn't.
>
> [You were afraid to?]
>
> Yeah, it was something you weren't supposed to do.
>
> [How did you know that?]
>
> I don't know. I don't know where I picked that one up. But it was something you weren't supposed to do. Way early on—now this might be an answer to that question—when we were real young, [about] four, five, or six, me and my sister and a neighbor girl across the street, we would—this is going to sound disgusting—we would play doctor, and I was pretty

young; I think I was about four, so my memory of it is sketchy, but we had a front porch on our house and we had a couch. We would go behind the couch, and what I remember is my sister and the neighbor girl would take sticks and insert them into my vagina, and they were playing doctor, and my mom came in one day and saw what was happening and was just disgusted, just mortified. MaryAnn was not allowed to play with us anymore unless she came over and had a discussion with my mom, and my mom told her this is not okay.

[And the feelings you associated with this?]

It was bad; you don't touch; those are private areas, and you don't touch them. It wasn't communicated that way. How I figured it was you don't touch your own body. And so, as an adolescent, when most people would start experimenting sexually with themselves, I never did.

If a little girl's natural curiosity about her body, her rather concealed genitals, and her sexuality is satisfied, she is likely to feel comfortable with her body as an adult (Renshaw, 1984). This is especially important for little girls whose parents rarely discuss their daughters' genitals or teach them the proper names (vulva, vagina, clitoris, urethra) for those body parts. Girls may learn to devalue their sexuality not because of the mysterious and concealed nature of their anatomy, but because of the mysterious and concealed nature of their parents' communication about it (Lerner, 1977; Pogrebin, 1983).

Pleasuring of the self, or masturbation, is a normal, safe, and readily available sexual experience that teaches girls about their own sexual anatomy and sexual functioning. The stimulation of her own genitals may start when a girl is very young. In fact, during the first week of life, boys can be seen to have erections, and an early equivalent of vaginal lubrication probably occurs in infant girls (Hopkins, 1980; Haas and Haas, 1993). Both are physical, involuntary reactions showing that a child's sexual development has begun. Although self-pleasuring has been found to be absolutely normal, some parents become disturbed when they notice any sort of sexual activity in their child. Some parents become almost phobic about touching their infants while washing, diapering, or dressing them. They do not want to brush up against the genitals because they have seen the pleasurable response this touch can evoke. These precautions are largely useless because youngsters will tend to touch their genitals as a normal part of their sexual development (Strong and DeVault, 1994).

The disapproval children feel from caregivers when they touch their own bodies has long-lasting effects. Gagnon studied parental attitudes toward children's self-pleasuring in the parents of three- to eleven-year-olds. In his sample of 1,482 parents, a large majority believed that most children do masturbate; a smaller majority believed it was all right to do so. Of mothers with sons, 47 percent reported their sons masturbated, whereas 20 percent of fathers reported that their daughters masturbated. Sons were more frequently told to do it in private, whereas daughters were more frequently told it was harmful or morally wrong. Both mothers and fathers report masturbation by their sons twice as often as by their daughters (Gagnon, 1985).

Virtually all sex researchers and therapists advise that masturbation is not harmful. Some also suggest that there are harmful physical and emotional effects from early sexual deprivation that can lead to psychological and sexual disorders in later life (Francoeur, 1991). Gagnon notes that masturbation is closely linked to the permission to feel pleasure in many areas of life. Looking at the common parental attitude toward young children's sexuality, particularly daughters' sexuality, it appears that the message "if it feels good, it's bad" is internalized, especially by girls, at an early age (Gagnon, 1985).

Of the twenty-four respondents in this study, five, with ages ranging from twenty-nine to fifty-three, reported that they masturbated as children or adolescents. Retrospective studies of masturbation, such as the one by Kinsey and colleagues (1953), indicate that most adult women do not report having masturbated prior to adolescence. However, a West German study on female masturbation showed that since the sexual revolution of the 1960s, there has been a marked increase in the percentage of women reporting masturbation prior to and during adolescence (Clement, Schmidt, and Kruse, 1984).

Those respondents in our study who did not masturbate said, variously, they "thought it was dirty," they "never thought of it," or they "never felt sexual" as they grew up. One respondent began to masturbate, but her mother found out, and she was shamed by her mother, so she stopped doing it. Respondent #12, age fifty-three, inadvertently found a way to pleasure herself as a teenager:

> I was quite a basketball player, and we had this wonderful basketball net and it was on a big pipe, about three inches in diameter, in our yard. And I would get the ball stuck between the backboard and the thing, and I would crawl up this pipe to get it. And this wonderful feeling would come over the lower part of my body, but I never knew that I could duplicate that in any way. . . . Yeah, and I'd get that ball stuck a lot.

Sexual ambivalence and discomfort may also be transmitted to children in the form of parents giving the children too much responsibility for learning and making decisions about their sexuality. Children hungry for information may be forced to make decisions, without guidance, that they feel unprepared to make. The result then may be that this sexual dimension of life simply happens to girls, creating situations to which they must react (Fine, 1988). Because parents may be uncomfortable about their children's developing and emerging sexuality, they may deny that it is happening. Parents tend to indulge in wishful thinking that their daughters are "not really interested in boys yet," so they tend to put off talking to their daughters about sex, waiting for the right time. Parents may raise the subject once, make their points, breathe a sigh of relief, and never mention it again. Thus, they forget that learning about sexuality, as with learning any important set of skills, is an ongoing process. Sociologist John Gagnon calls this the "inoculation" theory of sex education, or the "once is enough for life" theory (Gagnon, cited in Roberts, 1983, pp. 20-27).

On the other hand, parents may assume their children know much more than they actually do and that their children don't need permission to talk about sex. Because of the social discomfort that seems to surround sexual issues in most families, children probably won't feel safe initiating questions and dialogue without parental encouragement and permission. As a result, children are usually expected to learn an important set of behavioral and emotional skills through only one lesson.

Respondent #6, age thirty-five, describes her confusion:

> My mom had already been really up front with me about using birth control because her mother got pregnant with her when she was very young. So she was really adamant about me knowing about that and not denying that I was going to have sexual feelings. She told me that, so I just expected it. She told me it's natural and it's going to happen. . . . I remember masturbating from a very early age . . . oh, I just stumbled on masturbation. I knew it felt good to masturbate . . . I can't honestly say I connected it with what I was hearing about sex. . . . I enjoyed being sexual with Jerry (first boyfriend and first husband). We were very sexual. Sex was definitely a good part of our relationship. . . . Although part of . . . he turned me off. . . . And I think part of it was not even necessarily the frequency that turned me off, as lack of intimacy about it. That it was sex and not mixed with any intimacy, so I became disinterested. Then my relationship with Barry (second husband). I purposely chose Barry because he was a more emotional person. He liked to discuss feelings and showed an emotional side. He wasn't afraid to cry, so I think that drew me to him. To me, it seems like a transition to women, now that I look back on it . . . now that I am older. I feel that it [the education from mother] was even almost a license to go ahead and do it. . . . I never did get pregnant, but I could have. I guess I don't know if it's a good thing to be sexual—maybe not intercourse at that age when you can't be responsible. And you can't be responsible for a baby at that age. . . . She didn't encourage me to go do it, but she sure didn't make me feel like I should wait either.

In this previous quote from respondent #6, she says she did not realize that masturbation was connected to sex, which further illustrates the point that sex is sometimes taught to children, but arousal, desire, and pleasure are not. According to Whitfield, discussion of sexuality with children seldom includes any reference to sexual arousal. Sexuality is taught as a mechanical process and is associated with individual morality, victimization, and violence—but it is not associated with sexual desire (Whitfield, 1989). If something is not named, there is the implication that it doesn't exist or has no importance. As Michelle Fine asserts, "the naming of desire, pleasure or sexual entitlement, particularly for females, barely exists in the formal agenda in public schooling on sexuality (Fine, 1988, p. 33). She further notes that although boys and men are allowed desire, with the implication that they can't control their sexual impulses, desire for women is largely ignored, even by women themselves (Fine, 1988). Since all humans are capable of sexual desire by virtue of being human, the implication that desire doesn't exist or that it is wrong may tend to teach girls that they are bad because they feel it.

Girls are also made to feel ashamed about their developing bodies. In popular culture, much is made of women's breasts. They are admired and lusted after, but a young women may also be given a label such as "easy" or "slut" if she is attractive or her breasts are large. Susan Brownmiller notes, "Although they are housed on her person, from the moment they begin to show, a female discovers that her breasts are claimed by others. . . . No other part of the human anatomy has such semipublic, intensely private status, and no other part of the body has such vaguely defined custodial rights . . . her breasts belong to everybody, but especially to men" (Brownmiller, 1984, p. 41).

Respondent #13, age fifty-three, describes her lack of information and how she was shamed by her developing body:

> I remember being maybe twelve years old, and I had been curious all along about how women have children and all this, and I saw two dogs . . . I mean I saw two dogs basically humping in the backyard, and all of a sudden, I knew it. People don't do that! I could not believe that people could do something so animalistic. But it had to be. So that was the first realization. That was what sex was going to be like. And I didn't want to have anything to do with it. It's invasive. I saw the female dog trying to get away. Nobody was going to do that to me. I don't remember sex education. All I remember—what I remember from the one-room school—is sexual innuendos and chiding from the boys. I developed fairly early

and I didn't wear a bra. I can remember being kind of ridiculed that they could see my nipples through a blouse and going home and telling mom about it, and so then she got me a bra, but it was like that had to happen first. I felt awful. . . . I remember we had a witch's den at Halloween . . . the kids would create and the teacher would approve what was set up . . . . You know, you put grapes in there and then you put some slimy stuff on, and you'd wear a bandanna, and then . . . you'd walk a plank, and it was supposed to be innocent, and I'm sure it was, but what happened to me. . . . I remember getting a note somehow; it was put in my lunch or whatever, but it was clearly written by some boys who said they were going to peel me like a banana. The fact that I remember after all these years means it was pretty powerful, and I was scared silly to go in there. And I don't remember if I went through the witch's den or not. . . . I don't remember . . .

Myths and negative attitudes about menstruation persist as well. Girls may feel confusion and shame about menstruation, even if they do have knowledge of it before it comes. Negative attitudes toward menstruation have deep historical roots. The Bible describes women as "unclean," and in biblical times, women were not allowed to take part in festivals or ceremonies when they had their periods. Information about childbearing was limited, and birth was thought to happen by magic and was not connected to the menstrual blood. Fear of this "unclean" blood created myths about women's bleeding, and the bleeding was ascribed to magical or demonic power (Bell, 1987). Such myths persist for girls and women, leading them to believe that their periods are embarrassing, somehow a negative part of them and something they should hide, that their monthly hormonal changes render them unstable. Religions exist that continue to uphold some form of these taboos (Ussher, 1992).

Some young girls are given books and lectures at the time of their first period, and this marks the first time for them when the vagina is presented as a socially acceptable area of the body. However, according to Hopkins, "the message is still a mixed one since it is the reproductive role that is stressed rather than the sexual one." She further notes that many health books don't even show the clitoris in diagrams of the female organs (Hopkins, 1980, p. 5). Thus, many girls are not taught that they have a clitoris. Given the societal discomfort with teaching desire and arousal, many girls and women may learn only inadvertently that they have a genital part designed only for pleasure.

The relative ignorance regarding sexuality of adults in our culture is reflected in the misinformation that is passed on to young people. Whisnant and colleagues interviewed 171 girls regarding the use of sanitary napkins or tampons. Results showed that the vast majority of girls are given napkins by their mothers at the time of their first period. About half of the girls' mothers mentioned tampons to them, but most mothers suggested girls wait until their bodies were more "mature," or girls were told they could damage something inside if they used tampons while still a virgin (Whisnant, Brett, and Zegans, 1979).

Whisnant and colleagues hypothesize that the use of tampons may serve a role in psychosexual development. Mothers' discomfort with tampons could also be illustrative of parents' discomfort with their daughters' developing sexuality. They also suggest that the use of tampons may constitute a teaching moment, providing the first socially sanctioned opportunity for a girl to explore her genitals, to begin to form an image of the vagina, and to relate internal and external sensations (Whisnant, Brett, and Zegans, 1979).

Respondent #9, age fifty-seven, describes her first use of tampons:

> I was fourteen or fifteen and was baby-sitting at my cousin's. She had some tampons in her bathroom, and I was really scared and guilty and I felt ashamed of myself, but I put one into myself. It hurt some, and it felt really strange, but mostly I thought I was doing something wrong, something very wrong. I know it was my body! But it just didn't feel that way. . .

Respondent #13, age fifty-three, talks about starting to menstruate:

> I remember getting my period for the first time, and I remember Mom talking about it like her sick time, you know . . . but I was never prepared in the sense of . . . I mean I know there

weren't Kotex napkins lying around. . . . I mean nobody told me to start carrying them at a certain age, and this is why I think my teacher meant so much to me because I remember getting my period. I went to the outhouse. There were two bathrooms, and I went out there and I started to bleed and here I am in this one-room school, you know, and she finally realized that I was gone for a long period of time, and she was the one who came to help me then, you know, to do something because I was bleeding . . .

Generally, the respondents recalled in detail the rare and brief exchanges about sexuality and sexual information that they had throughout their entire childhood and adolescence. Because they were rare and brief and carried the implication of secrecy, the events had a powerful impact. Respondent #18, age fifty-one, recalls her sparse sex education. Her experience also illustrates how the media reflect the social constructions of sexuality. The media—in this case, magazines—both dictate and reflect the values and mores that shape behavior and attitudes:

. . . there is no way my family ever had a conversation with me about telling me anything about sex. So I remember, basically, it was the girl talk and, finally, in junior high or high school, when. . . . I would say, that I didn't have much information at all early on. I remember being very curious . . . so I read this one family health book, and I was very curious about reading the parts that had anything to do with anatomy or genitals or . . . also I read *True Love, True Story* magazines that were only at one relative's house, my dad's sister. And her daughter was maybe five years older than me, and both my aunt and her loved those [magazines]. They had stacks of them, and when I'd go down to see them, I was reading to see what all this romance and sex stuff was about. . . . I was pretty curious but had a lot of uptightness about anybody touching me. I really basically dated three different people in high school, but I didn't want to be touched and didn't . . . it was kind of remarkable that some of my friends were [interested] but I wasn't interested, and I didn't want it and that was sort of the beginning of feeling like there is something wrong with me, but I didn't want to. . . .

I remember once, my mother, when I was going out on a date with an older guy, tried to sort of—I'm going out the door and she's thinking, "I really should say something to her; I wonder if she knows not to let him take advantage of her" . . . and [my reaction was] "Mother! I already know. I know this stuff." That's the only time I ever remember her ever attempting to talk to me about sex at all. . . . I remember getting pretty much the message, not necessarily from my parents, but a societal thing about, basically, girls in high school who are sexual are bad girls. And that really comes from those magazines too because they were always describing the bad girls in town who had the babies and went out with the wild boys, and the girls who didn't were the good girls.

A girl's womanhood becomes apparent when she begins her first menses and her body starts to change. As adolescent boys develop sexually, they experience a compelling feeling of sexual excitation that they begin to believe they are entitled to discharge. Male sexuality with its genital/orgasmic emphasis has traditionally been viewed as the norm for all adolescents, both male and female. More recent writings are acknowledging differences between male and female sexual development. Sexual activity for females does not serve so directly as confirmation of womanhood. Females may have feelings of sexual interest and attraction, but girls' sexual activity is experienced more within the context of relationships rather than as the discharge of sexual tension (Notman et al., 1990).

"Many girls suggest that they have their first sexual intercourse because they want to acquiesce to the pressure of the boy's wishes rather than because of their own strong, internal and genital wishes" (Notman et al., 1990, p. 563). In fact, many girls feel alienated from their own experience of sexual desire. This alienation probably has to do with repressive socialization regarding sexuality for girls; that is, there is no cultural permission for girls to enjoy sex and feel aroused, and women are systematically taught to devalue themselves and their bodies. However, evidence also suggests that "desire" may be experienced quite differently by boys and girls. In addition, the boy's differing wishes and expectations, coupled with the girl's desire to place the *connection between them* at utmost priority, may lead the adolescent girl to feel unclear about her own needs (Notman et al., 1990).

Women are taught not to know their sexual arousal, or not to recognize it, and to be ashamed of it. If they don't acknowledge or know their arousal, how then are they to use the experience of sexual arousal to give them cues for making choices in their relationships? Because sex is taught as a mechanical process, it seems unsurprising that many of the women in this study did not recognize that among their early feelings for women, there was sexual arousal, for example, respondent #24, age fifty-three:

> . . . and one woman who was—we became good friends and she came there later—we were the RAs, resident assistants, on the same floor. And I figured that one out years later, and I even told her when we were visiting last summer. I said, "You know, I figured it out later; I really had the hots for you." And, of course, I didn't have any way to know. I had no concept. I never ever thought in terms of what was going on. I just thought I really liked her; I wanted her to be my good friend. I wanted to be with her. I remember feeling extreme jealousy when she was becoming close with some other person.

One study considers the link between sex and desire for women: In this study, women were shown pornographic images and asked if they felt aroused. Most of the women said no. However, data from the physiological tests, such as vaginal secretions, heart rate, and so on, showed they were experiencing sexual arousal (Heiman, 1977). According to Gonnerman (1994), the explanation for this lack of awareness is that girls develop an identity that splits into two parts—one side is the good girl, and the other side, the sexually responsive being—with these two parts strictly divorced from each other and neither part able to inform the other. The split is reinforced by parents who, because they don't want to know, pretend their girls' sexual development, sexual experimentation, and awareness isn't happening (Gonnerman, 1994).

Respondent #8, age forty-three, talks about her father's attitudes that taught her about sexuality:

> There was no . . . it was never talked about in the home. Except my dad would yell at my sister. He'd say all we ever thought

about was sex. He'd say, "stay away from guys cuz that's all they want." My dad trusted me because I was a tomboy. He didn't feel he had to worry about me with boys. My sister was. . . . If we were to go downtown and go to a play or whatever, he would badger her for at least an hour before, to the point where she would get so upset she wouldn't want to go. . . . She was very angry, and I later learned why she was angry. Later on, she came out with all this stuff as to—my dad raped her. . . . He said all we thought about was sex, but it was him.

Although the previous quote may not represent the experience of some respondents, it is clear that the quote is consistent with the sex role socialization in our society in general. Male sexuality is seen as active, initiatory, demanding of immediate gratification and divorced from emotional attachment (Spaulding, 1991), whereas females are accused of leading men on, teasing men, and creating sexual situations merely by being present (Brownmiller, 1975).

Respondent #13, age fifty-three, discusses her sexual learning about, and from, men:

My images of sex growing up and in high school were all negative.

[In what way?]

Very definitely. Well, the chiding by the boys. I heard a lot from my dad when he would be with his friends. There were a lot of sexual jokes that I found very upsetting and I would sometimes leave the room because I didn't want to hear them, and so sex was portrayed as this thing men did to you, you know? It was ridiculing, and I never . . . there were no positive images except in the movies, where everything was glorified, like, oh you're going to fall—Prince Charming stuff.

Respondent #9, age fifty-seven, describes a disturbing and confusing joke she was told by her husband when she was twenty-six years old:

I remember him coming home one day and laughing and laughing about this complicated story his friend told about a woman who was gradually chopped up—I mean her arms were cut off, and then her legs were cut off, so she could just be this hole, this vagina, that the men could penetrate, and she was tied to a pole. And he told me this story with the certain faith that I would laugh and think it was funny too. He was a good man, not a cruel guy, so I couldn't believe he would think it was funny, or that he'd believe I'd think it was funny. I remember I tried to explain to him how awful it was. He didn't get it. He thought I was being a prude. But I didn't even know exactly why I thought it was so bad. I mean, it was 1965; I didn't know about sexual exploitation or the denigration of women or anything. I wasn't sure I had the right to object. It was just a joke. But I just knew I did. What kind of a society did we live in that I didn't even feel justified in objecting to cruelty?

Since sexuality is a part of being human and a central factor in our everyday existence, but is also attached to guilt, shame, and violence, girls and women are caught in the wheels of a major paradox, as they attempt to learn who and what they are in this culture. Girls wanting to be "good" or "moral," as well as seeking to understand their sexual rights, are faced with many dilemmas.

Respondent #24, age fifty-four, confirms the confusion about sexual arousal. Sexual enjoyment was denied by her mother, although her parents said she could ask any question about sex and they would answer it:

My parents—probably it sounds insane—but they were really open, and any questions you had, you could come home [with them], and I remember talking about this "balloon" I had seen on the playground and why was it so funny. Why were the kids laughing about it? When I got ready to get married I was a virgin. My mother told me sex was something that a man enjoys and a woman puts up with. So when I was married and started enjoying sex, I thought I was perverted.

Respondent #5, age forty-one, describes how lack of information, combined with guilt and shame projected by adults, can present girls with a sexual quandary:

One of my earliest memories about sex is when I was trying on some clothes that my mom was making for me, and it looked like I had a little bit of a belly on me, and my mother freaked out and thought I was pregnant. She started yelling at me and said, "You've been fooling around with boys," and started pushing down on my stomach to feel if there was a baby in there. And I was totally . . . I had no idea at all what she was talking about. She just freaked. She thought I was pregnant, and I said, "There's no way". . . . So then I spent the next however many months until I got my first period afraid I was pregnant because I had a crush on the Monkees, because I didn't know how anybody got pregnant. . . . I thought, well, maybe if I just think about him. That was my first memory of sex and shame.

Respondent #17, age thirty-nine, describes the shame she felt as she attempted to learn about her own body and the shame her mother projected onto her:

Oh, I remember, you know, masturbating, but then I remember also getting candlesticks because I wanted to feel what it feel like to be penetrated. And I remember my mother finding the candles and confronting me about that and suggesting that I needed psychiatric help, that that was not, you know, normal . . . and me not knowing what to say, and her saying, "Well, do you need to see a psychiatrist?" I think that's what she said to me. I just remember psychiatrist was thrown in there, so it was clear what she thought of me . . .

As a young woman attempts to navigate sexual waters, she is confused by sexual double binds. Popular culture tells a woman that she is supposed to be alluring and arouse her male partner, but another aspect of her learning gives her no permission to have any erotic feelings herself. Therefore, she is usually forced to tell herself that sex is something that just "happens" to you, that she musn't plan for it. Her dilemma gives her limited choices: (1) to acknowledge her erotic feelings, plan for sex, and risk being thought of (or thinking of herself) as bad or promiscuous or (2) to be passive and "swept off her feet," that is, a nonresponsible, nonparticipant in the sexual encounter (Roberts, 1980; Kisker, 1986).

More than one study indicates that among sexually active teenage girls, those who regularly attend religious services are less likely to use an effective method of contraception than those who do not attend religious services. In light of their religious teachings, these girls appear to have substantial difficulty acknowledging that they are sexual beings (Singh, 1986; Studer and Thornton, 1987). They can't acknowledge their sexual desires and behaviors, so they may avoid using any contraception. To use contraception would only serve to remind them that they are indeed sexual, and not only that, but they planned to be sexual—it didn't just happen (Hafner, 1992).

Thus, the denial of female arousal and the "unsavory" reputation associated with it keep women from being full participants in their sexual lives. (In Chapter 6 on coming out—"Now That She Knows"—I will look more deeply at the cultural attitudes we hold about the evil of women's sexuality.) Popular culture and interpersonal feedback tell women that they are supposed to be sexy, but implicit rules say they are not supposed to have a sexual life. As adults, they may be censured for being "frigid" and not enjoying sex, but they spend years before they are adults being told that they are not allowed to be sexual, that good girls don't know or ask about sex. They are truly enmeshed in a series of sexual double binds (Kisker, 1986).

Until about 1980, it was commonly believed in the United States and Britain that sexual abuse of children and young girls affected 5 percent or fewer girls. Sexual abuse was considered an unusual occurrence. However, according to research by sociologist Diana Russell, 38 percent of women in the United States are sexually invaded before the age of eighteen without their consent; 16 percent, before the age of sixteen. Her sample of 930 women crosses income, class, and racial lines (Russell, 1986). Over the past ten years in the United States, as well as in Britain (Driver and Droisen, 1989) and New Zealand (Saphira, 1992), it has become clear that sexual abuse is more widespread than previously believed and that its impact on female sexual development must be considered. My sample reflects this. Eight of the twenty-four respondents had had sexually abusive experiences.

With specific regard to women's knowing about their own gender orientation, learning explanations for female homosexuality have pointed to aversive conditioning or being abused or "punished" by the other sex and, therefore, seeking relationships only with the same gender. Early studies reported that women who were raped had more subsequent lesbian experiences and that many female incest victims developed homosexual feelings. The evidence for this was anecdotal, and "given the male bias of the discipline [psychoanalysis] with its insistence on the male primacy of the penis" (Brownmiller, 1975, p. 177), the assumption seems predictable that women would choose women sexually only because of sexual injury or coercion by men. As Brownmiller notes, "the use of an intuitive approach based large-ly on analysis of idiosyncratic case studies allowed for no objective sampling (Brownmiller, 1975, p. 177).

Peters and Cantrell (1991) recently studied a large nonclinical sample of women who described themselves as heterosexual or lesbian. Results showed that the percentage of lesbian and hetero-sexual women reporting nonconsensual experiences with adults be-fore the age of twelve was comparable to that found in the general population. The hypothesis that lesbians would report a greater number of negative childhood/adolescent sexual experiences with males was not supported. More positive sexual experiences with females before age twelve was also not found for the lesbian group. Neither parental relationships nor parental attitudes about homo-sexuality were significantly different between the two groups. Therefore, the study did not support that lesbianism is caused by male aversion (Peters and Cantrell, 1991).

Research does not support a connection between sexual abuse and lesbianism. It is clear, however, that the sexual development of many young women is profoundly affected by sexual abuse. In the United States, only within the past ten years has there been public recogni-tion of the extent of sexual abuse. It would appear that the experience of sexual abuse reinforces the shame, silence, and passivity many girls feel about their own experience of sexuality, and intrinsic shame, silence, and passivity help to continue the sexual abuse.

Respondent #8, age forty-three, was abused by her uncle when she was in seventh grade, then age twelve:

> I thought he was my buddy, my pal, you know, the dad I never had. And I think he played on that . . . he again proceeded to molest me probably for six months for that period that we stayed there. He is an alcoholic. I really felt like I was two people at that point in my life. . . . After that, I felt like I wore a sign on my back that said, "I'm innocent and easy." . . . And I knew that if I had gotten a boyfriend at that time, maybe [my uncle would] leave me alone or think I might tell or. . . . I was afraid to tell my mother because I, she had gone through a lot and he was known for hitting on all the women relatives in the family . . . and then I started becoming pretty promiscuous as far as boyfriends, guys, because I felt what I got from him was what I was supposed to get and then that felt like love and so on. . . . I, he, you know, turned me on as to what orgasm was, and I really thought I was doing something to him that made him come on to me . . .

To complicate the issue further, when sexual feelings become a bigger part of the girl's life at puberty, she may "become aware of being out of step, of not having the same reactions as others, of preferring the company of her own sex, and of having little interest in dating boys or in the games of attraction that teenagers play" (Hinchen, 1988, p. 12). As she begins to understand that sexuality is involved—sexuality that is already confusing and problematic for her—and that her sexual feelings are different from what she sees around her, she may feel shame and fear (Hinchen, 1988).

About her interest in females, respondent #2, age twenty-nine, said the following:

> If I had questions about sex, my parents weren't hung up about it . . . although we didn't discuss it. . . . But I could have asked . . . I knew that sex was a normal part of life. But not with women.

Repression or even denial of same-sex feelings and attractions may result from societal and family expectations of heterosexual patterns. Because she operates primarily in the heterosexual and heterosocial world, which insists that female sexual satisfaction is dependent upon a male, a young woman is not likely to recognize her same-gender impulses. She may marry or become physically involved with a male (Gramick, 1984). Lesbian activist and writer Adrienne Rich (1980) labeled this societal training of women as "compulsory heterosexuality." One theorist of lesbian identity formation suggests that this training may cause women to disregard emotional cues, such as the depth of their attachments to women (Elliott, 1985). If women were allowed to understand their sexual feelings, to be unashamed of them, they might recognize that they want to seek out other women as more than friends, as potential life partners.

Assuming the adolescent girl recognizes that she is attracted to girls, this "heterosexualization" of desire may cause her to feel like a failure, a developmental failure, and out of step with her peers. At some deep level, or possibly at a more obvious one, she knows the stigma associated with same-gender attraction and will begin to feel shame about it (Hinchen, 1988). When, or if, she does experience her feelings of attraction for a female, she is likely to deny it, push it down and away, or she may miss the meaning or significance of it altogether. Although programs for gay/lesbian/bisexual youth have begun to appear in recent years, little validation was available for any of our respondents when they were growing up. This was also true for the youngest respondents, those in their late twenties, for example, respondent #2, age twenty-nine:

> I dated boys through high school. But I had a pretty clear understanding about same-sex attraction just for myself. There had been some experiences that I'd had during sleepovers in sixth, seventh, and eighth grade that were fairly erotic with other girls. Of course, that all got back to school eventually, and I had to use my wits and intelligence and popularity to scam the girls that were involved and make myself look OK . . . because I realized it wasn't OK. I just pushed all that down, but in rural Minnesota, you don't talk about gay/lesbian/bisexual stuff. There were no words for any of that, so all I knew was that there was something going on.

Consider also the comments of respondent #4, age thirty-three:

> My parents seemed to be oblivious to sexual things. Also, I had been taught that the Bible said it was wrong, so I didn't even know that it [same-sex relationship] existed. It sounds funny to say that I was taught it was wrong and also that I didn't know it existed, but somehow that's true. . . . And even through high school, I know there were girls that I was really attracted to, and I can say that now, but at the time, in high school, I didn't recognize that ever as being a feeling of attraction because (a) I didn't know that kind of attraction existed and (b) I never would have even dreamed of it in a million years. I would have thought boys were with girls and girls were with boys; that's it. . . . If I had known it existed, I think I would have known about me at a lot younger age. . . . I know I would have.

When much is made of success and failure in the development of opposite-sex relationships, the initial reaction of the adolescent who is aware of same-gender feelings is to hide—hide the feelings, hide the attractions (Martin, 1982). She doesn't see it around her, and she doesn't think it's normal, so she becomes a member of what Erving Goffman (1963) calls the "discreditable." She feels part of a minority. The minority status of the physically handicapped and racial minorities is obvious to others. Therefore, their problems and adaptation process are different from those of the gay/lesbian/bisexual. Same-gender attractions don't necessarily show, and those whose "flaw" is capable of being kept a secret must always struggle with this vulnerability: What would happen if this were known about them? At the same time, the punishments for possessing the stigma are all too obvious (Brooks, 1981). Still, society has not even perceived lesbians as such; the experience of lesbians has largely been kept invisible—economically, historically, socially, and psychologically invisible (Spaulding, 1991). Therefore, for women attracted to women, the hiding comes naturally.

Further, the girl's right to her own erotic feelings is denied, so when she feels something is missing in the usual boy-girl conquest that occurs in junior high school, she feels ashamed of her disinterest and believes there is no one with whom to discuss any other feelings she might have. In fact, she may overcompensate for her lukewarm interest because she wants to feel a part of the community of her friends, because she wants to "belong." The peer pressure to be accepted may encourage her to mimic feelings of attraction to boys, even if she doesn't have them.

Respondent #8, age forty-three, describes this feeling of acting to "fit in":

> [How did you feel about these boys (in junior high)?]

> I didn't like them. I didn't like it. I didn't understand it. I don't know. Maybe I just wanted a boyfriend. I wanted a boyfriend, but I didn't want to do all those things that they wanted to do all the time . . . stuff that was happening all the time, meeting behind the school buildings, kissing, going steady, you know. The girls talked about it. I wanted to be like them.

The sexual journey of women in this society cannot be transversed without encountering shame because shame is the inevitable result of this double bind: the shame bind occurs as a normally developing female sexuality becomes confused and constrained by mandatory ignorance. Women are thus hampered in their process of coping and in the pace of their self-discovery. How can they learn? The women in this study were nearly unanimous (twenty-three of twenty-four) that their understanding, their development as sexual persons, was restricted because they learned to be ashamed about some, or all, aspects of their sexuality. Gershen Kaufman describes shame as the "awareness of ourselves as fundamentally deficient in some vital way," along with the feeling that "there is no way to relieve the matter, no way to restore the balance of things," that is, no way to fix the deficiency (Kaufman, 1982, p. 9).

Respondent #14, age forty-eight, describes several of the shame-producing double binds and dilemmas she experienced when she was eight through twelve years old:

> . . . when I look back it was the house, the way it was divided up; the division between all the rooms was only a curtain. And I remember there being fights and being accused of peeking through these curtains, and I remember at that age having no clue of what the hell I would have been peeking at.

[Who accused you?]

My mother. So, and I must have heard . . . heard sexual things too. Most of those years I've blocked out. . . . He [father] was the one who went to the store and she was the one—she would point out to him when I started my period or when I started getting hair or when my breasts started developing. She would be the one to tell him all these things, and so they could talk about me, but there wasn't . . . like it wasn't OK [for me] to talk about sex. It was something that was really dirty and horrible, and it wasn't OK to ask questions about any of it. But she used to tell me stories about her wedding night that were really horrible . . . about bleeding, about hurting; it sounded like he was rough. . . . When I was thirteen, I told my mother about Dad having sex with me for years, and she told me not to tell anyone. She confronted him and it stopped, but she told me it would break apart the family . . . it would ruin his reputation if I told anyone. And then she started in on me, on how I was ruined forever, and no good man would ever want me, and I was not allowed to wear . . . not allowed to wear white, and I think it was mainly because it was a big deal that I had been . . . that he had spoiled me, quote, unquote.

According to Kaufman, shame originates interpersonally from many sources within the family and through relationships in the wider society. When the negative or shaming input is significant and consistent, the shame will become internalized so that one's self will continue to activate shame without any new event being required. Kaufman describes how "through this internalizing process, shame can spread through the self, ultimately shaping our emerging identity . . . that vital sense of who we are as individuals . . . leaving us feeling naked, defeated as a person and intolerably alone" (Kaufman, 1982, pp. 8-9). Once a person internalizes shame, she or he is vulnerable to it as a part of her or his identity. Therefore, if a girl grows up in this culture, she is highly likely to internalize sexual shame as a part of her identity.

Miller has described adolescence as a time "when girls begin to 'contract' rather than expand" (Miller, 1991, p. 19). Cultural pressures come to bear at the time of adolescence, and the girl takes on the characteristics of a woman. The idea of an appropriately social-ized woman in this society includes the surrender of her orientation toward confident self-expression of all thoughts and feelings. In fact, women are socialized to keep the most painful secrets, such as the fact that they are being abused or even the simple, everyday fact that they may regularly feel sexually aroused. Thus, by the age of ten or twelve, the girl is likely to have assumed sexual shame, as well as the culturally sanctioned orientation toward self-censorship for women (Pipher, 1994). This reduction in confidence and self-assertion prob-ably manifests sexually in a number of ways; for example, she is likely to be reluctant to pursue information about the sexual "differ-ences" she may feel; she is likely to hide interest in sex because it is linked to very painful emotions, such as shame.

Respondent #21, age thirty, describes an attempt to get informa-tion that created shame:

> I was scared of being gay, and I think back then I knew it, and one of the things that kind of pushed that back even further was I went to the library of my high school and I asked the librari-an—"Do you have," I said in a very low voice—"Do you have anything on gays and lesbians here?" and she said, very loud, or what appeared to me to be loud—"THE GAY AND LESBIAN SECTION IS OVER THERE, or you can look in the card catalogue." And I walked out of the library, and that was that.

In sum, then, how is a young woman to know she is different or to feel validated if she knows something is different? She is not given, indeed is not supposed to seek or find, sexual information, and yet she is supposed to know what to do when her body changes. She is expected to know what to do and how to act responsibly and what her choices are when she begins to experience sexual feelings. She is sometimes able to ask questions of adults in her circle, but she can sense whether it is OK to ask, can feel the atmosphere become tense when she does, so she is likely to experience discom-fort, or even shame, for being curious or direct about her interest. She is sometimes used sexually by the adults in her life, which teaches her to numb her sexual feelings and/or creates feelings in her of being of no value, except as a sexual object. She is given no preparation for the inevitable male attention she receives, but is accused of inviting and enticing the male attention when it comes. All women in this society are deprived because of these tight double binds, but women who feel same-gender attractions are at a particular disadvantage.

It is clear that to know they were lesbian or bisexual, the respondents in this study needed to know about sex and have permission to be sexual. Sex education and information, if provided, accessible, and sanctioned, might have assisted these women in teasing apart insidious, paradoxical sexual constructions and informed them about the possible range of normative outcomes for their relationship lives.

Chapter 2

Why Do These Women Marry Men?

The second major theme emerging from the interview data was that the experience of marriage was a seeming inevitability, not a life option, for these women. Over and over, most respondents, covering the entire age span, told of the implicit expectations from family and community that they would marry a man. It was clear to them that the only relationship option presented was that with a man, and if any other idea occurred to them, they kept it very secret.

The question of why women often marry without allowing themselves to consider the variety of ways they could live out their lives is deeply complex, far beyond the implications of a study about women who ultimately come out as lesbian or bisexual. However, for our purposes, the importance of the question persists. Numerous issues are germane, including female socialization and role expectations, the weight of tradition, as well as the prevailing societal definition of adult competency—marriage and child rearing—all within the firm framework of a patriarchal society.

Poet and writer Adrienne Rich (1976) captures the flavor of the feelings and thoughts expressed by the women in this research group. They were not told to marry; they just knew that it was a given that women married or were thought to be strange. They knew that if they did not marry, they would carry the weight of having violated a social rule throughout their lives. When they did marry, they felt somehow validated.

Rich says that from the time she was in her early teens, she felt like she was playing a role when she acted like a "feminine creature"; the part didn't fit for her.

She began the serious pursuit of poetry writing while in her teens and had fantasies of international travel as a journalist. Her plans to become self-sufficient felt very real to her. At the same time, she says, she practiced putting on lipstick with her girlfriends and talked about boys.

> There were two different compartments, already, to my life. . . . I felt that as an incipient "real woman," I was a fake. . . . This sense of acting a part created a curious sense of guilt, even though it was a part demanded for survival. . . . the day after I was married, I was sweeping a floor . . . as I swept that floor, I thought: "Now I am a woman . . . this is what women have always done." I felt I was bending to some ancient form, too ancient to question. *This is what women have always done.* (Rich, 1976, pp. 4-5)

Respondents #14, #24, and #15 all describe variations on the feeling that getting married is "what women do":

> [Why did you marry?]

> I didn't see it as an "option." It was—that's what I was supposed to do, and according to my mother, I was lucky if somebody asked me. I better snatch it up because no one else was going to ask. You're supposed to get married and have kids, and that's what I was expected to do, so that's what I did. (Respondent #14, age forty-eight)

> I met a person in psychology class. He sat next to me. He was real pleasant. There were five children in his family. They all seemed to get along. We started to date. He asked me to marry him. And I was really afraid that if I didn't take that one, nobody else would ask me. I know that as clearly today as I knew it then . . . it seemed a good way of . . . getting my life on track. (Respondent #24, age fifty-four)

> So we got married and had a couple nice honeymoons, and he was also very wealthy and so there were a lot of hints to that, too, the life of comfort and kind of thinking, well this is the way life is supposed to be, this is what you're supposed to do. Now, here the community is once again. I would be letting down my whole community who have given me so much, and

you know, all my ancestors and everything . . . it can be really big. So because in a Jewish community we are taught we are not just ourselves, we are everyone before us . . . there's a lot of responsibility there for family, family . . . (Respondent #15, age twenty-eight)

What do you want to be when you grow up? This question is familiar to every person since first being asked as a preschooler to confront the issue of adulthood, an issue that seemed remote. The pressure to make some acceptable life plan mounts during adolescence, when the onset of adulthood comes closer. The struggle to define ourselves as independent people with clear future goals is often viewed as the central psychological theme of adolescence. But are the choices for women's life plans really potentially unlimited?

The work of Erik Erikson provided a significant, prescriptive facet of society's view of women in mid-twentieth-century United States. Erikson's theory suggested that woman's "inner space" needed to be filled, that is, she needed to produce a baby to feel complete. His idea was that a woman's identity is completed through marriage and motherhood (Erikson, 1968). Erikson's ideas became well accepted as fact. Women who did not marry were viewed with suspicion, believed to be odd, or given the pejorative label "old maid." The dilemma for most girls was not would they marry, but who would they marry, and when.

According to social psychologist Esther Sales (1978), during early adulthood, marriage and parental roles—plus work roles—are the roles seriously explored as young women learn to perform the types of behavior expected for these roles. Most young women don't venture much outside roles that will fill the expectations of others. The nature of socially constructed sex roles is that they demand behavior compatible with the expectations that go with them. If a woman attempts to follow a role outside of those assigned to her, she may encounter people who are disconcerted by how her position is inconsistent with theirs. Taking a variant position creates stress in others, which creates stress for her. Friends, family members, or even strangers are likely to try to change her position so it agrees with theirs (Sales, 1978). The price of social discomfort or possible family rejection is so high that few young people are willing to pay it. Many young women acquiesce. In the perceived absence of another choice, and with the perceived threat of loss of acceptance by their community, they marry.

The pressure to conform to expected roles is described by respondent #16, age fifty-one:

> . . . in high school, I didn't really want to be around the boys. I wanted to—I had more fun with my girlfriends and again doing exploring, going around, just having adventures, camping overnight. I just enjoyed being with my girlfriends in high school. It was interesting because I felt pressured to look for a date with a boy. I remember when I was going to the prom, my folks were so happy when I was fixed up back then with this guy named Joe, and they were very pleased that I was finally going out with a boy. And then I didn't go out with another boy until next year's prom. And that happened, that boy that I went out with for my senior prom, Joe, the only person I ever really dated, was the person I ended up marrying . . .

Respondent #4, age thirty-three, describes the script that was laid out for her and how she sorted very pragmatically among her perceived options:

> [How did you decide to marry?]

> Mostly, because that when you graduated from high school, you either went to college or you got married. That was what you do. . . . I guess I really didn't have any aspirations that would involve college training of any sort. . . . I met a guy on a bus going to Florida. I traveled a lot, and I went to Florida for a couple of weeks and met this guy and just knew. I said, "Well, I pick you." Then we got engaged when I was in twelfth grade. We waited the proper year, got married, and that was my marriage. I had to do what I had to do. We got married because otherwise I had to go to college.

Respondent #6, age thirty-five, talks about her life script plus additional pressure because of her family's financial position:

> At that time, happiness was fulfilling all these stereotypes of being a married person and what it is like to grow up and be

married—What do you do with your life? You have a house and you have kids and you get jobs and you enjoy each other's company. I think that was encouraged for me as a girl growing up because, partly because I'm a girl and partly because my mom didn't have any money. I always thought college was unaffordable, and she didn't encourage me to have a life. She always told me I could do anything I wanted to do, but also, at the same time, I heard that was unaffordable. So I didn't even know what unaffordable was; I just thought it was out of my reach. I didn't even think about it. So I think, partly, I turned to marriage as a financial solution too. Even not knowing it at the time, that was the direction I was herded.

[That's an interesting choice of words—"herded."]

I guess I think of that as a societal thing. And I feel angry at society, at that now, because had I not been herded in that direction, I would have thought more of myself. I didn't have enough encouragement about myself . . .

Underlying all the assumptions about the rightness of heterosexual marriage are the assumptions of social laws concerning gender identity. That is, social law currently infers that marriage involves a man and a woman. It is being made perfectly clear through the passage of Defense of Marriage acts throughout the United States that marriage between two persons of the same sex is not yet socially acceptable. Marriages currently exist between biologically sexed males who identify as female and biologically sexed females. This has happened as a result of transgender males assuming the female gender through hormonal and surgical treatment. Is this, then, a marriage between women, that is, a lesbian marriage? Such a question is obviously beyond the scope of this book, but it highlights the shaky ground upon which many assumptions may lie. To suggest that gender need not be the only criterion for object choice, that is, choice of partner, is to shake the limits that provide organization and meaning to our human experience. These limits are not comfortably or easily changed (Burch, 1993a).

Sampson reminds us that any standard explanation—such as male plus female equals marriage—can become an unexamined term that provides the evaluative form within which comparisons are made. This can happen although the explanation itself—such as male plus female equals marriage—does not come under scrutiny. That is, some apparently neutral, objective descriptions that divide the world into categories, such as mind versus body or male versus female, are actually dichotomies that represent themselves as objective distinctions (Sampson, 1993). Burch suggests, for example, that an unstated corollary is behind the assumption that homosexuality is pathological. That unstated corollary is that heterosexuality is not pathological (Burch, 1993b). However, heterosexuality is usually unquestioned and unexamined.

An extension of this social law is the assumption that deep love— and concomitant generosity and gift giving—is appropriate and acceptable only between a male and a female. Respondent #9, age fifty-seven, describes her love for a girlfriend when they were in high school and the negative social reaction that resulted from her attempt to be generous to her friend:

> I adored this girl. She had a boyfriend and so did I, but I spent all my free time with her. I knew her parents were not getting this for her, so at Christmas, I had pants and a blouse on layaway and paid it off just in time to give it to her as a Christmas gift. I'll never forget the look on her father's face as he watched her open it. He said, "That's not the kind of gift girlfriends give each other." After that, he asked me to leave. I felt hurt, but was ashamed too, because I thought somehow he had figured out that my feelings for her were more than friends. I didn't know how that wasn't right or why it wasn't right, but I knew it was true.

The belief that reproduction and sexuality are inextricably linked has probably led to the emphasis of gender—male and female—as the principal criterion of sexual relationships and partner preferences (Ross, 1987). That is, traditional homophobic attitudes have placed the potential "death of the species" at the responsible feet of same-gender partners because their unions do not necessarily produce children. This fear that no children will be produced is probably the historical basis of the statement that same-gender relationships are "unnatural." However, what was true when most of these women married is no longer true. Artificial insemination has changed all that. A statement by respondent #3, age fifty-eight, reflects the bias that assumes if she hadn't married, she wouldn't have had children:

> It's too bad I couldn't have been more open back then, but it's probably good because I . . . probably would have realized much earlier my preference. I know I would have. And then I wouldn't have had the three children that I have. So it's just as well it was the way it was. Because I wouldn't have missed being married for anything because of what I have now.

In addition to these pressures, the social constructions of what constitutes "normal" womanhood and "normal" sexual expression are all too familiar. Psychoanalytic theory maintained a powerful hold on views of women and sexuality through the first seventy-five years of the twentieth century. As the fields of psychiatry and psychology developed, popular reasoning held that evidence of mature sexual development was marriage between a man and a woman. Sexual relationships other than between men and women were indicative of mental illness, arrested psychosexual development, or constitutional inferiority. For example, Falco cites Caprio who wrote *Female Homosexuality: A Modern Study of Lesbianism.* Caprio describes lesbians as jealous, unhappy, possessive, emotionally unstable, immature, narcissistic, guilty, sadomasochistic, insecure, and suffering "a multiplicity of neurotic health ailments." He states, "Psychoanalysts are in agreement that all women who prefer a homosexual way of life suffer from a distorted sense of values and betray their emotional immaturity in their attitudes toward men, sex, and marriage" (Caprio, 1954, cited in Falco, 1991, p. 19).

It is clear that patriarchal ideas, attitudes, and social structure have defined the context for expression of human sexuality. For example, psychoanalytic theory declared that the only "mature" orgasm was one that occurred vaginally, that is, when the penis was inserted inside the vagina. Through history, deviations from heterosexual life have met with social sanctions in many forms. In the fourteenth and fifteenth centuries, for example, both women and men suffered extreme retribution, such as burning, hanging, and beheading, for expressing homosexual preferences (Browning,

1984; Spencer, 1995). More recently, the Nazis sent thousands of homosexuals to the death camps during World War II. At the very least, same-gender expression has been, and remains, a form of expression to which social sanctions are applied in many or most settings. Therefore, a woman in the latter half of the twentieth century who was aware of same-gender feelings exhibited extreme courage if she resisted marriage.

Psychology and psychotherapists, allegedly those with knowledge of what is "normal" behavior, have not tended to lead the way to enlightened thinking. Psychotherapists are what Phyllis Chesler called "agent-clinicians" and tend to reflect the attitudes of society at large. Men are more often viewed as mentally healthy by society and their "agents" because the traits acceptable in men (confidence and independence of thought) are signs of mental health, although they are considered less socially acceptable and treated with less respect in women (Chesler, 1972; Enns and Hackett, 1990). Therefore, going to psychotherapy can still be a risky business for a woman. Respondent #15, age twenty-eight, participated in a year of couples therapy with her fiancé before they were married:

> . . . and [the psychotherapist] was a male. And Jeff and this therapist kind of came together, and I was the outsider, so it was kind of interesting. I was the—kind of a patient, and I needed to make the changes. . . . The psychologist did make me take an MMPI [Minnesota Multiphasic Personality Inventory] and I . . .
>
> [Did Jeff take the test too?]
>
> No.

Marriage among homosexual/bisexual women has been studied very little (see, for example, Coleman, 1985). In an investigation of male and female homosexuality carried out in 1973, Saghir and Robins state the finding that homosexual women married early after a "period of intense conflict and questioning in their lives which represents a further unsuccessful attempt at combatting their homosexuality" (Saghir and Robins, 1973, p. 256). Further, their report states that the marriages of these women were not made for love of the partner, were "doomed to failure" from the start, and were primarily unhappy relationships. Saghir's and Robins's respondents reflected the bias of 1973 attitudes; 1973 is the year that homosexuality was removed from the *Diagnostic and Statistical Manual of Mental Disorders*. Although Saghir's and Robins' research was carried out at the time when some of the respondents in this research were deciding to marry, these respondents did not reveal such harsh and negative judgments about their marriages. My present research reveals a picture of women's decisions to marry that are quite varied and do not reflect a clear picture of avoidance. Many of the respondents said that their marriages were satisfying at least some of the time.

Respondent #1, age thirty-six, describes her courtship and decision to marry:

> I guess in ninth grade would be about the time I really started wanting to; well, I suppose that's about the time that most kids would think about kissing a boy or whatever. And so it was like, well, that's what everybody is doing, so that's what we did, and it was really. fun. It was good, and then that summer, going into tenth grade, is when I met John, the man I married, and so all through high school we had dated, and when we started dating, it sure was fun and flirty and exciting. We were in the marching band together, so we went on events, and we have this in common, and so it wasn't too hard to make conversation about stuff and be together and have fun because it was already in place. You went to this parade and you got to go to this carnival and you had your group of friends around you, so it was kind of cozy, and it kind of felt connected. My friends started dating his friends, and it was fun and exciting and enjoyable.

Respondent #12, age fifty-three, describes the happiness she felt with her first husband:

> [Did you fall in love with him?]

> Oh yes, absolutely! I really did. He was the first guy who ever spent time getting to know me, enjoyed me. We had some intellectual equality. Socioeconomically we were very, very

different. I'd taken a class at the university on, you know—
what was it called?—Marriage and the Family, and there were
these questions that told you who you would be most likely to
have a successful marriage with. He didn't match any of it, but
God, he was cute, he was fun, and he was bright. And he paid
attention to me. So we really did fall in love, and we got
married.

Respondent #7, age thirty-two, remains married to her husband
and says she is not likely to end the marriage:

I don't know if I could get anybody better, male or female. . . .
We've got very similar interests. Each one of us will pick up
the slack when the other one needs it. I would be stupid to let
him go just because now I'm aware that I have female desires
too. I would hardly be able to find a female out there like my
husband.

In 1985, Coleman conducted a study of forty-five women, the one
formal research study carried out on married or formerly married
lesbians/bisexual women. He found that the women reported they
married because they were in love with their husbands, and they said
they married by choice. A pattern emerged that suggested their desire
for marriage was influenced by cultural expectations, but no more
than it is for heterosexual women. Coleman's and my present research concur that lesbian and bisexual women have difficulty knowing and becoming aware of their personal identity and gender orientation.

A number of researchers have observed that lesbian instrumental
behavior—that is, identifying and acting on same-gender feelings—
lags behind that of gay men. Spaulding suggests that this lag reveals
the effects of heterosexist gender ideology on women's development (Spaulding, 1991). As Coleman notes, hypothetically, the les-
bian/bisexual woman could avoid the pressure to marry and give
herself more time to consider other possibilities or to become aware
of her psychosexual identity development. However, to do this, she
would have to assert herself in an atypical manner, thereby risking
disapproval, loss of relationships with family members, societal
rejection, and alienation (Coleman, 1985). According to Gartrell,

parents may interpret a daughter's disinterest in marriage as personal rejection, failure, and social inadequacy (Gartrell, 1981). This potential failure to please parents is part of the pressure to marry that women feel.

Fifteen of the respondents in this study were not aware of same-gender feelings before marrying. Of those fifteen, thirteen of the women said that same-gender attraction never occurred to them before their marriages. Two said that they didn't know that lesbians existed; that is, they didn't know that some women have primary relationships with each other. They also said that they can see now that their self-awareness would have been different if they had known a category called lesbian existed.

Nine respondents described same-gender feelings or experiences before they married men. (See Chapter 4, "How Do Women Know?," for a more extensive discussion of this.) Two of these said that they had believed they were the only females who had these feelings, so they decided to ignore the feelings because they felt freakish and weird.

Of the seven remaining who did feel some same-gender impulses before marrying, all of them expressed some variation of denial of their feelings. Some women who denied their feelings *consciously repressed* the importance of these feelings; a few described a conscious or unconscious awareness that same-gender relationships were too difficult and, thus, pushed the feelings aside. Others said that they apparently went into denial of the feelings and were unable to retrieve them until well into adulthood. Note that denial is defined here in the psychological sense; that is, the feelings were so ego-dystonic or unacceptable to the women that for a period of time, they had no conscious awareness that the feelings ever existed. Denial differs from repression in that *repressed* feelings or thoughts can be called up if the owner of the feelings wants them to surface. Feelings or thoughts under psychological denial cannot be drawn from the person's consciousness at will. Denied feelings are only teased out very slowly and carefully—possibly in psychotherapy or as a result of many years of accumulated experience. (See "Discussion" in Chapter 6 regarding the critical accumulation of feelings that can overwhelm thoughts.)

Respondent #3, age fifty-eight, had a very important, four-year relationship with the woman she roomed with in college, but she either consciously or unconsciously repressed the feelings:

> My roommate in college and I lived together four years. And I think we definitely both had those feelings. . . . And I look back now on some of the letters she wrote, and now it's like, "Oh my God, why didn't I see that at the time?" But, you know, you put the blinders on so tight and you try not to see and feel and hear things that aren't according to what you were programmed to do. Even though I was a pretty free spirit, I still had a program to go to the university, graduate, eventually get married, and have kids. I was programmed by myself more than anybody, but of course, those were my role models. And so anything else, like falling in love with my roommate and having experiences there, would have thrown me off that track, and I wouldn't be the same person that I thought I was. So I put the blinders on. Imagine teaching Phys. Ed. and not having much sense of lesbian relationships. I had those blinders on so tight, it's funny I didn't run into brick walls. They were so tight!

Respondent #5, age forty-one, fought and resisted the feelings she had for women, thus consciously repressing them:

> I was twenty-two when I met him. He played guitar. We both played guitar. So we met at the Bible study, and we're both Swedish, and he was very cute. I was attracted to him. I thought he had great eyes, a great face, great body. I fell in love with him. He asked me . . . why did I marry him. I said, "Because I was in love with you." . . . He feels hurt for what has happened. "If you knew this, why didn't you tell me? I would have walked away from you."

> [You didn't know?]

> Well, I knew I had feelings for women, but I didn't know that that was a legitimate choice for me to make. I had friends who were lesbians, and I didn't judge them or think them any less than me, but for me, I wouldn't allow myself to have that. I

didn't want the societal—I didn't want the prejudice and didn't want the trouble. So I didn't consider myself. . . . I don't know if I considered myself a lesbian back then or not, or if I just figured the church says I could pray it away and I could get rid of it. And it wasn't real, and it wasn't part of me, so I thought that. [And so I married.]

Two of the respondents talk about how they married, but they knew, for whatever reason, that their weddings should not take place. However, they did not, or felt they could not, stop their weddings from happening:

I had just turned eighteen in January; we were married in February. . . . Looking back on the sixties, it was what else am I going to do, you know, if I don't take this opportunity, if I don't take this chance, what else is there? Because I didn't know what to do about my feelings, and I didn't know anybody else who had them, so I didn't do anything with them. . . . He was a nice guy . . . and the thing that was kind of flattering is that he was crazy about me, and probably about a month before the wedding, I thought to myself, "I don't think I want to do this," and then I thought, "I can't not do this. My mother would kill me. The invitations are sent; the dress was bought. I've got to go through this. Give up my life, but go through with it." (Respondent #19, age fifty-two)

So I got married in May, and Jeff's family came from Washington, and all these friends came from Washington and people from all over. The wedding had a life of its own, and it was a year and a half preparation, which I think is another reason I didn't stop it. Because if . . . my parents would have said to me, throughout the planning, "You can end it now and we won't be upset. You can end it now and it would be better." I would have done it. It was constantly in my mind. You can't go through with the wedding and then planning out—well, what would be the repercussions of that and what would I do with the gifts and how would I face everyone?—maybe it's better to just get married and deal with it later. (Respondent #15, age twenty-eight)

Several women talked abut the anxiety they felt that they might not be asked to marry. The fear of being a single woman, an "old maid"—viewed by society as a less desirable social role—was expressed by respondent #3, age fifty-eight:

> He would be a good father, a good provider, a very sincere, monogamous, honest hard worker; he had all of the Boy Scout traits that I thought at the time you needed to have in a husband. I had never been in love with any man, so this was just fine. I really had to decide whether I ever wanted to get married because I thought, "I really don't want to get married," but as I looked around the school—I'm using a small frame of reference—I saw these "old maid schoolteachers," and I looked and thought, "Hmm, I don't think I want to be that, but I really don't want to be married." I didn't know there were any other choices.

Several respondents described getting married as a form of relief from stress. Respondent #8, age forty-three, grew up in an emotionally and sexually violent home. She describes her plan to marry:

> I don't know; we started dating, and I knew Jim was safe . . . he was such a nice guy. . . . I knew that he'd never verbally abuse me. That was one thing I knew about him, and I knew that he'd never physically abuse me, and that was important to me. I guess I thought it was expected of me to get married, for being with anybody. This is who I should be with. And this person's going to get me the hell out of this town.

Respondent #23, age forty-seven, describes another kind of relief brought by marriage, the relief from the pressure to date men:

> [Were you in love with him?]
>
> I thought I was. I don't know if I was. I think I was sort of in love with him, but without being very emotionally close to him, if that makes any sense. He was a fascinating person too, and we were sexual, and that was interesting to me, and it was fun. . . . It was his idea to get married, and I just couldn't think of any reason not

to. . . . I was trying on experiences like people try on clothes. That was part of it. It was also a big relief to me in some ways to be married because then I didn't have to deal with guys anymore. It sort of took care of the whole thing. . . . I also wasn't very comfortable with the whole idea of dating and going out, and it was real convenient that I had that relationship, and it sort of took care of it.

Following is an excerpt from a memoir written by Colonel Margarethe Cammermeyer, formerly of the Army Nurse Corps, United States Army, who, in 1992, was asked to resign because she acknowledged her lesbianism to her Army superiors. This excerpt is particularly illuminating because Colonel Cammermeyer's achievements and basic personality are at variance with the traditional feminine stereotype, but she states, simply and directly, how she felt commanded by the rigid expectations to which females in the United States are expected to conform, regardless of their ambition, their ability, or their desires:

Harvey was a very personable, easy friend to everyone he met. When we showed up almost nightly at the officer's club, people exclaimed at how great the two of us looked together. The encouragement from all around us was not very subtle. . . . Yet there were times when I felt I couldn't breathe around him. Reconciling his constant presence in my life with my own needs seemed impossible. The only solution I saw was to stop seeing him; then maybe I'd get some breathing space. But that meant a confrontation, which I did not want. Finally, in January he developed a muscle spasm in his back and had to stay in the hospital for several weeks. This gave me an opportunity to escape.

I'm not proud that I told him I wanted to stop seeing him when he was on his back in the hospital. But it seemed my best opportunity to get some distance in order to think things through. I didn't have the courage or didn't feel I had the right to do it until he was in the hospital. Disappointing him because of my needs was very difficult. On his second day there, I came into his room, listened to how he was feeling and . . . then rather suddenly I told him I needed time alone. I told him, "I don't want to see you anymore. I am not in love with you, so why don't we just back away from this." He seemed crushed. He insisted I not do this. I needed time alone, but I compromised when he persisted. I said I didn't want to see him for thirty days and then I left. I got time off from the hospital and went [off] . . . for a few days by myself. It was a great relief to be alone in the mountains, walking, thinking, reading. . . . I wanted to become Chief Nurse of the Army Nurse Corps and a general, and that mattered more to me than becoming a wife.

When I got back to work, it started. Though Harvey honored my thirty-day moratorium on seeing him, I felt he conducted a rigorous campaign to get me to change my mind. I was astounded by his persistence. It seemed to me that he courted me from a distance in ways he never had while we dated. I got calls from his friends who said, "What are you doing to Harvey? He can't work; he can't eat." . . . I'd come home from work and there would be flowers at my door. . . . I'd go to my car in the morning and written in the frost on my windshield would be the words "I love you." I couldn't tell how much of this was because he wanted me, and how much was because he wanted to get his way. . . . His displays of affection were embarrassingly public; I'd been brought up to be a very private person, and I was frustrated by the continuous intrusion and bombardment.

But then, the heat increased. He called and politely, even sweetly, asked me to see him when the thirty days were over. . . . Then, at dinner, he asked me to marry him. I was stunned. I looked at him absolutely dumbfounded. . . . After a minute, I said, "I need to think about it." . . . I struggled to figure out what I was supposed to do or say.

I didn't believe I had any options. If someone had said to me back then that my decisions about marriage should be based on what I needed, I would have replied, "Well, I need to do what I'm supposed to do." My role as a daughter, woman, and nurse was to be there for other people. . . . I was losing control over my own life, and at the same time, agreeing to the most "normal" thing in the world. I felt both those contrasting forces; it was a price a woman paid. Though I was ambivalent about getting married, it meant doing what I was supposed to do and was a cause for happiness. That view would be confirmed by everyone around me in the following days. (Cammermeyer with Fisher, 1994, pp. 78-83)

It is clear that powerful social forces create a script, a plan for women's lives so pervasive that their own internal messages can be overwhelmed. Until very recently, a woman who didn't marry was risking a very negative assessment. Phyllis Chesler has said, "What we consider 'madness,' whether it appears in women or in men, is either the acting out of the devalued female role model or the total or partial rejection of one's sex role stereotype" (Chesler, 1972, cited in Ussher, 1992, p. 169). Like the default program on a computer, the expectation of marriage pervades the interviews for this research. Even now, are there really increased socially acceptable life outcomes, or does this default option need to be consciously and purposefully changed? As Ruth Baetz asserts, "We are talking simultaneously about two things—personal life decisions and culturally constructed minefields" (Baetz, 1984, p. 45).

To have the freedom to find their lesbian/bisexual identities, the women in this study needed to know that marriage is a tradition, a ritual, a religious ceremony, and a legal contract but that it is not a requirement for adulthood. Marriage is presented in our society as one life choice, necessary or inevitable and, except for those who simply cannot or who are very brave, not optional.

Chapter 3

How Do Women Establish Personal Identity and Gender Orientation in a Heterosexist Society?

THE FORMATION OF WOMEN'S IDENTITY

The third major theme appearing in the interviews was the struggle women had with the development of a clear sense of themselves and with acknowledgement of their *own* identifications, attributes, and desires. These women found that their personal assessments and judgments were often not accepted or taken seriously by parents, husbands, and friends. Their attempts as children, and as adults too, to experiment with a behavior or to discuss an attitude, feeling, or value at variance with those commonly expressed in their circles were met with resistance or were patronized. Often their experiences were not considered valid. Even for those with supportive parents, setting their own paths to a sense of personal continuity of self over time, to an identity they could embrace, was, at best, extremely challenging and, at worst, shame producing. The message they received was don't be who you are.

When the sexual aspect was added, the women found the going even more difficult. Where one's thoughts and ideas, feelings and impulses are not taken seriously, discussion and exploration of self and/or of sexuality are nearly impossible. In this society, in which heterosexual gender orientation is presented as the only acceptable outcome, many women (and men as well) struggle to fit in, hiding or ignoring their genuine impulses.

Ideally, a woman's sexual or gender identity (I feel like a woman) and her gender orientation (the gender to which I feel sexually attracted) informs the development of her personal identity as a woman. Her personal identity informs the development of her gender identity and orientation. Without an authentic interaction between these factors, a woman has the sense of something being "not quite right." She is likely to feel a sense of incoherence in her presentation of self and her subjective awareness. Many respondents in my research reported the unrest that this internal confusion creates.

Respondent #23, age forty-seven, gives a compelling description of that sense of incoherence:

> I was very strongly convinced that I wasn't OK—that there was something inherently wrong with me. I can remember that same guy I was telling you about . . . telling me that I just didn't see myself right and I think that was true. That it was sort of like being steeped in original sin or something like that. This was something that couldn't be fixed. And I just didn't want to deal with it at all. . . . I think it came from my feelings about my sexuality. I think that I . . . when I sort of came out to myself, decided that this was something I was going to have to deal with and that was going to be a part of my life, if I was to live, this was going to be who I was. It was almost like if you had two different images and it came into one image, like focusing, and that's why when you asked that question earlier about—was this something that I didn't recognize or that I knew and didn't know—it was like a ghost self all those years, and I would feed that ghost self, just enough to keep her alive. Music was very important to me. Women's music was very important to me. I went out of my way to go to women's concerts and so on. Usually alone. Through all of those years. It was sort of like, trapped, that I could feed this little self on the side. But still not really acknowledging the presence in me.

According to Erik Erikson, the foundations for what is referred to as "identity" begin at infancy. The basic task of infancy is learning to trust or mistrust that the universe is a place where one is able to feel safe and will get needs met. Between a basic sense of trust and the establishment of identity, the child passes through stages of development in which the ego strengths of will, purpose, and competence emerge out of the struggles of autonomy versus shame and doubt, initiative versus guilt, and industry versus inferiority (Erikson, 1968). According to Erikson, these stages progress in an order that is linked to social expectations and bodily maturation. The psychosocial crisis, or central issue of each stage, rests upon, and may modify the outcome of, all preceding stages, as well as the stages to come.

A significant task (and stage) of adolescence and young adulthood for many people is finding a person with whom one bonds in emotional and sexual partnership, that is, the task of intimacy versus isolation. Erikson (1968) places the task of intimacy versus isolation after that of identity, indicating that the growing knowledge of a coherent sense of self is a prerequisite to true intimacy in emotional and sexual partnership. According to Gramick (1984), "A strong sense of sexual identity, no matter how long it may take to achieve, is a prerequisite for the unfolding of psychosocial intimacy" (p. 33). Women who marry men and later find they want to bond emotionally and sexually with women may realize they have not felt that combination of authenticity, coherency, and self-knowledge that allows genuine intimacy with another person. The respondents in this study experienced many limitations on their identity formation processes that caused them to overlook or inadvertently ignore important information from inside and outside themselves. These women therefore tended to follow life patterns that proved inadequate or inappropriate as they grew and changed as adults.

Erik Erikson's (1968) work on identity formation provided a significant piece of psychology's view of women in the mid-twentieth century. Erikson believed interpersonal issues formed the core of women's identity, that is, interpersonal relationships with a husband and with children. A woman's identity was expected to be left partially open and flexible at adolescence, to accommodate the man she would marry and the children she would nurture. A girl's first temporary resolution of identity in adolescence, according to Erikson, consisted of a sense of her own attractiveness, an image of the mate she would seek, and a decision about the use she would make (or not make) of her body and its reproductive capacity. Her identity was thus to be completed in marriage and motherhood (Erikson, 1968). A woman who did not feel complete in marriage went against the tide of popular wisdom and was often censured for that resistance. This heterocentrist theory did not originate with Erikson, but the dominance and popularity of his theories reinforced the narrow lens of possibility through which women and women's possible roles were seen.

When she told her husband of her plans to separate from him, respondent #13, age fifty-three, was reminded of her role, how her husband perceived that role, and the challenge she faced if she attempted the determination of her own destiny:

> . . . that night I went home and asked Larry for a separation . . . his response that night was to hold me. But the next morning, it was "get out of here" . . . and so I just took my things . . . and stayed at that motel . . .

> [Was it a given that you would be the one to go?]

> I felt too bad. I felt too much guilt . . . and he was, thank God, confiding in George, his best friend. And George was also a good friend of mine . . . and finally George called us and said, "You have got to talk to each other. . . . I'll be there as a mediator if you want me to be . . ." but there was a session before that where Larry and I met, and I allowed him to treat me like a father with his child . . .

> [Because you were being a naughty girl?]

> That's exactly right . . . and then he asked Marion to take care of me. You know he wanted to make sure I would be OK . . . so not only was I a bad girl, but I couldn't take care of myself . . .

Erikson (1968) decided that women became complete through motherhood, and although that edict does not hold for all women, it is certainly true that many women enjoy mothering. However, motherhood has been idealized in this culture, and women have often been pressured to choose between having children and having a personal life. Women who may enjoy motherhood but who, nevertheless, choose to pursue work or education in addition to their mothering (i.e., women who choose to be full persons) have often lacked family support and felt family resistance to their activities and ideas. Respondent #1, age thirty-six, describes the feeling of limited options—almost an inevitability—she had when she ventured to imagine her own future:

> So my daughter was born when I was twenty and I was an at-home mom; I didn't work. When she was about four and the kids were getting ready to go to school, I said, "OK, now what am I going to do with my life?" Kind of a transitional thing. I decided to have another baby. So we had two more, actually, two more boys, so I have the four children, the two older and the two younger, so there are two sets and I was an at-home mom the whole time. . . . When the kids got older, and I'm looking at my life, like, "Well, I'm not going to be an at-home mom forever. I want to do something," and I chose to go to massage school. . . . I decided to enroll and go to school there. I got a lot of flak from my family, not necessarily the children, but my husband, my parents, his family. It was like, "Well, what do you want to do that for?" And my husband's statement was "Well, I really wanted to start investing in some stocks and so I think that's what is more important to do with the money than to send you to school."

The struggle to establish her own path begins for a woman in adolescence. It certainly makes logical sense that the adolescent life stage can provide young people with the optimal situation for defining a sense of identity, providing that all the possible models and outcomes from which to choose are readily available to the adolescent and that all those models are socially acceptable. Not yet firmly tied down by adult commitments, the adolescent may sample a variety of possible occupations, beliefs, and attitudes, eventually adopting a more or less permanent sense of who he or she is. However, even at the close of the twentieth century, we find that the range of socially sanctioned outcomes for the female is limited. If a woman's identity develops in line with the expectations of her family and social circle, she can feel affirmed by others, comforted by her "fitting in." However, if women are not free to consider fully what their intuition, their bodies, their motivation, and their intelligence might be telling them, their choice may be that to fit in, they must feel incoherency, emptiness, a sense of things "not being right." Women with same-gender impulses have experienced an additional level of limitation and, therefore, an additional layer of inauthenticity.

Because of the paucity of sex information, scarcity of role models, the pressure to marry, as well as a lack of permission to exercise their individuality, many women in this study reported that their sense of themselves felt somehow "off," until they moved into a life in which they saw women as potential partners. At that point, the pieces began to fit.

It is important to note that despite the pressure of popular wisdom and expectations, there have always been female adolescents for whom marriage and/or motherhood never felt right. In addition, there have always been women who experienced a pull to their same gender with such a power that it could not be denied, despite the societal pressure against it. The women in this study, formerly married lesbians or bisexuals, do not necessarily fit into these categories. For these women, relationships with the opposite sex and marriage to a man have either felt right at the time they were entered into—they believed that there were no other options—or experienced as an inevitability.

We have already discussed the pressure American women feel to marry a man. Marriage is a social ritual and religious tradition, as well as a legal contract, but it is just one way society can choose to organize relationships and raise children. Whitehead has pointed out that the social gender dichotomy—male and female—is present in all known societies in the sense that anatomic sexual differences observable at birth are used to start tracking the newborn into one or the other of two social role complexes—male or female (Whitehead, 1981). The social meaning given to the physical differences between the sexes is constructed and designed by the society in which the two role complexes are found. Anthropologists such as Whitehead have been instrumental in bringing the concept of social constructions out into the open. Anthropologists originally identified the differences in social meaning given to marriage, sex roles, and other constructs in various cultures:

> There are apparently two biological classes, male and female, and two social classes, men and women, and the ideas which

make social relationships between the sexes appear "reasonable and appropriate" are actually socially constructed. What are called "natural processes" are actually social processes which have evolved to shape and determine sexual identity, sex roles and even eroticism itself. (1981, p. 83)

What does it mean to say, as Whitehead does, that sex roles are "socially constructed?" We are shaped as sexual beings, shaped in our identities, by our perceptions. The shape of our perceptions is not unlimited. That is, most of our perceptions come from a common world of social practices and institutions so embedded in our shared reality of power, language, and identity that they are invisible to us. These shared perceptions, that is, these perceptions about which many people agree, are social constructions. For example, marriage is a social construction, and much of how motherhood is perceived is socially constructed. Social constructions may seem to be reality, but what they truly are is a shared way of seeing something that some people have agreed upon. The effect of naming social constructions is to make the invisible visible. People who are not aware that they are determined by the specific cultural meanings, the social constructions, of their culture will not be free to be fully who they are. They will not feel free to explore the many ways one can live and experience life.

Beyond the social sense that marriage between a man and woman is a given, a few women in the study identified an additional layer of social constructions that may limit perceptions and behavior. The "you can only be gay or straight" dichotomy has been as limiting for some women as the man and woman partnership dichotomy has been for others. Respondent #2, age twenty-nine, had been aware that she felt an emotional and sexual pull to both sexes, but she found it difficult to sort out her feelings because there was no place to talk about them:

> [Until the last couple of years, you were saying, you primarily identified as lesbian. When did you realize, "Hey, bisexuality is more the way I see myself"?]
>
> The social network I had was very antibisexual, very disbelieving that it was a real state of mind or a real identity, so

there was a lot of pressure there to just not talk about it. And
Mary was particularly threatened by that identity and just
didn't want to hear that, although I was constantly reassuring
her that it didn't mean I couldn't be monogamous or that I was
even interested in anybody else . . . [as time went on] . . . I was
in a lesbian relationship, but identified as bisexual, and learning that those were two different things. . . . I was learning it
was more than sexual acts that make you who you are. But it
was taking me a long time to understand how that fit with
myself and my own beliefs and my work and my own relationships because I wasn't having a lot of opportunity to discuss it
. . . because my friends didn't want to talk about it. They didn't
want to go there.

As has been noted previously, this writing is occurring at a time
when questions regarding the meaning of gender are being hotly
discussed. One salient aspect of gender, of course, is gender orientation. Maggiore has wondered if homosexual identity is an essential
identity or a socially constructed one. That is, has there always been
a lesbian identity, or is it a phenomenon of the late nineteenth and
twentieth centuries (Maggiore, 1992)?

It is important to note here that social constructions work on the
consciousness on levels other than the cognitive. Therefore, social
constructions can limit a woman's knowledge of herself, her needs,
and her desires without her awareness. For example, "If I'm taking an
antidepressant, I must be crazy." This makes no sense, and it isn't true,
but many may tend to believe it. Another example, "I'm into nice
clothes and wearing makeup so I can't be lesbian," or "I also have
feelings about men so I can't be lesbian." These social constructions do
not bear up factually or logically under scrutiny. That is what makes
them social constructions. Social constructions are powerful because
they're pervasive and, often, unquestioned.

A consideration of the ways in which social constructions have
limited women's options and self-awareness must return to Erikson
(1968), who was an early proponent of the identity concept. Paradoxically, Erikson conceptualized women's identity as *her construction* of the experience of womanhood, of living in a woman's body,
and of living with the gender-based role prescriptions and proscrip-

tions of her culture. He failed to recognize and take into account the social constructions concerning women's roles. However, Erikson's conceptualization could be interpreted as sympathetic to women's struggles to define and control their reproductive power within a patriarchal culture. According to Patterson, Sochting, and Marcia (1989), Erikson appears prescient in his concern that feminists should not ignore women's reproductive power because that could further devalue women, as well as devalue the care and nurturance women usually provide.

Nineteen respondents in this research had children; most had two, one had three, and one had four. The ages of the five who had no children were twenty-eight, thirty, thirty-two, thirty-nine, and fifty-three. Nearly all the respondents made incidental positive references to their children during the interviews. A few referred to their children's role in their lives or in their identity process. However, we did not specifically discuss the role that motherhood had played in their identity process toward same-gender relationships. I leave that research for others to pursue. Although I will not go deeper into this issue, note that in Mardy Ireland's book *Reconceiving Women: Separating Motherhood from Female Identity* (1993), she posits that "[t]here is no normative female identity for the woman who is not a mother" (p. 104).

Many women in this research group experienced joy in their childbearing and child rearing and identified strongly with their roles as mothers. The power of the mother role and the idealization associated with it is suggested by respondent #3, age fifty-eight:

> And you didn't know how you were going to feel for those children until you had them. Everybody in the world that you knew that had kids could tell you, "This is going to be the most momentous occasion of your life. This is going to be a love that you cannot find anywhere to the depth of that love." And you think you understand. But you have no clue. It's like, have you ever known someone that you just willingly—and I get teary because it is such a cool, neat thing—willingly and without second thought put yourself in front of a truck for that person? This is the way we feel about our kids. Even when they disappoint us, we still feel that way.

Women who have believed they needed to follow carefully the American social constructions of motherhood may have sacrificed the pursuit of their own goals for the sake of their children. Indeed, given the strength of idealized social constructions associated with motherhood, how could they have not, at least, modified them? Although the respondents in this research didn't name it as an issue, given the extent of women's responsibility for child care in this society, the energy devoted to children could indeed have delayed and/or created some barriers to women's self-discovery.

Respondent #1, age thirty-six, describes the tension between her mother self and her individual self:

> So that was how I went to work, just part-time, a little bit here and there, and the kids kind of got plugged into other programs, and I didn't make all the conferences, and I didn't make all the programs, and I was kind of sad, but at the same time, it was kind of freeing to say my kids are involved in this, and my thought process around it was "I'm not always going to be there, but my support can be there." I can send them with my love and my concern and my care and not feel like a bad mom because I can't be there for every concert or play or whatever it is I had to miss because now I'm at work. . . . I had a lot of thinking to do around that because "I'm a home mom and I'm going to support my kids through everything; I'm going to be there for them always." But there are different ways to be there for your children, and one way to be there is not to be there and let them experience something with your support, but not your presence. And it was a big learning lesson for me too . . .

Despite the variety of identity-shaping factors that clearly apply only to females, no identity development theory was devised specifically for women until Ruthellen Josselson's appeared in 1990. Prior to the 1990s, Carol Gilligan (1982), Jean Baker Miller (1976), and others were writing about differences in a woman's development, but most developmental theorists tended not to separate men and women and wrote about *adult* development of identity. Building on the basic identity formation theory of Erikson (1950), James Marcia (1966, 1980) developed the identity status approach to studying the process of identity formation. His theory has become the dominant paradigm for research in identity formation. Marcia describes four points that are reached as a person explores attributes, desires, and commitment to various identifications. Marcia calls these points identity statuses. These statuses are both outcomes of the process of identity formation and structural properties of the personality. Each portrays a dominant mode of experiencing the world and represents the point that an individual has reached in her or his life. Each should thus affect and shape future identity formation and the passage through subsequent life stages. Developed through studies of white men, this research holds true for women in a limited way only. The following is a description of the four statuses developed by Marcia:

> *Identity diffusion* is the least developmentally advanced status. In *diffusion*, commitment to an internally consistent set of values and goals is absent, and there is little exploration. People in identity diffusion tend to present as having a carefree lifestyle and/or as being empty and dissatisfied, but they may actually be following the path of least resistance and/or avoiding the identity formation task.

> *Identity foreclosure* represents a high level of commitment to a set of values and goals following little or no exploration. For some, identity foreclosure is a state of lesser development, a developmental starting point from which a period of exploration may ensue. Marcia considered this a less developed state than that of *moratorium* or *identity achievement*. Those following the foreclosure pattern adopt a single set of values and goals, usually those of their parents, without considering carefully whether those values and goals are their own.

> *Moratorium* status refers to the process of forging an identity—occupational, interpersonal, and ideological commitments—from the myriad possibilities available. The person in moratorium is intensely preoccupied with exploring options and working toward commitment, although the identity is not yet fully formed. Some people remain in moratorium over many years. Some go on to identity achievement.

Identity achievement represents an autonomous resolution of identity, incorporating a set of commitments adopted during a period of exploration. Marcia says the exploration of the moratorium period, which generally precedes identity achievement, distinguishes the flexible strength of identity achievement from the rigid strength of identity foreclosure. (Patterson, Sochting, and Marcia, 1989)

Patterson and colleagues also note that Marcia (1966) suggested the foreclosure status was "adaptive" for women because girls and women were not supported in the process of exploration necessary to form self-chosen commitments (Patterson, Sochting, and Marcia, 1989). Rather than seeing this as a problem that society creates for women, Marcia's theory followed the pattern of most scientific psychological research. Researchers have seen the experience of women as woman's natural path, and they have attempted to fit what they saw into research frameworks developed with males, thus creating the impression that woman's identity development was somehow inadequate. In the same way, Marcia's theory acknowledges that women are not supported in following their own path, but the explanation given is that this is a limitation to which women must adapt. Finally, sliding over the contradiction, the theory describes women's tendency to be less risk taking and to live their lives as their parents did.

Ruthellen Josselson (1987, 1996) applied Marcia's identity status model to women's identity development and found that women differed consistently from men. Faced with the choice often experienced by researchers studying females, since she was the first to do identity research with females, she could choose to develop a new instrument or she could utilize something already available. She chose to use Marcia's identity status interview as she interviewed women for her study because she wanted a basis for comparison with previous research. Josselson's initial study was with college-age women. She found that women fit the various identity statuses, but the reasons they fit there and the negative implications drawn about women in this process were inaccurate. She found that women's identity development is different from men's.

Hopefully, the assumption that adult development is largely similar for men and women is changing and clarifying. However, it is not encouraging that a major book on adult development published in 1990, which is described as "on the cutting edge of innovative research and novel understanding" (book jacket note) does not specifically separate adult development of women from that of men (Nemiroff and Colarusso, 1990). Thus, the mythical assumption is perpetuated that all healthy adults are free to explore intensely all options, or that if they are women, their charge is to accept a less complex and rewarding level of development because that's what they will have.

The mother of respondent #10, age fifty-one, communicated her awareness to her daughter that limited avenues were open to her and to women in general:

> . . . for my mother and for that generation, and particularly given her background, you got where you wanted to go by finding a man who would take you there. And when I got a degree, she said she hoped I would get certification to teach because if, God forbid, someday [my] husband should die—and it never occurred to me that I would work my entire life or that was an option besides marriage. And I married somebody who seemed to be the right socioeconomic class and [religion]. . . . I didn't always like him very well but . . .

The psychoanalytic perspective of "maturity equals autonomy" was the foundation for previous identity theorizing, including Marcia's. This means that all identity research previous to that of Ruthellen Josselson was based on the assumption that a person has reached maturity only to the degree that he or she has attained autonomy and independence from others. The cruel irony is that women are not socially granted the autonomy and independence that allows them to explore all the interpersonal, occupational, and ideological options, then they are called less mature for having failed to explore those options. Carol Gilligan has done groundbreaking research exploring women's development, as it naturally evolves and as it is socially shaped within a crucible of concern for others and their opinions, especially men's (Gilligan, 1982; Brown and Gilligan, 1992). Josselson describes the attempt to study separation-individuation in women as a "disorienting task because women tend to grow within rather than outside of relationships" (Josselson, 1987, p. 189).

Josselson describes women's lives as based developmentally on a balance between the self and the self in relation to others. Women tend to think of their futures in terms of who will be in their lives and how. As Josselson notes, autonomy and connectedness for women are kept in balance, and the fundamental difficulty with a clear explanation for this balance is that language has not yet evolved to define the nuances of intimacy and mutuality. We have tended to look at development in agentic terms; that is, what will I become? Only recently has language and theory begun to be developed that explains the achievement of female identity and its basis in the value of the questions "What will I be, and what will I be for others, and how will they connect to me (Josselson, 1987)?

This research on women's overall development is particularly important for our purposes. If Josselson, Gilligan, and others are correct, if women normally develop in connection with who they are in relationship to others, then the "others"—the "models," or people in their lives, especially the socially sanctioned models—who are present at each stage will have a major impact on the maturity of the developmental commitment, as well as on the maturity of the relationship and intimacy commitments a woman is able to make at each stage. (See Chapter 5 for a discussion of lesbian/bisexual role models.)

Before describing the identity statuses as Josselson developed them for women, an aside about self-in-relation theory is important here. The self-in-relation aspect of women's development should not be idealized. It would appear that women have developed this component not necessarily because they are more generally kind and generous than males but because they have been the primary caretakers of children. Caring for children and parents and, by extension, developing the natural capacity to respond to others may have become hardwired out of survival necessity, or, perhaps, the training girls receive as caretakers has become a social construction. In any case, once again, the questions are raised: Does child care and child rearing delay the process of self-awareness and self-discovery for these women? How does a woman's concern for the welfare of others, the opinions of others, shape the formation of her commitments?

A few of the study participants expressed reservations concerning their parenting. For example, respondent #10, age fifty-two, is able to describe her parenting without sentimentality:

> I don't even know if—I didn't really even choose to have children. I would never have chosen . . . I think pregnancy prepares you to lose control over your life. You lose control of your body; you have no say over that development or about childbirth or about a baby needing you for the rest of your life, and I think I went on automatic pilot from the time I got pregnant, for a lot of years, while the kids were little. I don't remember joy in my life. If I have any regrets . . . I think I was a good mother, again in very technical ways. But if I had to do it over now, I would do it with a whole lot more joy. It was a "should."

Examining Josselson (1987, 1996) and the identity status theory, a number of questions find answers. (It should be noted that Josselson's first research [1987] used the names for identity statuses assigned by Marcia. By 1996, Josselson had changed the names, as she said, "to make them more descriptive and less evaluative" [1996, p. 275].) Josselson's research applied the identity statuses to women and found that women seemed to fit into the same criteria as men. However, the reasons they arrived at or moved through their identity statuses were different from men's.

Josselson (1987) found that *foreclosures* (in 1996, she called them "guardians"), as young girls, had harmonious, gratifying relationships with their families. They were "good girls," doing what was right. For them, the adolescent task of self-definition jeopardized that harmonious inner balance between connection and autonomy, so they sought to avoid the psychological tasks of adolescence. They liked the old balance, and they experienced no push to individuate. However, notes Josselson, her research showed that many *Foreclosures* experience a surprising level of fulfillment because rewards are found in carrying on the family rules and traditions.

It should be noted that many of the respondents in my research described themselves as "good girls"; that is, during their childhood, teenage years, and for some, well into adulthood, they did what their family expected, often just what their family had done. Only five respondents made early, clear efforts to be different in choices and goals from their families. Finding the reasons for these women's, for any women's, tendency to acquiesce to these and other external influences is a major focus of this research.

Those who have reached the status of *identity achievement* (later, "path makers") value competence more for its own sake than for its role in pleasing others. They do experience some guilt at their breaking away from their prevailing family model (if it is different from their own), but they also tend to have more capacity to tolerate anxiety and guilt. When they do not please others or do not meet their own inner standards, they experience more stress and pain, but because they tend to persist in following their own road, they become more flexible than *foreclosures* tend to be and seem better able to detach from and process that pain.

For example, respondent #9, age fifty-seven, describes the paradoxical messages she got from her family about following her own path:

My mother always said, from the time I was a little girl, "Hitch your wagon to a star," so she wanted me to have big ambitions, do great things, make her proud, make myself proud. Dad, too, but he wasn't so verbal. But they also let me know they were upset when I changed careers, when I sought more education, when I wanted more from life than they seemed to want. The way they showed me they were upset was that they didn't ask about it, any of it. After awhile, a new job, my raise, the trips I took, the people I met became this big invisible blob that was always there, but they seemed to pretend it wasn't. . . . I don't know. . . . Were they jealous? or threatened? or worried about me? I don't know, but it really hurt me, and we never talked about it. I wanted to; I tried to. But they just wouldn't talk about it. About my kids, oh yes. About our house, yup. But I just learned that I wouldn't get support from them around my work life so I found it else-where.

Moratoriums (later called "searchers"), among women, attempt to break out of their family template completely. The previous quote may be a good example of how a mature woman handles this issue. But the younger *moratorium* cannot quite bring herself to give up the experience of being "good," and so she tends to swing back and forth during late adolescence. *Moratoriums* try to hang on to what Josselson (1987) interprets as the comfort that comes from doing what they have been taught is "right." The extremes of identity confusion among the young *moratoriums* indicate the intensity of the internal separation-individuation struggle, although they will deny their experience of it. Josselson notes that external circum-stances play a strong role in the outcomes for these women.

Swinging back and forth between doing what one wants to do and doing what one is expected to do is described by respondent #15, age twenty-eight:

> We got married in May of '93, and I had started graduate school in September of '92. We moved in together in the middle of the graduate school year, and I see a big turning point for me was starting graduate school . . . it's kind of a sheltered life and Jeff worked on Sunday . . . and I was living with my parents, and so it was kind of out there in [the sub-urbs] and kind of outside anything going on, which was not me, because all of my life I had been active in the world and in college. I was involved with everything and a million different people. And friends from college started saying to me, from undergrad school, during the time I was engaged to Jeff, and then through part of my marriage, "What's wrong with you? Where are you? You're not the person I know. You're walking outside, Suzanne, but your soul's gone."

Several respondents established a career or personal path that differed from their parents, but, as Josselson predicts, the price they paid was high. One respondent needed to break ties with her family:

> I met my husband at college. Became a nurse. The day after I graduated as a nurse, we went around the country. My husband

and I did a bicycle trip. . . . We kind of did the clean cut from my parents, which was good. . . . Actually I'm from a very tight-knit German family. If you do anything to break the family rule by . . . if you break the silence [and reveal secrets] which I did. . . . You know you're supposed to do everything in family to protect the family. Also, I have more education than in my family so that's a step out too and it's significant that I have moved on. . . . It's just the way it is. You know, you just don't . . . . It's just rules that I know. Just family rules. You don't break the silence, but I did. (Respondent #7, age thirty-two)

Those women who stay at the *diffusions* identity status (later called "drifters") seem to lack the building blocks that the other statuses are trying to rearrange. They are not necessarily avoiding this developmental task. They are searching for parts of the self that they failed to develop at earlier times in their lives because of emotional damage and lack of support (Josselson, 1987, 1996).

For example, respondent #14, age forty-eight, survived sexual abuse by her father. For many years, she fit the diffusion identity status. She describes part of the long path she followed to heal and to find her self again:

[You were a feminist first, then you became a lesbian feminist, then identified as a lesbian. What do you consider the identification piece if you had not been involved yet with a woman?]

For me, it was switching over. It was recognizing what I'd been taught and started to challenge. Things like patriarchal values and religious systems and institutions, starting to. . . . I just couldn't absorb enough feminist, lesbian feminist literature because it felt so true, and it helped put names or words into what I already felt or believed, and I became what I . . . the switch was when I . . . I really felt woman centered instead of male centered. And the more woman centered I became, that became part of what I now consider lesbian identity.

[So it's a female identity rather than an attraction-to-female identity.]

Yeah.

[Are you saying, do you think, that your decision or your process was partly political?]

Partly, in the beginning. Now that I've lived a lesbian life for this many years, it would be more complicated than that because it's . . . it's emotional, it's, you know, all kinds of things. But I think my initial drawing in was political and that helped me to . . . it was easier for me to justify being political . . . than being sexual.

In addition to the specific ways women approach autonomy and independence, it is important to note that there is real contradiction in the socialization of females. Girls receive ambivalent messages in early childhood that create dependence but also encourage autonomy at the same time. When girls reach adolescence, they are expected to be "feminine," to plan to be wives and mothers, and to abandon the behavioral patterns of independence that had been encouraged at an earlier age (Brown and Gilligan, 1992). In the relational sense (the relational sense is what Josselson calls the "central organizing force" in women's development), this places women in a double bind (Josselson, 1987). Contentment and relational harmony tend to remain the uppermost values for women, but it may prove difficult for them to remain in harmony with others and also foster their independent actions. The feminist movement has created new role models for independent action among women, which may help as time goes on. However, the respondents in this research—including the youngest ones—tended to talk about the limits on self-assertion set during their development.

Respondent #6, age thirty-five, describes a scenario that was repeated by many respondents, as they discussed their attempts to establish their own unique paths and the responses they got from significant others:

[I was] excited about going back to school and . . . I also enjoy that part of myself, and it doesn't make me less of a person to want these other things, that I am still a mom and I am a good mom.

[That you could do both?]

Right.

[You didn't feel that understanding from Barry?]

No. I started taking one class at a community college. He didn't say much about that. Then the next quarter, I told him I wanted to take two classes. He said, "Isn't that a bit much?" That was pretty clear to me at the time. That really bothered me. It bothered me because he wasn't the supportive person I thought he was—only when I fell within a certain ground of what he wanted me to be.

It is clear that women and girls are shaped and reinforced for fitting the mold and socially punished if they don't (Gilligan, 1986). However, despite the high value placed on relationship and equanimity, adolescent girls are not always totally agreeable. Girls can have rebellious periods as well, but they may tend to work at learning ways to manage differences in such a way that everybody's interest is represented and relationships are maintained. This may include subterfuge. Whereas boys seem to overemphasize separation and rebellion, the risk for girls may lie in a tendency to submerge differences—and hence submerge authentic experience—to avoid conflict and to preserve harmony in the relationship (Gilligan, 1982). In addition, the young girl is often aware of her own sense of things, for example, fair rules and desirable friends, which may well run counter to what she is told by those in authority. At adolescence, girls become subjected to a kind of "voice and ear training," designed to make it clear what voices girls should use and what girls can ask without being called stupid or rude (Gilligan, 1987).

An example of the "voice and ear training" that teaches women to submerge their differences is articulated by respondent #16, age fifty-one. As she recalls a turning point in her marriage, she describes the slow-growing awareness that she was submerging differences between herself and her husband so that the household would continue to run smoothly:

. . . I had gotten a full-time job directing volunteer services down at ———— Hospital in [large city], and I was gaining more confidence. I was also earning my own income; I was meeting a lot of people, and I was feeling very valued, something I didn't feel much in the marriage. . . . I started about 1982 feeling very restless, uncomfortable. Something is wrong with me—I should be happy—and I don't know what it is. Started seeing a counselor to try to figure out what was wrong with me, of course. Joe was very unhappy, very threatened.

[You mean he was threatened by the fact that you weren't happy?]

Yes. I wanted to buy a car, on my own. I changed my hairstyle and I got rid of my glasses and went to contacts, and he didn't like those types of changes. They were very threatening to him.

[So the style in your marriage was that for you to do something, you asked him if it was OK?]

Yes. And get his permission to do it.

[Did he check things out with you before he did them?]

No. Let's put it this way. I would be in a meeting in a boardroom, talking with people who are listening to me as well as I was listening to them. I was making decisions. I had some influence; people were listening. I'd come home, and it would be the little wife role again, where dinner was supposed to be on the table and he made all the decisions, and I think some of that was starting to not sit well with me. I was beginning to think, "Wait a minute. I can contribute more here."

Other theorists have explored how girls and women develop intellectually, that is, how they learn and how they feel about themselves as knowers. Belenky and colleagues (1986) delineated the special quality of women's ways of knowing that affirms the self-in-relation ideology. They showed that knowing for women involves a "connected knowing," an "orientation toward relationship," rather than separate knowing that emphasizes objectivity. Connected knowing depends on taking an empathic attitude toward that which is being understood; girls are typically more highly developed in empathic skills than boys of the same age, particularly skills involving emotional responsiveness and engagement rather than detached, objective knowing. Cognitive skills for females, then, may not undergo the same shift in level of abstraction during adolescence as they do for boys. Rather, girls may experience a more continuous line of development, with an increase in well-developed empathic attunement. During adolescence, this divergence in ways of knowing may become more apparent "because educational systems reward adversarial, objective, abstract, dispassionate approaches to problem solving" (Notman et al., 1990, p. 567). To consider this, think about how science and math are highly valued, whereas literature, art, and music tend to be valued less. Girls can and do learn the adversarial, dispassionate approaches, but, as Notman and colleagues note, "they may then feel inauthentic and mechanical in their academic work and vulnerable to self-doubt and a sense of alienation from their own accomplishments" (Notman et al., 1990, p. 567).

Carol Gilligan has done extensive research on girls in the United States, identifying a major reduction in confidence and lower level of self-assertion in girls as they grow from ages eleven to sixteen. She concluded that adolescence poses a "crisis of connection for girls coming of age in Western culture" (1989, p. 9). "Sacrificing the self for others, although endorsed by the ideals of 'feminine goodness' in our culture, undermines authentic connection by excluding the self" (Gilligan, 1987, p. 82). Excluding the self may engender suffering and confusion. Girls attempt to solve these attachment problems by finding creative ways to stay connected to others and also include themselves and their needs in their relationship equations. Girls' creativity constitutes an important "resistance" to the prevailing societal norms of both femininity and detachment.

The change in level of confidence and self-assertion and the self-sacrifice to which Gilligan refers during ages eleven to sixteen is described by respondent #12, age fifty-three. I have included an additional set of quotes describing some of what was happening in her home around that same time:

In grade school, I was just a shining student, but it was easy. I was, in fact, a leader, got along well, a negotiator. I hit seventh grade, and the bottom sort of fell out. I hated it. At the same time, my face broke out, I was skinny, and everything changed, sort of. I mean I was bored stiff with school. And I couldn't make myself study. I just didn't care . . .

. . . from junior high, seventh grade, age twelve or thirteen, until probably just a few months before she died . . . she [mother] was a very angry person. Angry toward me. I couldn't make this woman satisfied or happy or feel fulfilled, whatever she wanted. . . . [I think] she sort of wishes that I had been, looked different, probably had more boyfriends. I mean, I think what she really wanted me to do was live her life. And I couldn't do that . . . it hurt a lot. The anger hurt. . . . I walked on eggshells to keep this woman from being angry at me. I didn't like anger. I didn't like loud voices. I was uncomfortable with it. . . . I think what I did with it was—it set me up to fear anger forever after. So I was a good girl everywhere.

The central importance of mothers in the process of identity formation was confirmed repeatedly by the women in this research. They consistently made reference to relationships with their mothers, sometimes with frustration, at times with affection. With relation to the autonomy versus dependence issue, Josselson points out a further misunderstanding about women that has been espoused by traditional psychodynamic theorists. Psychological theory that bases itself on the importance of a woman's development of autonomy, as evidenced by separation from mother, is simply inaccurate (Josselson, 1996). Any sound theory of the separation-individuation process that underlies identity formation in women must appreciate that, for good or ill, women never fully separate from their mothers. The relationship with their mothers is crucially important to women, at least through their early adulthood. Whether women feel close to their mothers or not, mothers' internal influence (e.g., as first role model) and external influence remain powerful. A woman may appear to reject her mother and/or rebel completely against her mother's ideology, but, writes Josselson (1996), a woman's relationship to her mother "continues as a central axis of identity definition" (p. 226). "Whatever a woman is, in a deep psychological stratum of her being, [she] either pays homage to or disavows her mother (p. 229).

Women may find it difficult to encourage their daughters to vary from "mother's way of being" in the world, despite the fact that mothers are women who have been subjected to the same social limits as their daughters. Here is an example of a woman/mother who, despite her own personal experiences of limitation, seems to enforce the social limits on her daughter. Respondent #1, age thirty-six, discusses what evolved with her mother as she attempted to define her identity as a woman:

> Yeah, . . . I started looking at myself, and that's when I really first started turning the wheels about what am I all about. What do I see as making myself happy in my life? How would I picture the perfect life? . . . It was like, all of a sudden, instead of saying this is how a perfect life is because this is how you're told a perfect life is, I gave myself some freedom to go—How would I live my life if I got to just choose how I wanted to do it? And started fantasizing . . . and following that path in my mind and concerning where it would lead me to and how that felt and trying it on and writing about it. . . . I always thought it was, "This is how you're supposed to" and never gave myself the opportunity to go, "Well, how do you want to?" . . . and that just started opening more and more doors for me; my voice became stronger, I finished school, and I decided to go to work. . . . My mom's comment to that was, "Who is going to take care of the kids?" And I thought, "This is such a ridiculous statement from my mother" because when I was a child, my mother worked, and at that time, it was very backwards. I went to a babysitter, and my mother worked when most moms were at home . . . and so, for me, to have her make that statement to me, was just like—I wanted to laugh, but at the same time, it did hurt. It felt like total nonsupport and—that actually just made me go, "Well, I'll show you . . ."

Of course, the entire process of identity development for women occurs not only with mothers but with a family in which development of identity may be constrained or enhanced according to the circumstances. It was earlier believed that there was, as a matter of course, a dramatic deterioration in the quality of parent-child relations during adolescence (Fullinwider-Bush and Jacobvitz, 1993). More recently, however, work has shown that this rupture occurs in only a small percentage—between 5 and 10 percent—of cases. However, optimal development is best fostered by parents who are able to redefine their relationships with their children so that they balance closeness with encouragement toward relative individuation. Many researchers have found that adolescent development difficulties occur where closeness and connectedness between parents appears to be absent. Fullinwider-Bush and Jacobvitz describe the dissolution of boundaries between parent and daughter, that is, too much closeness of certain kinds, as causing difficulty in identity development of the adolescent girl. For example, if a parent expects a girl to listen to his or her problems or turns to the daughter rather than the spouse for emotional fulfillment, the child's own needs for support and guidance are compromised (Fullinwider-Bush and Jacobvitz, 1993). Several respondents described parent-child role reversals in their families. A typical example of this type of role reversal, where the child is expected to parent the parent, was reported by respondent #17, age thirty-nine, as she described the relationship between her mother and father:

> It was not an affectionate, overly affectionate, or loving relationship. It was probably more reserved, definitely more reserved and silent. As opposed to fighting, I think, more often than not, there was the silence between them. That was pretty typical. My father would have episodes where he would be very accusatory or antagonistic, and I don't really remember. I mean, it takes two to get into that, but I don't know what her responses were other than to say things like "Your father's giving me the silent treatment again," and she would tell and retell disappointment stories about my father.

In sum, then, at both conscious and unconscious levels, a woman's identity is grounded in developmental changes but keeps an implicit and explicit connection with the family, as well as the larger society in which the family develops. Social values and constructions set down paths and create barriers to discourage truly original thinking for women. However, during adolescence when the ability to think abstractly and hypothetically is new, she can make self-determinations. If she feels permission to do so, identity can include understanding her own personal ethics, what constitutes personally meaningful behavior, and the freedom she may feel to pursue that behavior. Identity can include choosing the people with whom she will relate and sorting out what is important to the self from what is not important.

In addition, more commonly for women than men, identity involves the sense that she may, and will, tend to take the feelings and opinions of others into consideration as a normal part of her development. In other words, some external locus of control will be normative for her. Ideally, she will not feel guilt about this. However, she is likely to feel guilt because society expects and values autonomy, and she will differ from males in the level of autonomy to which she aspires. At the same time, she may not be encouraged to act too independently because of the limits set on appropriate behavior for a female.

Hoare (1991) suggests that it is in adolescence that potential roles are identified and "the infinite array of the possible" presents itself (p. 248). How can the young woman in a society driven by sexist, heterosexist, gender ideology establish for herself a coherent and authentic identity if she is not shown the infinite array of the possible to which Hoare refers? She may be exposed to only a limited set of normal outcomes. If a woman is to have a sense of ownership of her personal experience, she must feel the sense of agency that comes from self-knowledge, which, in turn, comes from the ability to impact her environment in a personally meaningful way (Glodis and Blasi, 1993). In addition to the limitations on freely chosen identity that are true for all women, what happens when a woman experiences a subjective identity that she perceives is not found anywhere outside the self? The desire to be "normal," or not different from most others, is felt most strongly in young adulthood, but remains strong throughout life. How can she feel that sense of agency? Can she listen to herself and what her emotions, her intuition, her body, and her perceptions are telling her? Is she forced to repress or hide her own experience out of shame? Is she forced to deny her experience because that experience cannot be validated outside the self?

THE DEVELOPMENT OF GENDER ORIENTATION

The evolution of a lesbian or bisexual identity in women cannot be examined or considered without placing that evolution in the context of women's general identity development in this culture. Having looked at this general identity development, having seen how women are carefully guided toward certain behaviors and socially constructed heterosexist outcomes, the next step is to examine theories that consider the development of gender orientation.

Theories and models of lesbian identity development exhibit wide variation, including biological, learning, psychodynamic, and the "stage" models. Each category has its own set of problems, one of which is that many have been adapted from models of gay male identity development. It would appear that the assumption that women and men develop similarly, even that gay male and lesbian women develop similarly, is erroneous. This assumption reflects the sexism implicit in much scientific research and needs to be challenged. However, the purpose in this writing is not to evaluate these models of sexual identity, but to outline them briefly, particularly where the propositions they espouse illustrate some aspect of the respondents' experience in this research.

Considering the development of gender orientation, during the adolescent years, some girls explore sexual and affectionate relations with members of their own sex. Cook (1983) and the Kinsey, Pomeroy, and Martin (1948) surveys suggest that 45 percent of boys of college level report some homosexual experience if they are "early maturers," and 25 percent report this if they are "late maturers" (Kinsey, Pomeroy, and Martin, 1948, p. 315). In younger teenage girls, about 14 percent of orgasms reported come from same-gender contacts, with no differences in age of maturity (Kinsey, Pomeroy, and Martin, 1953, p. 461). The Kinsey data are forty-five years old and whether they are still completely accurate, for most girls, these early contacts will cause a good deal of anxiety and guilt because they do not reflect the usual path. These experiences may be the beginning of a lesbian or bisexual orientation. For other girls, adolescent experimentation with sexual feelings and behavior in relationships with other girls is one way of exploring their bodies' sexual responsiveness and is part of a developmental process leading toward heterosexuality (Notman et al., 1990).

Respondent #15, age twenty-eight, describes her earliest sexual memory, which she apparently didn't take very seriously at the time:

> [My] earliest sexual memory is at the age of nine, playing house with a friend in my parent's basement and having an orgasm. Well, then it was with a girl.
>
> [You were having sex with each other?]
>
> We were pretending to have sex with our clothes on.
>
> [And you had an orgasm? What did that tell you?]
>
> What did it tell me then? I don't know. I don't think I've ever thought about it. That we get along playing house? [laughter] That made sense. Yeah, let's do this again. But I was always the boy, playing any kind of . . . playing anything. I was always the boy because I was taller. I don't know what that means.

On the other hand, respondent #9, age fifty-seven, took an early same-gender experience very seriously. It caused her intense pleasure and intense shame, which put her memory of it into a place of denial for many years:

> I met Jane out in the alley in the summer between sixth and seventh grade when the kids were all playing kick the can. She was a year older and very athletic, but musical too, so we hit it off immediately. The ways in which she was different from me were very appealing to me, I think. I was not a physical person, not good at sports, so I was very drawn to her strong body. We both felt a pull to each other right away . . . ended up being practically inseparable for a year or so. Played piano, listened to music, went to movies . . . I used to sleep overnight at her house, kiss, touch breasts, . . . God, it was so sexually exciting for me. But her friends began to harass us about spending so

much time together . . . and I couldn't stand the pressure anymore of feeling hidden and ashamed. I don't believe I thought about it much. I just *felt* about it. I felt so much pleasure, but I felt utterly ashamed—partly because the pleasure was sexual, which was a no-no, and partly because she was a girl and I knew that wasn't right. One day, I just cut it off. I wouldn't see her or talk to her. I know now how cruel that was. I should have talked to her, but I needed to just forget it . . . let it go . . . and I did. For about twenty-eight years.

Current theorizing about whether homosexuality is an essential condition or a set of behaviors, and about whether gender is the critical determining variable in a sexual relationship, is beyond the scope of this writing (see, for example, Butler, 1990; Ross and Paul, 1992; Rust, 1993). However, it is important for our purposes here to note the assumption underlying this research, that is, that homosexuality is a "normal" condition, with normal taken to mean independence of mental illness rather than normative social or moral values (Ross, 1987). According to Jung and Smith (1993), "the moral debate about whether or not gay people are by their very orientation imperfect, defective, diseased, evil, or good continues to be necessary. It must simply be joined with identical inquiry regarding straight people" (p. 3). They argue that this is "the legitimate and necessary consequence of reform" (p. 5) and that "there is no painless way to dismantle heterosexism" (p. 168).

A lesbian or bisexual orientation is framed here as two outcomes among several normal possibilities for women (Brown, 1995). That is, when the term orientation is used to mean preferred gender of sexual partner, there may be an implication that "normal people" choose to be sexually attracted to persons of the other gender, whereas lesbians and bisexuals choose to fall in love with persons of their own or both genders. Although it is true that a girl may or may not act on her orientation, she does not *choose* her gender orientation (Francoeur, 1991). I am not saying that gender orientation is innate—the evidence for causation is not clear. Several theories about causation are outlined throughout this chapter. I am saying, however, that whatever causes her to be attracted to women, more than simple choice is involved. She either experiences the capacity for this orientation, or she does not. Just as she either experiences sexual attraction to men, or she does not.

Respondent #5, age forty-one, felt attractions to women beginning in high school:

> [I was] . . . attracted to women and coming on to some women, but being rejected . . . then in college, my first year of college, same thing. And I had never dated anyone in high school. And never dated guys. Nobody. And then being rejected by women, too, at this point of rebellion, not finding anybody interested in me as well. . . . One was my best friend, and I was afraid, so I stopped hanging out with her because I was attracted to her, but I felt if I came on to her that would be bad, so actually I just didn't talk to her . . .

The search for an explanation of homosexuality should really be an attempt to understand the roots and development of all sexuality, but, as I have said, this has seldom been the case. Heterosexuality was, until recently, relatively poorly investigated. This neglect probably reflects the view that heterosexuality is a given and requires no explanation. In actuality, homosexual orientations are likely to be explained best when the nature of all sexual needs and directions is understood (Money, 1980). Current research points in several directions, but as yet, no comprehensive explanation is satisfactory to all (Haas and Haas, 1993).

As has been previously addressed, the luxury of expressing the feeling and enjoyment of her own sexual arousal is a gift society tends to deny a woman. Sexual arousal comes as a result of a complex interplay of innate predisposition and early experiences and reinforcements. If she doesn't feel sexual interest when she is supposed to feel it, that is, with her husband, a woman is punished. The punishment is just as likely to come from herself because she has absorbed heterosexist assumptions along with everyone else in her culture. For example, respondent #18, age fifty-one, talks about the messages her body was giving her when she was married; her body was not responding sexually to her husband and she blamed herself:

I thought that being in the Twin Cities would make me happy and happily married. I don't know what I thought. I was denying all the sexual incompatibility, but, you know, I need to back up and say mostly what I felt all the time I was married was inadequate as a woman. Not like there is something wrong with me that I am not enjoying sex . . . that we are not enjoying it together. . . . It was more that there was something really wrong with me.

At this point in her life, this respondent had no idea that she was sexually attracted to her own gender. However, it's possible that she knew she bonded emotionally with women, and, perhaps, she was even aware of fantasizing sexually about women. (I wish I had asked her.)

Writers and researchers differ in the descriptive label they use for same-gender attractions. Moses' and Hawkins' description is what I use in this paper. They have said that the development of what is commonly called sexual orientation is actually a gender orientation consisting of three parts: (1) affectional orientation—the gender of persons we bond with emotionally, (2) sexual fantasy orientation—the gender of the persons with whom we fantasize having sex, and (3) erotic orientation—the gender of the persons with whom we prefer to have sex. Even though these are interrelated, they are distinct aspects of gender orientation (Moses and Hawkins, 1982). Reinforcing the validity of the separations among these three aspects, two respondents in this study commented that they will not pursue relationships with men again, but they still fantasize, at times, about sexual experiences with men.

Several women in the study talked of their attractions to both genders, and three respondents specifically stated that they consider themselves bisexual. Bisexuality is considered here as an identity of its own, not necessarily a transitional phase from heterosexual to lesbian. According to Rust, bisexual identity challenges a dichotomous view of gender orientation. She suggests that shifts in gender orientation may be a "normal outcome of the dynamic process of identity formation that occurs as mature individuals respond to changes in the available social constructs, the sociopolitical landscape and their own positions on the landscape" (Rust, 1993, p. 74).

However, bisexuality is only recently beginning to be investigated, and research is very sparse. One interesting idea about the development of a bisexual identity is proposed by Ross and Paul. They suggest the existence of a continuum, with, on one end, those persons for whom it is very important which gender they relate to sexually—those for whom "gender matters"—and, at the other end of the continuum, those persons for whom the gender of the person they relate to sexually is less important—those for whom "gender does not matter"; it is other aspects of the person that stimulate the attraction (Ross and Paul, 1992). This contrasts with the traditional Kinsey continuum, with exclusive heterosexuality defining one end of the continuum and exclusive homosexuality the other. The Ross and Paul continuum is defined at one pole by "gender matters" (homosexuality and heterosexuality) and at the other by "gender doesn't matter" (bisexuality).

Respondent #20, age fifty-four, is apparently implying that gender doesn't matter to her:

> Actually, I'm dating a man right now. I said we have a lot in common because we are both looking for the woman of our dreams.

Although it is just now being openly acknowledged in the 1990s, bisexuality has been recognized for many years. Alfred Kinsey did landmark research into sexuality in the United States about fifty years ago. According to Kinsey's data, half of all American males were exclusively heterosexual in their experience and fantasies, but 4 percent of them, and 2 percent of the females, were exclusively oriented to persons of their own gender. The remaining percentages of Americans had varying proportions of sexual fantasies or experiences involving both males and females (Kinsey, 1948, 1953). Kinsey's research suggests that occasional fantasies or daydreams of sexual contact with one's own gender may or may not be a sign of same-gender orientation, but it could suggest a potential for bisexuality if the person felt that interest.

Respondent #6, age thirty-five, describes her first sexual attraction to a woman:

. . . I took classes. . . . I became sexually attracted to this woman, and that was the first time I'd realized in my life that I was sexually attracted to a woman. I was twenty-eight. I was totally infatuated, and I spent a lot of time with her. I shared all the things I did at school with her. I tried to share [my school activities] with [my husband], and he wasn't interested . . . this woman was not sexually attracted to me, did not identify herself as a lesbian. . . . When she would tell me I'm beautiful, she was very seductive, and it was not a healthy situation. . . . She later agreed we had a lesbian relationship. It was lesbian in all other senses than being sexual.

The majority of these women (seventeen of twenty-four) had no conscious awareness of same-gender impulses until after marriage. However, Bell and Weinberg did extensive interviews with self-identified gay and lesbian people and found that in almost every life, they could trace the awareness of homosexuality or heterosexuality to very early ages. That is, for most people, evidence suggests that orientation is developing even in early childhood (Bell and Weinberg, 1978). Research indicates that same-gender attraction is as deeply ingrained as heterosexuality, so that the differences in behaviors or social experience of prehomosexual girls and their preheterosexual counterparts reflect or express, rather than cause, their eventual homosexual preference (Haas and Haas, 1993).

Respondent #8, age forty-three, tells a story of childhood and adolescent crushes, one that was repeated by five women in the study:

From kindergarten to seventh grade, when we left California, I played every seasonal sport. . . . I think I fell in love with every recreational leader I had. I didn't understand that. As I got older and got into recovery, I started looking back at, you know, am I, do I think I'm gay because these people gave me something my mother couldn't give me at that point in my life . . . . This one gal, Laura, she became a kind of role model for me. I always looked forward to her coming by and picking me up, and she was our coach, and I just, I would get flustered when I was in her presence. I wanted to be with her all the

> time. I think, from the grades, I knew something was different
> . . . and she's still my friend today . . .
>
> [Is she a lesbian?]
>
> No, very happily married to a man.

At this point, no clear understanding has yet developed that explains why some people are sexually attracted to the other gender and some to their own. Until the early 1980s, psychoanalytic explanations of homosexuality dominated the thinking of many researchers and writers. Sigmund Freud and psychoanalysts who followed viewed homosexuality as the product of a seductive, dominating mother and a weak or passive father. Freud spoke little of the development of lesbianism (Gay, 1988). Later psychoanalysts, particularly Freud's daughter Anna, attempted to correct this omission. Lesbianism was viewed as a mirror image of male homosexuality, that is, the outcome of a distant and ambivalent mother. The result is that, supposedly, because of the lack of love from her mother, the daughter is led to seek such love from another woman (Wolff, 1971). Psychoanalyst Nancy Chodorow (1978) posited that the center of female personality development can be found in the mother-daughter relationship. These approaches are intriguing when considering the development of a lesbian or bisexual identity. However, they may raise the issue that if same-gender attraction begins in the mother-daughter relationship, why don't more women develop same-gender attractions (Brown, 1995)?

Biology is an obvious place to look for an explanation of deeply ingrained behavior such as sexuality. Current research does suggest that the development of gender orientation may begin months before a baby is born. David and Barbara Bjorklund note that evidence indicates that prenatal hormones already determine one's sex and that evidence is accumulating showing hormones influence which sex one will be attracted to (Bjorklund and Bjorklund, 1988). A number of studies have examined the hormones associated with femininity and masculinity. Do boys and girls, adolescents and adults, have different amounts of estrogens and androgens determining their gender orientation? Lesbians may have more testosterone than heterosexual women, but the evidence has not been consistent because some lesbians have more estrogen than heterosexual women (Goodman, 1983). However, is this a cause or an effect of their orientation?

Garfield Tourney (1980) reviewed a large number of research studies and found the results much too contradictory to support or exclude a role for hormones in gender orientation. He also notes that the most telling argument against hormones playing a direct role in determining adult gender orientation is that neither homosexuality nor heterosexuality has been consistently altered by hormone injections.

In addition to hormones, the brain appears to play a role in determining sexual direction. Tentative evidence suggests the hypothalamus may be involved. This tiny seven-gram organ has a number of important functions, including regulating involuntary body processes, helping coordinate thinking and emotions, and relating pleasurable feelings. LeVay (1991) reports that the size of the hypothalamus differs in men and women and that it differs in heterosexual and homosexual men. Whether this observation will be confirmed, whether it also occurs in women, and whether convincing structural correlates exist await further research.

Brown notes that biological models of homosexuality development assume a nonchanging sexual self for lesbians. Biological models are thus inadequate to explain the evolution of a lesbian or bisexual identity, as found in the subjects of this research. However, she does suggest further that it may be tempting to embrace biological models because they suggest the essential, inborn nature of gender orientation, thus confirming that gender orientation is truly out of a person's control. Such a perspective supports legislation against discrimination (Brown, 1995).

Nine of the twenty-four respondents described serious attractions to women after they were married but before they came out. In some cases, the attractions occurred before they realized what the attractions might mean. The respondents were all ultimately rejected by these women. Respondent #13, age fifty-three, faced the ambivalence (or perhaps a shift in gender orientation, such as that referred to by Rust [1993]) of a woman with whom she tried to have a relationship:

One of my good friends was named Sister LuAnn, and she was real special to me. She was a nun. I think of all the women that I met before I really realized that I wanted to come out, LuAnn was dearest in my heart. We studied together; we'd go on walks together . . . when I left that program, . . . LuAnn said she was going to come and see me for a weekend, and I was just so excited. I thought, hot damn! This is unbelievable, you know. She's going to come and spend a weekend with me, and this is very telling that I probably should not have gotten married . . . well, I guess I really married him because I didn't think I would find a woman who would want to be with me for the rest of my life. I just didn't; I didn't think they were out there. I mean, I felt like that about LuAnn, but I knew she was not a lesbian. And she is no longer a nun, which I find interesting . . . but I think I kind of had—given up is too strong of a word maybe— but I wanted to spend my life with somebody, and I really didn't think I would find a woman. . . . Anyway, what happened is that [when she was visiting] she came on to me . . . . and my husband was upstairs in bed. And I flipped out. It was so incredible. It was so wonderful. [We had sex] and the next morning, well . . . Larry went off to work, and it left her and me at breakfast, and once again, it wasn't talked about . . . just like it never happened! And I was married and I was going crazy. And I had to take her to catch her bus out of there . . . and eventually we did talk about it later. She was not a nun then . . . because I wanted to be physically intimate again, and she basically said, "I am just not comfortable with it at all; this is not who I am. I can't do this . . ."

Carla Golden, a feminist psychodynamic theorist, suggests that women's sexuality may be an aspect of identity that is "fluid and dynamic" as opposed to fixed and invariant (Golden, 1987, p. 27). The idea of women's sexuality being fluid and dynamic would certainly be supported by the experience of the women in this research. For example, many of them had important relationships with men in addition to their husbands before they turned to relationships with women, and others continue to entertain possibilities of significant sexual relationships with both genders.

For example, respondent #22, age forty-five, expressed an awareness of her sexuality and orientation as potentially fluid and dynamic:

> I have been single for the last couple of years, and they [lesbian friends] say, well, you know, "Are you out looking?" And you know, somebody is going to walk into my life, and I'm fine with that, and actually, it could be a guy and they say, "What do you mean it could be a guy?" and I say, "You know, if a person walks into my life and it's somebody I fall deeply in love with, I'm not going to ignore that opportunity just because it's a man." . . . I'm extremely proud to be lesbian . . . it's just that in this life, if that opportunity presented itself, I wouldn't turn my back on it because I am a lesbian. I would look at it. . . . I would look at him as a person.

As we discuss gender identity, we enter an arena that could alter entirely the issue of heterosexual/homosexual/bisexual identities. Much current writing and theorizing focuses on what is meant by gender and gender identity. Some authors present the idea that "the category of gender itself is a social construction, the terms of which are decreed by patriarchal law" (Burch, 1997, p. 48; see also Butler, 1990.) Gender and culturally dictated sex roles thus assign certain "appropriate" behaviors to men and to women that are violated or ignored under social penalty. For example, many lesbians say they were tomboys as children or that they are, or were, not properly feminine in some way. Burch suggests this raises the question, then, of whether some heterosexual women have felt atypical or unfeminine:

> Awareness of gender *improprieties* often precedes awareness of sexual interests. Possibly this experience shapes or reinforces sexual choice in some way without exactly determining it, but surely the reverse is true: Awareness of [nonstereotypical] interests affects one's gendered self-image, although not in a readily predictable way. (Burch, 1997, p. 48).

Respondent #8, age forty-three, says she knew she committed gender "improprieties" because she never has felt feminine enough:

Well, you know, they told me I had to put my blue jeans away when I was in about sixth grade. I wasn't comfortable with that. I never liked wearing a dress. And, you know, you got to start acting like a lady now, and that was very difficult for me because my sister is two years older than me, and Sue, the baby, was seven years younger than me. They were very feminine . . . they liked doing their nails. I've never liked doing my nails. Don't do them. I'll make sure they're clean or groomed, but I'm not into putting on make up, and I've always had to do what I've done to get by.

Current theorizing about gender and gender identity poses questions about homosexual and bisexual as well as heterosexual identities. For example, if gender itself is a social construction, what does it mean to say that a female is attracted to females? Is it attraction to the culturally dictated sex role or to the physical body of the person? In addition, if gender identity is not as firmly defined at birth as was formerly believed, it is possible that gender is not an organizer of experience, that is, that a woman has this or that experience because she is female. Rather, perhaps experience is an organizer of sexuality, that is, she has this or that experience, which then nudges her sexually in one direction or another (Whitfield, 1989). Inner sensations may participate, but it is now known that gender identity is much more psychological and less biological than had been thought previously and, perhaps, that is particularly true for girls (Kirkpatrick, 1990). Theoretical ideas about these fascinating questions concerning identity are only beginning to appear.

Regarding "gender improprieties," about half of the respondents in this research state clearly that they identified as tomboys as children. In a 1981 study by the Kinsey Institute (Bell, Weinberg, and Hammersmith, 1981), "tomboyism" was found to be the only childhood factor even slightly related to lesbianism in adulthood. Nichols and Leiblum (1986), as well as Burch (1993a), suggest that girls and women who eschew sex role stereotyped behavior may be more autonomous and independent people, but that may not necessarily correlate with lesbian identity. Burch (1997) notes that "both lesbian and heterosexual women may experience themselves as masculine in important ways that do not have anything to do with confusion about their [gender orientation] and that may be either highly valued or felt as deviant. . . . Being 'butch' . . . was a way to say 'I'm identifying with the power here'" (Burch, 1997, p. 53). At a conference I attended years ago, the speaker (whom I can't recall) said that being a tomboy correlates with being a lesbian only for women who don't like to climb trees.

Several respondents either stated or inferred that they preferred to play with boys or do activities associated with male role behavior as they grew up. Respondent #6, age thirty-five, describes her childhood experience:

> I would summarize my childhood as happy. I was a tomboy. I played a lot of sports. I wasn't interested in playing with girls at all. They didn't interest me because it seemed boys did more of the things I was interested in and their activities were more exciting.

What role does learning have in the development of female gender orientation? According to behavioral psychologists, most human behavior is learned. Learning is a way of acquiring behavior through experience and interactions with others. Behavior that is reinforced tends to be learned, and learning also occurs through imitation. That is, people tend to behave in ways that resemble the behavior of others who serve as models. Learning advocates also suggest that what is sexually arousing, or what "turns us on" sexually, is largely the result of early experience. Could gender orientation be learned? Bell, Weinberg, and Hammersmith found that two-thirds of the homosexual men and women in their sample had a same-gender experience before age nineteen with someone older or of their own age. Adolescents have an incompletely formed sexuality and are ready to learn any number of patterns. If a pleasing homosexual experience is one of the first physical encounters for a girl, that reinforcing relationship could set in motion a pattern that could persist (Bell, Weinberg, and Hammersmith, 1981).

As discussed earlier in this chapter regarding identity formation, this culture discourages young women from consulting with themselves to draw conclusions about anything. They are expected to listen to others. Along with homophobic attitudes that are likely to discourage same-gender impulses, young women are not consid-

ered valid sources of information about themselves or for themselves. In light of this societal attitude, it is easy to understand why
respondent #21, age thirty, had difficulty taking her same-gender
impulses seriously:

> [When you had all these crushes, interest in females, attrac-
> tions, what did you think about them?]
>
> In high school, I was repulsed by them. In junior high, I did have
> sexual thoughts about other women, and pretty heavily . . . and I
> just thought, "Oh, this is bad, really, really bad" and then I
> remember thinking, "This is not OK," and I drank a lot. I tried
> not to think about it. I used alcohol a lot of the time when John
> and I were married. I was part of a feminist group, and I thought
> these thoughts I'm having about other women are just natural,
> and I think straight women have them too, you know, especially
> when you are part of a feminist group and you see it all the time.
> But I remember the first time I saw two women kiss; I was just
> appalled. It was at a retreat with my feminist group, and I was
> walking down the hall and these two friends of mine were kissing
> . . . "Oh, excuse me!" I ran off . . . yeah, it's OK, but . . .

It has been suggested that aversive conditioning—that is, being
hurt or punished by the other sex—may cause women to seek relationships only with their own gender. Early studies reported that rape
victims had more subsequent lesbian experiences and that a great
number of female incest victims developed homosexual feelings.
However, many early studies were biased because they viewed homosexuality as an illness or abnormality and focused their research
on limited clinical populations.

To investigate this issue, Peters and Cantrell (1991) recently
studied a large nonclinical sample of women who described themselves as either heterosexual or lesbian (see also Chapter 1 on sex
education for treatment of this issue). Results showed that the percentage of lesbian and heterosexual women reporting nonconsensual sexual experiences with adults before the age of twelve was
comparable to that found in a group of women from the general
population. The hypothesis that lesbians would report a greater
number of negative childhood/adolescent sexual experiences with

males was not supported, nor was the idea that the lesbian group would have more positive sexual experiences with females. Neither parental relationships nor parental attitudes about homosexuality were significantly different between women from the general population and women who identified as lesbian. Therefore, the study did not support that lesbianism is caused by male aversion (Peters and Cantrell, 1991).

Many theorists have seen homosexual identity formation as a linear process and have proposed developmental stage models of the process. The developmental model defines progress as movement through the stages and eventual replacement of a heterosexual identity with a homosexual identity. These models assume that once it is embraced, the mature gay/lesbian identity is permanent.

Several models of gay identity development have been proposed. Evans and Levine (1990) summarize the models well. They indicate that some emphasize the internal psychological processes involved (Dank, 1971; Plummer, 1975; Troiden, 1979; Coleman, 1982; Sophie, 1987). Sophie's (1987) and Cass's (1979) models concentrate on lesbian identity development. Cass's model takes into account both psychological and sociological factors and has six stages. However, for our purposes, a weakness in Cass's model is her implication that once an individual suspects lesbian tendencies in herself, any step short of identity synthesis represents a partial failure (Elliott, 1985). The idea of identity as a goal rather than a process does not fit with the apparently fluid and dynamic nature of women's sexuality as found in this research.

Although the number of proposed stages in these models vary, four steps are generally identified:

1. An increasing acceptance of the homosexual label as applying to one's self
2. A shift from negative to positive feelings about this self-identity
3. An increasing desire to inform both gay and nongay individuals of one's gay identity
4. More frequent and closer involvement with the gay community

According to Evans and Levine (1990), other models focus more exclusively on the coming-out process, that is, the process of identifying as gay/lesbian, both to oneself and to others (Hencken and

O'Dowd, 1977; Lee, 1977; de Monteflores and Schultz, 1978; Lehman, 1978; Moses and Hawkins, 1986). These models suggest a progression that moves from self-acknowledgement to coming out to significant others to identifying oneself as gay to the public at large.

Although Sophie (1987), Cass (1979), and Lehman (1978) are discussing the gender orientation of women, most of these models assume that the formation of a gay identity is identical for men and women. However, other researchers (de Monteflores and Schultz, 1978; Marmor, 1980) have noted the following:

1. Women tend to develop a lesbian identity later than men develop a gay identity.
2. Women tend to develop a lesbian identity before becoming sexually active with women.
3. Emotional attachment is more important than sexual activity to women.
4. Homosexuality seems to be less threatening to women than to men.
5. Sexuality tends to be more contextual, relational, and fluid for women than for men.

Another lesbian theorist, Ponse (1978), places more emphasis on consistency of feelings, behaviors, and cognitions than she does on sequence of events or linear progression. Her model suggests that there will be/can be a certain amount of moving back and forth among the stages before a lesbian identity develops. Marmor (1980) notes that the experiences of lesbian women are more similar to those of heterosexual women than to those of gay men. That is, current models of women's development emphasize the relational strengths of women (Enns, 1991; Miller, 1991). In fact, Bridges and Croteau refer to a recently developed lesbian identity model by McCarn and Fassinger (1991) that points to how sexual identity development is intertwined with relationship development for many women (Bridges and Croteau, 1994).

Many respondents in this research talked about wanting to be just friends with boys and finding dating boys awkward. Respondent

#23, age forty-seven, reveals an early sense that relationships with males were problematic for her:

> My intention throughout my adolescence was to be a nun, which I think was very self-protective for me.

[Self-protective in what sense?]

> Self-protective in the sense that I didn't take dating and adult kinds of things very seriously when I was in high school, although I felt very different in a number of ways, socially it was sort of my context that . . . oh I don't know . . . it kind of let me explain it to myself during those years, I think.

[Explain what to yourself?]

> Not being socially interested. Not being interested in dating and feeling very different and not in the sort of suburban mainstream.

Although all these stage models have value, they elucidate the process of gender orientation primarily after awareness has begun. Missing from the discourse is what happens inside a woman's emotions and perceptions at the earlier stages, that is, before she knows. Plummer's model may come closest to considering this earliest stage of preknowing. He takes a symbolic-interactionist approach. That is, he suggests that the process is awakened or modified depending on the experiences available to a person as she or he goes through her or his life (Plummer, 1975). Plummer's work may foreshadow that of Paula Rust.

Paula Rust (1993) has investigated the coming-out process, attempting to develop a nonlinear model of identity formation that names bisexual identity and homosexual identity as equally valid alternatives to heterosexual identity. She found that when she presented her information as the calculated average ages at which milestone events occur in the women's lives, her data concurred with earlier stage models; that is, the data seemed to say that coming out is an orderly, stage-sequential process. However, Rust found that the statistical distributions behind the averages revealed that individuals often switch back and forth between sexual identities and experience periods of ambivalence, during which they wonder about their sexual identities and sometimes express no sexual identity at all. Rust suggests that "the developmental model must be replaced by a social constructionist model of sexual identity formation in which variations and change are the norm" (Rust, 1993, p. 68). Rust appears to be saying that a woman may find that changes in her sexual identity or gender orientation may be necessary to describe accurately her experience in her particular social context. That is, the conceptualization of same-gender attraction has changed from the pejorative category of the past to a category in the 1990s that has many social and political meanings.

The present research respondents tended to "try out" their same-gender attractions as they went through the process of discovery toward coming out. Respondent #16, age fifty-one, describes the confusion she felt as she divorced and was learning to know herself. She reached out to a friend who seemed available, but who did not want a mutually loving relationship once the respondent declared her feelings:

> One [woman] in particular became very supportive . . . this particular person had been divorced and had two children. She said, "If you just need to get away for a few days and just take a break, you can come on over and stay at my place." Which I did do one time. Anyhow, we developed a very close friendship. To make a long story short, I realized that I loved that person and that I guess . . . I loved her! I mean, I loved her more than my friends and that was, I was—was trying to hide it for a year, year and a half . . . it's hard because you know a good Catholic girl can't have these feelings. It's with men, you know, and you shouldn't have . . . either. At that point, I wasn't thinking about anything physical. All I knew was I had these overpowering feelings of just—it was incredible the way I felt about this person. . . . I wanted to be around her, and we just had such wonderful times. We connected so well; we were supportive of each other. When she was down, we just—she was more shy and bashful and she said, "You just bring things out in me and make me laugh," and we had such great times

together. Anyway, when I realized how I felt about her, it was one of those greatest moments in my life . . . but that was also the beginning of thinking, "No, this can't be; you can't feel this way about another woman . . ." She said, "You know, a man—if a man and I were as close as you and I are, he would probably want to take me to bed . . ." So she said this . . . and I thought, "I feel so much for this person, and I think if I tell her I am going to lose her, and I don't know if I can handle that." Besides thinking I can't feel this way about another woman . . . What is wrong with me? . . . finally she and I were talking one evening, and I said—she said, "Is something wrong?" And I said, "There is something I'm going to tell you" . . . so I told her how I felt, which is basically no expectations, nothing. I just said, "This is how I feel about you and I do love you. I really do love you." And anyway, within five minutes, there was total rejection. She didn't want me to come around anymore. . . . She said, "I need to see my minister. . . . We need to split up. . . ."

Rust's (1993) model would propose that coming out is the process of discovering oneself in terms of social constructs—that is, what or who is available to identify with, what or who is available to model oneself after—rather than the process of discovering the lesbian within. For some women, there is, and always has been, awareness of the lesbian within. For the women in this research study, however, before marriage to a man, seventeen of the twenty-four had *no conscious awareness* of their same-gender impulses. Seven had varying degrees of awareness, from a fleeting thought to full same-gender experiences. Of these seven, some tried to hide it, primarily because they believed there were no other women like them. Others didn't consciously repress their feelings; they simply did not know. What do we mean by "know"? The issue of "knowing" for women, that is, what and how a woman knows, will be considered more fully in Chapter 4.

Even as she describes the social constructionist model of identity formation, Rust (1993) adds that individuals themselves do not generally experience their identities as socially constructed. Women generally experience their own sexuality as stable and essential, regardless of their history or location in life. Rust reiterates that this social constructionist model of sexual identity formation will be useful only if those who experience the search for sexual identity see it as a goal-oriented process of discovering and accepting the possible fluidity of the goal. That is, she reminds us that sexual identity (or gender orientation, as I prefer) is indeed constructed. Individuals experience their subjective reality. Then they are able to pursue their goals from the outcomes they perceive to be available. If heterosexuality is the only perceived outcome, women are unlikely to identify themselves in terms of a social category such as lesbian or bisexual, as long as they are unaware that these categories exist (Rust, 1993).

Half the respondents had an early, strong attraction to a woman that was rejected but that could have provided them with significant information about themselves had it developed. However, the outcome of a full relationship with a woman was not, in Rust's terms, an outcome they perceived as available. In the confusion of new feelings, and the lack of awareness that such a relationship was a valid one, respondent #25, age fifty-three, describes a painful adult relationship that evoked the same-gender feelings and then sent them down into denial again for a number of years:

> . . . I started doing music at church, in my neighborhood church, the parish where my kids were going to the school. So we were involved in that church. One woman—the whole group of musicians were all women—who played piano, one day I just said to her, "I love you as I've never loved any other woman," and it just came out of my mouth, and we were just hugging at the end of church and saying good-bye for the day, and we just hugged, and it was Christmas and so it's a celebrating type day, and this came out. I had no idea. I had not thought of that and her, ever. That I was aware. And so I went home, and it was Christmas Day, and I remember that, and the rest of the day was a total wreck, thinking, "What is that? What did I say? What does that mean?" And I was such a mess, and I didn't know what to do with it. And here I am, something like forty-one, and . . . so finally I talked to her about it, and I told her how I felt, and she cried; she didn't want to hear this, and she didn't want that to happen. She was

married with five kids, and I was just totally enamored. Then there was no denying it. I couldn't just take it back and say, "Oh well" . . . so we went round and round about this and continued to work together, and then I stopped doing the music, and I couldn't be around her. Then there were times that she got so upset, she said, "[We] can't be friends anymore. I can't take this." I even went out one time for coffee and to talk with her husband about this . . . then finally we became friends again, and I really thought I could do it. Just be friends. Then I just pushed aside any thought that I could be a lesbian. I just sort of shoved it down, thinking, "Well, this is just a weird phase or something that I just went through. And now it's gone." I would laugh about it to myself and say, "Oh, my God, what were you thinking?"

As part of the development of her model, Rust (1993) studied women who identified as lesbian or bisexual, who were unsure, or who preferred not to label themselves. Thus, her research participants are similar to the respondents in the present study. That is, many of these respondent women were attracted to men at some point in their lives and attracted to women at others. Rust's model seems to validate another sexual self-identification that will affirm the previously unacknowledged experience of these women. Of course, only each woman should be allowed to provide the label for herself, should a label be desired. For example, as I have said, three respondents stated that they identify themselves as bisexuals:

[Do you identify with bisexuals?]

In my head I do. I tend not to say it because the majority of my friends are lesbians now. They consider that a cop-out. I am settled enough in my life and in a circle of friends that I don't have to use labels very often, so it doesn't come up. I do think of myself as someone with an affectional preference for women, who is for sure bisexual. Sexually, I'm probably more heterosexual than bisexual, than lesbian. I miss sex with men sometimes, and I fantasize about it a lot. It doesn't mean I want, that I certainly don't want them around, but I always have had wonderful sex with men, so has [my partner]; we talk about that. (Respondent #10, age fifty-two)

A number of the respondents in the study said that when they felt validated in their same-gender attractions for the first time, they felt whole for the first time. They felt as if they were finally "at home," that this knowledge made them feel complete.

[Is there a moment you remember when you knew that something had changed or had to change?]

The closest I can come to that is when I realized I was in love with Jill and I felt that I was home; it felt like a big relief. And that's where I belonged. I didn't go through an identity crisis about "O, my God, what am I going to do?" I went through a crisis [but not about that]. (Respondent #22, age forty-five)

Erikson defined identity as "the accrued confidence [in] the inner sameness and continuity of one's meaning" (1950, p. 235). The women in my research slowly gained a sense of wholeness, of completion, of "inner sameness."

However, to recognize the potential of their evolving lesbian/ bisexual identities, these women needed to recognize sexism and heterosexism and to be aware of how the evolution of their overall identity and gender orientation is affected by sexist and heterosexist gender ideology. Because they tended not to be aware of these influences, barriers remained in their paths to self-awareness.

Chapter 4

How Do Women Know?

A fourth issue surfaced in the analysis of these interviews, but it was a theme in a different sense than the others and requires an explanation and a context. By now, it is clear that women who ultimately become aware of their lesbian or bisexual status after they marry have not known of this status, or they have denied or consciously repressed this knowledge. To allow themselves this knowledge, they needed to transcend significant sociological and psychological barriers to their awareness. However, besides needing specific pieces of information to facilitate their knowing, what is meant by saying, they "didn't know"? What did they need to know in order to "know"?

We've already addressed three major themes that surfaced in the analysis of these interviews:

1. The women needed to know about their bodies, know about sex, and have permission to be sexual with themselves, as well as to have sexual relationships with others.
2. They needed to know that marriage is a tradition, a ritual, a religious ceremony, and a legal contract, but that it is not a requirement for adulthood.
3. They needed to recognize sexism and heterosexism and to learn how the evolution of personal identity and gender orientation is affected by sexist, as well as heterosexist, gender ideology.

Knowledge in each of these areas can remove and lower barriers to experiences that could have marked the path toward this particular self-awareness. However, a further barrier issue encompasses the previous three and provides a pattern that can be separated from them: that is, to what degree is a woman able to act autonomously, to self-determine her own path toward sexuality here in the United States of America?

Normal behaviors are exhibited by many women that could contribute to the impression that women do not act on their own. In Chapter 3 on identity development, discussion focuses on how it is normal for a woman to consider other people, and especially her connections with others—family, partner, children—as major factors in everyday decision making. It is normal for a woman to place limits on her self-assertion—at times, because she chooses to preserve relational harmony and, at other times, because she will be ostracized for stepping beyond the sex role stereotyped behavior of submission if she does not. This is not to say that a woman cannot assert herself in every situation. She can if she is willing to deal with the consequences. This is true for any adult. However, a woman may submerge her differences with others, at times, because she estimates the relational cost to be too high. Although men may also do this, it is generally less typical male behavior. In any case, it is important to compare the differences between men and women because the prevailing idea of "normal" has consistently tended to be a reflection of how men are (e.g., see Broverman and Broverman, 1970; Showalter, 1987; Ussher, 1992). Women have been thought of as not normal rather than different.

The barrier issue to which I refer is more extensive and cannot be explained by normal women's behavior. Within these twenty-four interviews, the women revealed a sense of the need to acquiesce to some external authority in response to nearly every transition in their lives. In the narrative, this is reflected by comments such as "doing what I'm supposed to do" and "not thinking about what I wanted to do." These responses are typical of an oppressed group. Since authenticity of experience and consistent subordination are incompatible, these women found themselves in yet another double bind. They could either be authentic, acting on their true thoughts and feelings, or they could behave in ways they knew would be accepted, often being inauthentic. Self-determination is clearly limited under these circumstances.

I belabor this point because we live in a patriarchal culture. And, while we ponder what has kept these lesbian and bisexual women from becoming aware of a crucial piece of personal information, such as their same-gender attractions, one crucial assertion might be that their limited self-awareness was not due solely to inadequate self-searching or "faulty internal programming" (Nickerson, 1992). In defining their attractions for women, they would have been defying the patriarchal social structure of male and female and risking the censure of the dominant group. That is, no matter how many changes are presently, slowly occurring, maleness still carries more power than femaleness. This was even more accurate ten or twenty years ago, when most of these interviewees were getting married. Women have traditionally been accused of lacking decisiveness and of seeking external validation for their behavior, among many other criticisms. This kind of externalizing behavior is a result of what Jean Baker Miller calls "their training as subordinates; for anyone in a subordinate position must learn to be attuned to the vicissitudes of mood, pleasure and displeasure of the dominant group" (Miller, 1976, p. 110).

Freire has pointed out that the major characteristics of oppressed behavior stem from the ability of a dominant group to identify their norms and values as the "right ones" and to use power to enforce their views (Freire, 1971). Indeed, the overall thrust of this research has been to investigate the ways in which women are socialized into behaviors and roles—actually externally programmed—that do not support their growth and development as unique individuals, but instead keep them dependent on the approval of others. Change is occurring, but it is very slow.

Even respondent #2, age twenty-nine, whose parents are supportive, experiences ambivalence:

[Do your parents accept you?]

No. Yes and no. In their liberal way, they have to, but still, and to this day, they're more excited when I've got a guy in my life than if I have a woman.

A crucial realization for these women is that at some point, whether before or after their marriages, they perceived their same-gender impulses to be so threatening to acceptance in the community, so threatening to family and other relationships, and therefore so threatening to material well-being and to the balance of power in their lives, that they could not "let" themselves know or act on these feelings. In any case, the women represented by this study did not feel the freedom to determine their own path, regardless of whether they "knew" what it might be.

Respondent #9, age fifty-seven, describes the emotional risk she took in coming out to her mother:

> As soon as I realized that I had to leave my marriage, that I had found the path I had been seeking all those years, I told my mother. She knew I cared for my husband, so I couldn't tell her I was leaving because we weren't getting along. . . . I'll never forget the look of revulsion on her face when I told her. She looked disgusted. And this was a woman who taught me all my life that all people are valuable no matter what, that we should never be prejudiced. Well, I took her home and dropped her off, and she didn't look at me or speak to me for about six months. And after we began talking again, our relationship was never the same. It was . . . strained and just different.

I have mentioned elsewhere, and it is important to point it out again, that there are women for whom the pull toward same-gender attraction was so clear and unavoidable throughout their lives that they knew that they must pursue those relationships regardless of the societal pressures against them (Faderman, 1991). These are women for whom the gender of the persons they relate to sexually is a crucial factor, that is, for whom "gender matters," in the terms of the scale proposed by Ross and Paul (1992). The women represented in this research, on the other hand, are apparently those whose gender orientation is potentially more fluid. That is, they have been able to have sexual relationships with both men and women. Three women in this research describe themselves as bisexual.

Respondent #7, age thirty-two, describes her bisexuality in the context of her present marriage:

> [Is your husband aware of this?]

> He knows I am bisexual.

[How does he feel about that?]

It makes him a little nervous. We have talked a lot about that in some fashion, and some of it, a big part of it, is Christianity too. And the other piece is that he is afraid that I will go out and have a relationship with a woman. He's known for a couple of years now. I told him shortly after I was sure that was what I was. And that I wasn't going to change my mind. And I assured him that I have no plans to change anything that is going on.

[You mean that you married him and your commitment was to him and to that relationship? Does he feel fairly secure in that?]

Yeah. It's not something we talk a lot about anymore. I think it's just kind of there. Oh, I bring it up now and then.

[Every relationship has—there's always the idea, the risk, that if a person wanted to, he or she could have a relationship with someone else. In this case, it's a woman, and in some cases, it might be a man. So in some ways it's not different. But it sounds like for him it feels different.]

. . . He doesn't want me to have a relationship with anybody else. . . . You know, the bigger deal to him is that it is a woman attraction, though. . . . More for him to have to get used to.

It should also be noted that there are women who come to be woman identified as a result of their frustration at the injustices men have committed against women. They believe that men see or treat women like grown-up children and that they would be forced to fill that role if they succumbed to becoming the male image of womanhood. Their relationships with women are seen as a political challenge to sexism and heterosexism (Faderman, 1981). The women in this research group, however, did not appear to be making political decisions to love and partner with women. One woman (respondent #14, age forty-eight, see Chapter 3, pp. 82-83, for her quote) of the twenty-four talked of being drawn initially to women through a feminist perspective, but her later awareness was more emotional in nature. The remaining twenty-three appear to have evolved their awareness of the power of their same-gender attractions through a series of emotional experiences that finally resisted or defied cognitive explanation.

Although they had no support, these women did make attempts to negotiate their own life direction in general. Many described attempts to do so which were emotionally wrenching but which gave them strength as they went through them and came out the other side. Respondent #1, age thirty-six, describes the process of change she experienced as she began to realize she did have some ability to determine her path if she was willing and able to deal with the consequences. This developing awareness of her power supported her later when she left her marriage and came out:

> . . . Once I made that first decision to go to school and go against how I was supposed to do things, many more things started happening . . . so I realized I can say, "No, I want to do it this way." That created a big turmoil within my family because—I almost feel sorry for my husband for what happened to him with me, all of a sudden. . . . We were just supposed to do things the right way. Now all of a sudden I was doing other things differently, and he didn't know what hit him. It was like, "What is going on with you?" In one way, he was used to me being very passive, until all of a sudden I just started my persona going. I was unstoppable. This is what I want, and this is how I'm going to get it. He tried to go against that, so things started happening, with difficulty between us, with that being an issue. One thing led to another, and I started spending less time at home and more time working; also, the other thing that I had never really done is have a real social life. I had been at home, done the kid thing, watching the movies that were on TV. So all of a sudden, it was fun to go out with friends and my peers and visit and play . . .

Some women do risk self-assertion, regardless of the consequences. For example, one of the younger respondents, #2, age twenty-nine, knew early in her marriage that she had erred in marrying and was able to assert herself very competently:

. . . I was just becoming a youth worker; I had just begun my career, working with kids. I was learning a lot about the community and figuring out that there was a lot more to this than only relationships. I was starting to see the political end and starting to understand some of that. Twelve days after we got married, I met Mary at work . . . and it didn't take me long to realize that I was really attracted to her and that I wasn't attracted to [my husband], and he knew about my being bisexual, but we didn't discuss it at all. So I told him it was a mistake and that I couldn't at this point in my life be in a monogamous marriage. I couldn't do it. I hadn't finished figuring this thing out.

This short marriage was unusual among the respondents; the majority of the women were married for many years before they made a change. Although most had clues about their gender orientation early on, they tended to stay in the marriage, trying to make it work. Six were married twenty or more years, ten between ten and twenty years, and the remaining eight stayed married from one to ten years. The three youngest respondents were married the least amount of time (one to two and a half years). They had less time to be married because they were younger, but their shorter marriages also probably reflect a gradually increasing flexibility in attitudes regarding marriage and divorce, as well as the increased availability of lesbian and bisexual role models in the media and the larger community.

Several women said they stayed in their marriages after they knew about their gender orientation because they were unfamiliar with making decisions that took account of their own needs and desires. We have discussed the usual range of women's behavior that includes the self-in-relation theory, that is, that women normally consider their actions in light of other people's needs, feelings, and perceptions. However, even a relatively well-functioning woman may have self-boundaries that are too permeable; that is, she may be so sensitive to the needs of others that she ceases to act in her own best interest. The response of respondent #23, age forty-seven, reveals how she was able to regain her subtle loss of self as she grew in self-awareness:

There was a gradual process that I went through, I think, over a number of years, of sort of reclaiming within myself who I am. Not the role I had thrown myself into as a physician and as a parent and as a wife, but sort of more an essential "who I am is me" kind of thing and I had really—I don't think I had given it up because there were a lot of things that I did that were self-nourishing that were in my own interest all through my marriage, but I certainly didn't view it as important, and I sort of viewed anything that was my own desire as a secondary kind of thing, and so I had let huge parts of what my normal life was go.

[Secondary to what? You said your interests were secondary to . . .]

To everybody else's needs but my own. And I think, basically, what those years in counseling were about for me was reclaiming my own space.

As a group, these women ranged from erudite to plain speaking, and many expressed a sense of self-empowerment, yet they had all been significantly affected by the social rules and prevailing realities hampering their self-knowledge and had felt limited in their ability to take risks and make decisions, especially about their relationship lives. By educational and experiential standards, they were a rich and varied group. Nineteen went to college. Fifteen had bachelor's degrees, four had master's degrees, two had PhDs, and one had an MD. Four women had some college or post-secondary school training. All were employed—most had been employed throughout their adult lives. Two who had no formal post-secondary education had gained supervisory positions in their companies. Before they became aware of same-gender attractions, they expressed that their weakest area of functioning concerned intimate relationships. This would fit with Gramick's (1984) assertion that until identity has been firmly established, psychosocial intimacy is not possible.

Going beyond the customary tendency to consider their actions in light of others' needs, some of the women actively sought or wished for external validation, that is, someone to help them figure out what to do about their relationships. Indeed, as women, they had been taught not to listen to themselves and had grown accustomed to being told what to do, for example, respondent #5, age forty-one:

> My family really wasn't interested in being involved in Bible studies and whatnot. But I kind of went that way.

> [What was that about for you?]

> Black and white. I think it was about what do I do? I just felt like it gave me a lot of answers that I just didn't want to make decisions about myself. There was direction there. And there was safety. I just felt safe.

> [You mean, if there is a clear answer for everything, then I don't have to think about my feelings about all these things?]

> Right. Exactly.

Seven of the twenty-four women specifically mentioned the angry, controlling behavior of their fathers as an aspect of their childhood that had a strong impact. Their fathers' treatment taught them not to talk, not to assert, and not to trust themselves. For example, respondent #13, age fifty-three, describes the atmosphere at home and her parents' relationship:

> I think part of our family upbringing was you don't talk about things. And the secrets. . . . The messages I heard were mainly from Mom, if something went wrong at home she would say, "Don't tell Dad." And so a kind of fear of Dad was instilled. Even though it was something stupid like a broken washing machine. Don't tell Dad.

> [What would Dad do if he found out?]

> He could get angry, but he never did anything physical that ever hurt any of us that I'm aware of. But he had a temper, and I think Mom may have been—I don't know if she was afraid of what he might do—but I know that there was a message. . . .

My mom was very dependent upon Dad forever . . . for money, for transportation. He basically did everything. She couldn't work outside the home.

[Why not?]

He didn't want her to.

Respondent #25, age fifty-three, talks about the effects on her that did not encourage any independent thinking or action:

[How did that affect you, to have a father you felt was controlling?]

If affected me very, very much. We walked around on tiptoe, and feelings weren't allowed. You couldn't get angry. You couldn't fight. You couldn't disagree. It just wasn't allowed. And in this home with nine people, there was total order.

[You mean, order like robots?]

Well, not . . . not all my siblings were like me. I was an extremely fearful type, perfection perfect, "don't get in trouble" type kid. Probably more so than any of my siblings.

The conditioning that discourages women from listening to themselves and/or acting independently reinforces their doubt of their abilities, judgment, and competence. They realize that they are often not promoted, not highly represented in positions of leadership, and they tend to blame themselves. Until the past few years, theories of human behavior produced by psychologists have not focused on how the larger sociocultural context affects behavior, except very peripherally (Brehony, 1983). According to Jean Baker Miller, women have been ignorant of the sociocultural factors because they have compared themselves with men. She says women come to believe that there is some special inherent ability, some factor that remains inevitably beyond their reach that allows success (Miller, 1976). Since women tend to be discouraged from pushing themselves in their careers, and also because responsibility for child care, household management, and so forth, tend to present obstacles to their careers, women have needed to believe that the playing field is level. They have avoided acknowledgement of these unfair arrangements. Therefore, women have needed to believe that men must have this special quality that makes their life success more possible. Miller asserts that the conditioning women experience all their lives encourages belief in this myth (Miller, 1976).

These women tended to doubt their ability and competence and were afraid of making independent decisions. Respondent #10, age fifty-one, echoes the statement of nearly every respondent in the survey—that she married because she believed marriage was the only option. This respondent includes another theme that also repeated through these interviews—fear of making a decision:

> And I got married three weeks out of college, went right from a dorm to my parents' house for three weeks and into marriage. I think deep inside I knew it was a mistake . . . because I think I wasn't committed enough to George. But if I'm really honest, and I sometimes am almost too good at being honest, my motivation, I think, I got married because I was afraid to face the world after college. I didn't know where to go. It gave me too many options.

Respondent #19, age fifty-two, says her options were limited and she knew which ones were permitted, believing at the time that that was "how it was." Without awareness that society limited her options, she accepted all responsibility for feeling the need to stay within those perimeters:

> I didn't know what I was going to do with my life. Sounds stupid now, but, you know, 1961, you went to college, and I didn't want to do that, and you get a job as a secretary, and I took kind of a general course in high school, so anyhow, I thought, fine.
>
> [So you didn't see a lot of options?]
>
> No . . . so I did everything that I was quote supposed to do unquote . . . very into being like everybody else.

These women tended to doubt their ability to make judgments and to take care of themselves. After she had been married for about fifteen years, respondent #24, age fifty-four, describes how she was reluctant to leave, although good reasons, such as her husband's verbal abuse, alcohol abuse, and financial irresponsibility, were accumulating for her to end her marriage. This was true despite her own career success and other evidence that she was well able to take care of herself and her children:

> And I even sat at my desk thinking about leaving him and realizing there was no one else for me to live with in 1979. Who would be eligible? I also just couldn't see in my mind that I could support a family on my own.
>
> [Even though you had been doing it (supporting the family)?]
>
> Even though I'd been doing it for years, and the business that he was running now . . . he had his own little business now. He started gift-shopping franchises . . . but he drank all the profits . . . I was making at that time probably eighteen to twenty thousand, and in the seventies, for a woman with no education, that was big money. I was making more than the vice president of the bank; when I applied for a house loan, he said, "You make more money than I do." . . . But I can't be alone, and there is no other eligible person in this city, and I was terrified of raising kids alone.
>
> [What is it that you were afraid about specifically? Do you know?]
>
> Even though I had a strong image at work and was a very confident person at work, [I was] always being diminished [at home] and I was looking at myself based on what he was telling me. He was telling me that if I ever [gained weight] he would leave me [and that] I was not nearly as smart as he was—that kind of thing. [I] drop something, and to this day, I expect somebody to yell at me. The first time I dropped and broke something when I was living with Laura and she didn't yell, I just couldn't believe it. I stood there, and she [asked]

"Did you do it on purpose?" And no! "Then it's an accident. No big deal." But wasn't that important to you? "Not as important as you are."

This research shows that these women were blocked in their realization about their gender orientation to make early, clear moves in that direction. In conflict with these findings, a number of writers have suggested that individuals with same-gender attractions go through a lengthy, painful process of avoidance, self-deception, cure seeking, and "playing it straight" before they finally accept homosexual attraction as part of their identity (e.g., see Troiden, 1988). Although this assertion may be true under some circumstances, it assumes that information about same-gender relationships is readily available and that the individuals in question are completely free to trust their own judgment and accept or reject this information as they see fit. One finding of my research is that many women with same-gender attractions are blocked in fully "knowing" about their attractions because they are living within a sociological context that limits their information, as well as their outcomes. Nichols and Leiblum (1986) appear to support this latter premise, suggesting that heterosexism and sexism make avoidance behavior more likely to occur. Without the full range of sanctioned relationship outcomes, women are most likely to accept those outcomes that they see modeled, ones which are not likely to threaten their network of other relationships. The heterosexist ideology which drives our society has made positive same-gender relationship models unavailable.

Many models of gender orientation development tend to represent the process of this development as primarily one of "willingness to know this about myself" (see Chapter 4), but other writers have been critical of linear models of gender orientation development, stating that the process is more complex (see, e.g., Ross, 1987; Rust, 1993). My present research also suggests a relatively complex picture of gender orientation awareness.

As stated in Chapter 2, of the twenty-four women interviewed for this research study,

1. fifteen did not know of their same-gender feelings before they married,

2. and the remaining nine had same-gender feelings or experiences before they married. Of these last nine,

- four consciously repressed their impulses because they thought they were unacceptable or they didn't know how to interpret them;
- one failed to know because she combined psychological denial with conscious repression to deal with her feelings;
- two thought they were the only women who had these feelings and so consciously repressed them; and
- two experienced total denial of the feelings; that is, in the sense of psychological denial, they didn't know that they didn't know.

Following are examples of each of these categories.

Respondent #8, age forty-three, consciously repressed her same-gender feelings because she didn't know how to interpret them:

> [Relating to boys] I did what was expected of me. I had, like I said, Sister LuAnn and Gina. Those were the people I really wanted to be with.

> [Did you ever think of those relationships as sexual?]

> I felt about wanting to be with them. I don't know if at that time in my life, I was really into thinking I could ever have sex with them. I mean, I grew up and I was expected to live a certain way, you know, and when I left California and moved to a small town, if I had told anybody that that's what I was about—I was having those thoughts, you know. I don't know what the fear, what that would have been . . .

Two of the four who appeared to repress their impulses (ages twenty-nine and forty-one), may have had enough information about lesbians and lesbianism before they married so that it could be said they made a choice to avoid investigating their same-gender feelings in the sense that Troiden (1988) describes, for example, respondent #5, age forty-one:

[When you were in high school, did you date?]

No, I was an athlete. I did my athletics. I was really into school. I loved math. . . . I played sports and guitar, and I did some music, and then I did my schoolwork. And that was it . . . and I was attracted to women too.

[When did you first notice that?]

When I was very young. Eight, probably. Dreams of little girls that I knew from church or teachers I had crushes on or my cousins. I just stayed in the evangelical, going to Bible study and doing that. I tried to push it down, pray it down. Whatever, . . . I knew I had feelings for women, but did not know that was a legitimate choice for me to make. . . . I had friends who were lesbians, and I didn't judge them . . . but for me, I wouldn't allow myself to have that.

What did "lesbian" mean to these women—before they came out, as they came out? What were the images and stereotypes that led to lack of fit with them? Why couldn't they see themselves with those images? In her writing from 1978, Lee Lehman describes the contradictory assumptions made about lesbian women. Although the writing is twenty years old, the myths and misperceptions are just now beginning to change. On the one hand, notes Lehman, there is lesbian invisibility. When two women live together for years, the neighbors may choose to accept them as good friends, as roommates, as two "old maids" who get what little comfort they can from each other. Society has recognized that women are very capable of giving each other emotional support and can accept that two women may live together and care for each other. However, a sexual relationship between these two women is either unimaginable or unthinkable. Therefore, many lesbians and lesbian couples remain unidentified and, thus, invisible. On the other hand, there is the paradox that once a woman is labeled lesbian, the society thinks of her almost exclusively as a sexual being. Despite the lack of scientific evidence to support this, studies surveying opinions have shown that lesbians are believed to be far more sexual than other women.

Lehman (1978) describes other myths that have grown out of this misperception. For example, lesbians are child molesters; a lesbian only needs sex with a man to "cure" her; lesbians hate men; and, of course, lesbians are sex crazed. All they want is sex. It seems likely that these images and impressions were the ones with which our research respondents couldn't identify and also why they couldn't imagine they might be lesbian or bisexual. (More discussion about role models is in Chapter 5.)

Respondent #17, age thirty-nine, didn't "know" about her feelings because she combined psychological denial with conscious repression, due to personal repugnance about sex, as well as difficulty with the lesbian identification issue:

> I remember him taking me a place called _____ in [large city], which was a gay bar, and being fascinated by the—what would I call them—leather dykes, I suppose, with the really weird short hair and black biker jackets, biker wallets, you know. . . . It began a series of fantasies about these women who were tough.

> [Were you drawn to these women?]

> [Nods] Scared the death out of me, too. . . . I never imagined . . . . I look at people today, and they act upon this instinct, you know; they go out, they seek, they find, . . . and I don't remember even thinking that I could allow myself to do that. I don't know whether I thought it was perverse or dirty or twisted or. . . . I can't remember.

> [Are you talking about these women or sex, period?]

> Sex with women. I don't remember thinking about any social issues. I don't remember thinking my family will disown me or any of that stuff. It was not about any of that. . . . I think for me, maybe the bottom line has always been, how I function sexually.

> [What made sexuality so difficult for you?]

> Probably because it was presented as distasteful and dirty. And I think my experimentation, which was pretty normal, was discovered and cast in a pretty negative light.

Two respondents, ages fifty-two and thirty, thought they were the only women who had these feelings, so they believed they were very unusual and could never find women to share a relationship with them, for example, respondent #19, age fifty-two:

> I loved high school. I loved playing sports, and as far as my orientation, I knew; I didn't know I was a lesbian, but I knew I felt differently about girls. I was young. I'd been having these crushes on schoolteachers and crushes on girls, and yet, when I was in high school, I had crushes on a lot of my friends but I . . . I didn't know what to do about my feelings, and I didn't know anybody else had them, so I didn't do anything with them.

Respondent #21, age thirty, had similar feelings and used alcohol to try to deal with them:

> I think I started crushing out on teachers when I was really young, and I didn't know what that was about. I think back to it then, and was I looking for a mother or was I crushing out because I was gay and didn't know it? In junior high, I really fell for a history teacher, really bad; it got obsessive, and she distanced herself from me, which I look back now, and that was a healthy thing [for her] to do. . . . I remember she made a comment, "So when are you going to start dating boys?" and that just threw me for a loop because it was like, God, you know, I got to do this dating thing. I was scared of being gay, and I think back then I knew it. . . . [In college] I was pretty bad, and I think one of the reasons I drank so much then is because I was having these feelings for Sue and I was trying to mask them. If I were drunk and I was affectionate with her, it was excusable because I was drunk. Drunk people are affectionate.

The remaining two were in complete psychological denial of their impulses. According to Rust, a presumed heterosexual identity "serves as a perceptual scheme that filters and guides the interpretation of experience; experiences are given meanings that are consistent with heterosexual identity" (Rust, 1993, p. 71). Respondent #23, age forty-seven, articulates the "knowing but not knowing" mental state:

I couldn't quite identify as a lesbian.

[You mean you had thoughts that maybe you were?]

Yeah, but without going as far as the maybe. I don't know how to explain that really. I read everything that had the word lesbian in it. I started going to Amazon Bookstore and buying books like crazy. I bought Del Martin's *Lesbian Woman*. . . . I started understanding what my relationship with my roommate had been . . . but I said I was doing all this without being very overt about it. I've had other experiences with the same kind of thing in my life, where you know something, but because you don't name it, it's like it doesn't exist in a way to you. . . . I journaled all those years . . . on and off . . . and I never wrote anything about this in it, ever. On the other hand, I wrote love poems to my friend Geri—tiny little handwriting. It makes you want to cry. But I never named it. I never said it.

[Have you ever thought of that as denial?]

That's what it is.

In another example of psychological denial, the words of respondent #9, age fifty-seven, are a reminder that much experience goes unacknowledged, particularly experience that doesn't have social approval. For this woman, the unacknowledged experience apparently included feelings of sexual arousal along with general attraction to women:

You know, when I look back now, I'm really mystified about how I had these experiences and these feelings and yet I didn't register them internally as significant. One woman I sang in church choir with, I loved with all my heart. I know now I was turned on in her presence all the time. And a young woman I interviewed once when I was doing my job. She and I were really drawn to each other, and she invited me to her house for dinner. She and I talked after dinner, and then she went and put her nightgown on before I left. We stood in the front entry of her house and talked for twenty minutes. When I left, I felt electric and excited. But I still didn't get it. There are others too. One girl in high school I connected with when we were adults. She said she remembered the feelings we had for each other in high school, and she knew—at the time—what they meant. But I didn't. It was sexual arousal that was unfamiliar, I guess. Or was it OK to be aroused? Or did I know it was sexual? Or was it just sexual?

Once again, it appears clear that the women represented by this study did not feel supported in determining their own paths. Even if they had had good sex information and awareness, even if they had known they didn't have to marry, and even if they had understood the broad potential parameters of their identity development as an ongoing process, they would still have been living in a patriarchal culture in which, paradoxically, these three issues would have been socially managed and controlled anyway.

We need to remember that patriarchy's chief institution is the family and that women tend, in general, not to do things that rock the boat, especially the family boat. The family is both a mirror of, and a connection with, the larger society, a patriarchal unit within a patriarchal whole (Millett, 1978). Women do tend to limit themselves with alliances that they tend to foster because of their cooperative nature and their interest in harmonious relationship connections, many of which originate in the family. These limits and alliances have indeed kept them from "knowing."

More important, however, these women have been subject to ascriptions of temperament and role as defined by their society. These ascriptions originate in patriarchal ideals, about which Millett wrote, "under their aegis, each personality becomes little more, and often less than half, of its human potential" (Millett, 1978, p. 44). Perhaps no governing ideology has ever exercised such complete control over its subjects as has patriarchy. As long as patriarchal ideals disallow independent thinking for women under penalty of social punishment and do not include permission for same-gender relationship arrangements, women (and men) will find it difficult to "know" and act on their same-gender attractions.

Chapter 5

Where Are the Lesbian Role Models?

As the respondents moved through the process of learning to know about their gender orientation, in addition to the issues discussed previously, restraint was placed on their knowing by the lack of healthy images and serious role models available to affirm their same-gender feelings. This was the fifth theme identified in the interviews. Many respondents in this research became aware of their same-gender attractions long before they acted on them or left their marriages. However, once these women had a sense of their attraction to women, they did not see many women around them with whom they could identify, from whom they could learn, or after whom they could model themselves.

Women tend to become what they know they can become, based on what they see around them. That is, we know that throughout life, much learning takes place as a result of what is modeled by other people (Bandura and Walters, 1969). Paula Rust has said that "self-identity is the result of the interpretation of personal experience in terms of available social constructs" (Rust, 1993, p. 68). One could argue that the social construct of lesbian/bisexual could exist for a woman but that she would find it very difficult to act in terms of that construct without role models. We learn from the behavior, attitudes, and values of those people who happen to present themselves in the landscape of our lives. They represent models for emulation. Models—in this case, women who are comfortable with their identity or orientation—provide encouragement, guidance, and validation. They will show a variety of responses to situations, giving cues to the range of normative behavior and feelings a woman may have as she experiences same-gender attractions. Models normalize. When models are available, women becoming aware of their changing identity feel less alone and more supported, validated, and normal. As we have seen, identity, at least in part, evolves as a reflection of the social world.

Significant sources of models are the images seen in the public realm. These public images tend to show what is possible, but public images in the media, advertising, films, and so forth do not freely and spontaneously appear. As with all aspects of an organized society, acceptable images are managed, parceled out by society's gatekeepers, such as the legal, medical, psychological, educational, and informational institutions. These agencies have much control over which images or models can appear. Society, in general, reflects those attitudes, and legal and institutional oppression reflect and enforce the attitudes, assuring that they continue.

If categories of people—such as lesbians—are represented as undesirable, then women who become aware of their inclusion in that category will feel undesirable too. The general attitude of American society has been consistently pejorative and distorted toward lesbians. Lesbians, gays, and bisexuals are prejudged, by definition, "bad" or somehow "evil." Women who think they might be lesbian or bisexual will need exposure to stable, balanced lesbian women who express pride in their identities and abilities to deal with homophobia. As Bohan (1996) notes, "prejudice involves negative attitudes toward a group based on preconceptions and stereotypes which lead one to judge individuals within the group not by their personal qualities but by their membership in the stigmatized group" (p. 42).

Six women in this research group knew as they grew up and before they married that lesbians existed as a group. Two of these (ages twenty-eight and fifty-four) described lesbian family friends. The other eighteen said, variously, they "didn't know lesbians existed" or that after they were adults, they had some vague sense of lesbians, usually as a stereotype of masculine, tough women, very unlike themselves. Most of the women only learned about lesbians and relationships between women through great personal effort and/or by searching for a community. Respondent #25, age fifty-three, describes the impression she had of homosexuals when she was a child:

[Did you know any lesbians growing up?]

No, absolutely not.

[Did you know what lesbianism was?]

Well, I know that certainly, and I know that. . . . I remember my mom talking about—homos and fairies were the two terms that I would hear her use. She didn't use them a lot, and she wasn't that . . . it was certainly said with an air of that's not good. Homo, or he's a homo. . . . So I did know that this existed, and I knew it had to do with two men and two women, but I sure didn't spend much time thinking about it . . . and then at [college], there were two women roommates that others used to gossip about, that they thought they were—queer. . . . It was something that I—well, when I was younger and in high school and college, I am sure my attitude was that that is something that, thank God, I am not. I didn't have curiosity about it, and I did not—and because of Catholicism or whatever, I'm sure I just thought it was bad, bad . . . sinful.

The forces that have created these prejudices, distortions, and stereotypes of lesbians have grown out of complex networks of sexism, sexology, psychoanalytic thinking, misogyny, fear of difference, and so forth. It is important to begin with an understanding that these women were restricted in their knowledge by a dearth of positive lesbian role models and certain exposure to homophobic myths and stereotypes. One bedrock of patriarchy is that women and men are paired and that women need men to care for them. In the interest of preserving patriarchal institutions, single women who live without men are vilified and ridiculed or they are ignored, which makes them invisible.

In the social and family context of lesbians as bad, sex crazed, tough, or otherwise objectionable, respondent #23, age forty-seven, says she didn't know what to think about her growing same-gender feelings:

I had close girlfriends. . . . I had crushes on them. I had a friendlike relationship with them, but had a really profound crush on two different women whom I followed around, but I didn't talk to myself very much about what I was doing with that or what I would do with that if anything ever happened . . .

[Did you think of it as an option? You are saying you didn't name it. Isn't there a difference between not naming it and not thinking it was an option?]

I think it was both. I didn't think of it as an option because I was married. And I didn't think of it as an option partly because I couldn't envision myself as a lesbian. I didn't have much experience. I didn't know what the reality was, even apart from reading articles, and I didn't have any context to fit it in.

To examine stereotypes, Faderman (1981) traced the history of Western society's treatment of the lesbian from the seventeenth century to the present. By examining the portrayal of lesbians in literature, especially novels and magazine articles over the past century, she discovered a major shift from acceptance of romantic friendships between women at the beginning of the century to a vilification of those women and their relationships later. These romantic friendships of two women sometimes evolved into shared lives, but no labels of lesbian or homosexual were applied to define these relationships, and they were not stigmatized by society (Faderman, 1981). However, Freud's focus on sexuality as central to human development and experience stimulated a growing interest in sex. This interest spurred the formation of the science of sexology. In the late nineteenth century, a group of sexologists undertook to research and clarify what were called perversions, cross-sex identity, a third sex, "the riddle of love between men" (Bohan, 1996, p. 17). After the perversions were listed, heterosexuality was left over and, thus, was considered normal. Since the medical model begged biological and medical explanations for all nonheterosexual identities, homosexuality was ultimately considered a medical "condition," not normal, but amenable to treatment (Bohan, 1996, p. 17). After the popularization of these psychoanalytic concepts, lesbians were vilified and feared as sick individuals (Faderman, 1981).

The field of psychology apparently transferred this pejorative view of homosexuality from psychoanalytic theory to the psychological canon without change. However, in 1973, homosexuality was removed as a mental illness from the American Psychiatric Association's *Diagnostic and Statistical Manual of Mental Disorders*. In 1975, the American Psychological Association issued a resolution of agreement with this stance, saying that homosexuality implies no impairment in judgment, reliability, or general social and vocational capabilities and that mental health professionals were encouraged to show leadership in removing the stigma of mental illness long associated with homosexual orientations (Gonsiorek and Weinrich, 1991).

However, change occurs slowly, and inconsistency shows itself in institutions as well as individuals. A study conducted in 1982 showed that 38 percent of social workers, clinical psychologists, and psychiatrists who responded labeled homosexuality as sexual deviance and stated that their intention in their treatment of homosexuals was to change their gender orientation (Hetrick and Martin, 1984). Hopefully, an alternative view is evolving: the problem is not the individual's discomfort with her identity; the problem lies in the societal attitudes that condemn that identity and therefore make its acknowledgement and personal integration painful. "It is those attitudes, not the identity, that need to be repaired" (Bohan, 1996, p. 19).

The experience of respondent #1, age thirty-six, illustrates her struggle with the conflict between her love for one woman and then another—and the homophobic lesbian prejudice she had absorbed from her society:

I had fallen in love with Ann and then made the decision that—I have my family. This is what my choice was, but we then remodeled the house to have a place to vent all my energy, and then these thoughts were occupying my mind that I was saying, "Nope, I can't think about that; nope, can't do that, nope, nope, nope, nope, nope." And my [other] friend Joan was calling me up while I was going through this, and she says, "I'm going out to [restaurant]; do you want to meet me there?" "I can't; I'm painting. No, I can't; I'm wallpapering. No I can't." Then one day, I said, "Okay, I'll meet you" . . . and

I didn't say a word to her about what was going on with me at that time and, I didn't know why I didn't. I went home and looked at it, and the answer I came up with was if I had said something to Joan about that happening, what was going on with me, it would open a door, or a gate, a floodgate actually, for my feelings for [Joan] that came through on a real big level, and I didn't want that to happen. I had made the choice; now I'm going to stay married. I'm going to stay raising my family in the traditional way.

At the close of the twentieth century, it is tempting to think that there is widespread belief in the need for changed attitudes. There is hope that the progress of the lesbian/gay/bisexual movement in the United States will yield greater acceptance and more positive role models and images. For example, a few years ago, when Ellen DeGeneres came out to millions of viewers on prime-time television, hope developed that the life event of this apparently ordinary woman could educate the American public to greater awareness that lesbians do indeed exist and that they are similar in appearance to their friends and neighbors.

However, Ellen's coming out was not really an innocuous as it was carefully portrayed on TV. To be more palatable to the American public, being lesbian was portrayed as having little effect outside of its own quiet existence. The show did that well and probably convinced some people that lesbians can be acceptable. However, the high number of viewers probably indicated curiosity, voyeurism, and, in some circles, revulsion rather than genuine interest. That is, it is clear from many sources, plus my research, that the category of lesbian and lesbian existence, however ordinary, challenges patriarchy (Ussher, 1992). Two women together as loving life partners who are living full lives without men are a challenge to the carefully constructed institution of patriarchy. "Being a lesbian is inevitably political, whatever Ellen says" (Amussen, 1997).

One respondent's experience illustrates our society's judgmental attitude toward lesbians and gays. When her family reacted to learning about her brother's orientation, respondent #21, age thirty, realized that her family viewed his being gay as an extremely shameful secret:

My brother is gay and came out to the family, and they were having a heck of a time with it. My mom, shortly after my dad died, he came out to her, and she was freaked. . . . When she first started freaking out, I didn't know what was going on . . . and then I found out it was about my brother. And I thought, "What's going on? Somebody tell me please." And my family's attitude was, "Don't tell the kids; they don't need to know." Finally I cornered my other brother, and I said, "What's going on? Is something horrible happening to Alan?" He said, "OK," and he takes me to my room. I remember he was wearing his uniform at the time; he was a weekend warrior—army reserves. He sat down on my bed and said, "I don't know if you know this about Alan. I'm sure you've suspected . . . your brother is gay." And I went, "Yeah, and?" He said, "Your brother is gay." I said, "Is that all?" I thought he had a horrible accident. I thought someone broke his heart. I thought he was dying. I was thinking all these things. And he's gay . . . glad he's OK, whatever. Left it at that.

Voyeurism and judgment are certainly not limited to the United States, but these attitudes toward sexuality and sex-related issues are highly prevalent in America. On the day after Ellen DeGeneres' coming-out show, a reporter on National Public Radio interviewed a woman and man who write for Belgian and German periodicals, respectively. They were asked if they reported to their audiences about the *Ellen* issue highly publicized in the United States. The reporters said they had not reported on it because their audiences would not be interested in such news, except as an example of American attitudes. They said their readers took less interest in issues of gender orientation, lending the whole phenomenon more of a live-and-let-live attitude in their countries.

Because much of American society reacts to lesbians as freakish and aberrant, generally, the women in this research study found it very challenging to accept that they might be lesbian. For example, respondent #17, age thirty-nine, talks about how difficult it was for her to see herself as lesbian and also normal:

But I remember . . . going to a lesbian therapist, finding a therapist, and having her ask me, "Are you lesbian?" and I denied it. You know, I wasn't prepared to say that I was.

[What was stopping you?]

I think the fear of the label of being identified and not knowing what that would mean, not knowing many people who were lesbians, and not having a sense of the normalcy that I understand now. Even in spite of our connections, I think my scope was fairly narrow, fairly limited in terms of who I knew who was lesbian.

We shouldn't be surprised by the public outcry against Ellen and her coming out because for hundreds of years, patriarchal attitudes have created the impression that women without men are sick; in fact, women, by definition, are either powerful temptresses or evil, with the potential to be both. One hundred years ago, the Victorian woman was expected to emulate the "angel in the house." This prescription was a double-edged sword. Ussher (1992) tells us that the Victorian woman was credited with natural goodness, but was also called a weak, infantile, mindless creature in constant need of male supervision and protection. To provide examples of the extreme and dichotomous references to women in the nineteenth century, some authors (e.g., Martin, 1987; Showalter, 1987) have examined the Victorian novel. They have analyzed the young and pure Jane Eyre and her counterpart, Rochester's first wife Bertha Mason, the madwoman locked in the attic. These authors suggest that raving, aggressive Bertha is locked up because of her sexuality, her transgression of femininity. Their analyses posit that Bertha's worst attacks of rage and violence come, as the author said, when the moon is "blood red" or "broad and red" (Showalter, 1987, p. 67), thereby inferring she is a prisoner of her menstrual cycle. She has the "moral insanity" associated with women's sexual desires (Ussher, 1992, pp. 63-93).

Ussher (1992) writes further about the links between misogyny and mental illness. As she points out, representations of women as sexually out of control could be a reflection of men's ambivalence about their own power, as suggested by Simone de Beauvoir (1953), or a dread of maternal power and control (Dinnerstein, 1976) arising from their early experiences as infants. In any case, Ussher states, "what is certain is that these representations exclude women, mark us as the Other, dividing us and categorizing us through labels of 'witch,' 'madwoman,' 'whore.' Only as 'wife' is one safe" (Ussher, 1992, p. 87). In other words, only a woman who is submissive to a man is socially acceptable.

The misogyny and sexism described by Ussher also elucidate a deep link between sexism and homophobia that is often underemphasized in analyses of lesbian prejudice. Homophobia—especially men's fear and hatred of women who are strong and independent and women's fear of being perceived as one of "those" women—remains an important part of the fight against equal rights for women. Ussher notes that during the nineteenth century, all women were considered deviant, but the woman who was believed to be the most deviant was the woman who preferred the sexual company of women—the lesbian. As with the celibate woman, the lesbian doesn't need men. Rather than denying her sexuality, however, she enjoys it. The woman who chooses to be sexually active, but not with a man, is also deeply threatening to reigning patriarchal values (Ussher, 1992).

The research respondents show by their responses that they have absorbed the homophobic attitudes rampant in this society. Respondent #14, age forty-eight, describes her reaction when she and a friend were accused of being lesbian:

[During your marriages, who were your friends?]

Usually females, and that was one of my first clues. And in between, it would be females, and when I look back, a couple [who were] probably lesbians that I can point out and one that was married. We were especially close, and I remember being accused all the time when we were out and about of being lesbians, and I'd be terribly offended by that. And a roommate I had in between. I think that's when we really started, started realizing, you know; it was like we both frantically went into short-term male relationships after we were trying to prove we weren't [lesbians]. Either I knew enough about it or heard enough about it to think it was a pretty bad thing.

[A bad thing?]

Um, from my family's perspective, yeah. It was a sin or some perversion, sexual perversion.

In sum, lesbians have been feared and reviled for the past 100 years. During the last twenty-five years, our respondents began to become aware of their same-gender attractions. Although progress has been made in the positive visibility of gay/lesbians/bisexuals, numerous sources warn that acceptance is not imminent. The talk from the religious right that granting civil rights to gays and lesbians constitutes special privilege, the hate speech coming from Washington, DC's political arena as well as local political sources about homosexuals who are "destroying the fabric of American family life," and the Defense of Marriage legislation being passed in many states all serve as a reminder that the very success of the gay/lesbian civil rights movement is producing a backlash (Vaid, 1995; Zimmerman and McNaron, 1996). This troubling homophobic backlash also slows the production of positive lesbian images and role models.

Homophobia thus continues to limit positive public and private views of lesbian women and is part of the tightly knit web that holds all women in their places and keeps them from seeing one another clearly. It is in the interest of patriarchal value maintenance that women be threatened by one another and see one another as dangerous. Adrienne Rich (1980) writes eloquently of the loss of women's mutual support for and to one another that is created and maintained by lesbian prejudice. Although the supposed danger and deviancy of lesbians has been part of the misogynistic discourse describing women for hundreds of years, it was in the nineteenth and twentieth centuries that the lesbian became officially pathologized, with her sexuality considered part of her supposed "condition." Jane Ussher (1992) suggests that the Victorians were so fearful that innocent heterosexual women could be led astray by the knowledge that sexual relations between women were a possibility, that in England, they made homosexual acts (sodomy) between men illegal, but did not publicize the deviancy of sex between women. They did this, in effect, by not mentioning it. Sex between women was unimaginable to the Victorians, just as it remains so to much of American society today. In any case, no one had a name for what women do together sexually. Therefore, sex between women was legally deemed not to exist and, thus, could not be officially regulated. It remains true that a significant part of homophobia is the attitude that lesbians/gays/

bisexuals don't exist. For the women in this study, therefore, an additional level of paradox appears: lesbians are deviant and dangerous but/and they don't exist.

As I have noted, most of the research respondents had no concept of lesbians. In her career as a teacher, respondent #3, age fifty-eight, had many colleagues and friends who were lesbians, but they were invisible to her at the time. She had no idea "who" they were:

> Although I know that teaching phys. ed.—I had some phys. ed. teachers that seemed to figure out all these fun other choices, but I didn't understand them. It's like we were great friends when we were teaching, but when it came to parties and social things, they never invited me, which I couldn't understand. I was just crushed by that because that hadn't ever been my experience.

> [How did you respond to that?]

> I didn't at the time. I should have confronted them and said "Why don't you ever invite me?" I was just bewildered because I usually am a pretty social person. I'd get invited everywhere. So I couldn't figure out what I [was] doing wrong; they were older, and I thought, well, maybe being older. They had more fun than anybody in my age group. I came to find out, now, I look back, they were all gay. And I didn't think that I was or at that point, I wasn't, or whatever I was. But I was not a comfortable person to invite to their parties because I was "dating." I was going with other straight people on the faculty, and now [that] I look back, and it makes complete sense.

In this heterosexist, homophobic society, who did these women have as role models? Two constellations of problems exist regarding the availability of lesbian role models. In Chapter 3 on identity, we began a discussion on the societal attitudes toward, and the stereotypes of, lesbians. First, lesbian invisibility has not changed in the past thirty years: two women together are thought of as two good friends, sometimes pathetic, who are lonely and living together because they haven't got a man. This invisibility of known lesbians obviously reinforces the mistaken idea that lesbianism is rare.

Most people say they don't know any lesbians. Lee Lehman describes the revelation of her lesbianism to her parents. When they said they didn't know any lesbians, Lee notes,: "I couldn't help thinking of the 'roommates' and 'friends' I had been introduced to, and the 'best friends' with whom my parents used to play bridge" (Lehman, 1978, p. 24). This lack of role models, and the invisibility of known lesbians, reinforces in women their lack of worth in society and leaves them always seeking to find a place in a community that appears unaccepting and disapproving.

Respondent #2, age twenty-nine, describes the powerful influence of one woman who dared to identify herself publicly. The respondent recalls her persistent memory of the woman who apparently was willing to identify herself publicly as bisexual, giving this respondent an image, a potential role model:

[When you talk about the process of realizing that you are bisexual, what things, what events, or what were the people or thoughts that made you realize "Hey I'm not just straight; I'm bisexual"?]

Well, something was making me curious. I was trying to get my hands on any kind of reading. I don't know what triggered it at first; I don't understand that. I still don't know. I know that there was a woman in the town where I grew up who came to work at the school for about three weeks. I don't know what happened to her, but she came out there as bisexual, and that did not happen, ever. But she was getting married to a man, and I remember the day I heard that little rumor, and I remember looking at her and thinking, "Wow, okay," just for a brief minute and totally accepting this. None of what may have been other people's judgmentalisms had crept into my mind at all. I was like, do it! But just for a second. And I never pursued talking to her anymore. She was an administrative assistant there, and she didn't last very long. I don't have a clue what happened. Maybe this got out. I don't know. But I remember that moment and hearing that word. And understanding what that meant for just a second, and I must have been fifteen. But then it was gone again, and I never listened, never heard about it. Now there's some good stuff out there. In the last five or six years, but even ten years ago, there was very little.

The second problem is that once a woman is believed to be, is labeled as, a lesbian, she is no longer invisible and harmless; she is thought to be obsessed with sex. Our society promotes the homophobic distortion that since her sex life can be separated from procreation or "wifely duty," the lesbian may be seen as *only* sexual. As we have discussed, our culture deals paradoxically with sex: We are surrounded by sexual imagery in magazines, television, films, advertising, and all popular culture. At the same time, acknowledgement of the significant role of sex in a normal life is rare. Serious, intelligent discussion of sexual issues in the media or between adults is rare. Therefore, paradoxical constructions result. This particular paradox suggests that a woman who has a sex life in which the major function of sex is the giving and receiving of pleasure is a whore, a tease, a prostitute, or a bad girl.

One flagrant example of a paradoxical construction is revealed in comments by respondent #14, age forty-eight. She describes the skewed and distorted attitude taken by her family toward her lesbian identity:

> [Does your father acknowledge that he did this to you (the incest)?]
>
> He acknowledges it, and he says he is sorry. The—at one point in my life, I was doing some incest treatment kinds of things, when I was around thirty, and they agreed to come in for an hour and, you know, that's it. It's solved. It's done with. Why do you keep bringing this up, and why do you have a problem? What's wrong with you? If you would just be a Christian and join the church, you know, and blah, blah, blah, blah. And then since I came out as a lesbian in the last ten years, what's come out with the family is that my being a lesbian is worse than his being incestuous with me . . . and that he's not incestuous anymore but that I'm still—I'm a lesbian.

Research results show that people with more negative attitudes toward homosexuals also express more rigidity and guilt toward their own sexual impulses (Margolies, Becker, and Jackson-Brewer, 1985). Oppressed minority groups are often seen as more sexual, and so gays and lesbians are viewed as expressing sexual impulses in the extreme. In the United States, with the vestiges of the Puritan ethic framing sexual discourse, this is not at all surprising. The result of all this homophobic misogyny is that these twenty-four women were exposed to very few healthy images of lesbians. However, some women were fortunate enough to have lesbians in their family or friendship circle.

Because of her parents' close lesbian friend, when respondent #15, age twenty-eight, was ready to come out, she had somewhat fewer negative perceptions to overcome than most women might:

> As I look back, I felt what was going on in my head—this was the starting of my thinking, even though years before I had basically been co-parented by a lesbian in my home, which was the woman who founded the women's studies department with my father.

> [Co-parented?]

> She lived with us and it was like there were three parents. She lived with us; she had a partner in [large city] who would come visit.

> [So, she was a close friend of your parents.]

> Right. We never really talked about her being any different because it wasn't different as far as my parents were concerned. So, just Nicky. Nicky lived with us, and she had a female partner who lived out of town, and nothing clicked with me until I think it was about the—I think while I was in college, I called my mother and said, "Is Nicky a lesbian?" And my mother said, "Well, yeah." And I said, "Why didn't you ever tell me?" And she said, "Well, it didn't matter. Why should we have said anything? Nicky is Nicky and she just lives her life, and she has a partner and I have your dad." And that's just how it was.

As she was becoming aware of her same-gender identification, respondent #4, age thirty-three, connected with her sister who introduced her to a new community. Having a sister who was lesbian provided a powerful role model who helped validate and define what this woman was learning to know about herself:

[When your sister said that she was lesbian, was she the first lesbian you had known?]

Yup. And then she would point out people. And I'm like, "You're kidding." Or even people on TV and I would go, like, "No way!" I didn't even know it was such a big area that so many people were involved in this; that's so cool. Because at first, I could be supportive for her. Because I didn't know that I was going to try it, and I felt that was kind of my attitude, "Well, maybe I'll try it." And once she started taking me out to the bars and stuff, and I just felt so comfortable; it was like, "Oh, this is it." So I guess it was mostly at her coming out that I realized and then became comfortable with it and started meeting people, and I made it a very big part of my life because I knew that it was my life too. That was who I was inside.

[That was your community?]

Yup.

During the 1970s and 1980s, if these women were consciously or unconsciously hunting for lesbian images in the media, there were few role models to be found. Prior to 1969, no gay/lesbian/bisexual images appeared on TV dramas, situation comedies, radio and TV talk shows, or in magazine articles and broadcast and print news stories (Vida, 1978). Since then, a few more appear every year. Early on, the film images were negative—primarily very lonely, unstable and/or sex-crazed women (*The Killing of Sister George* [1969]; *Windows* [1980]). Since 1990, several TV shows have had fairly neutral gay characters. However, game shows especially seem to thrive on tasteless jokes around the words fruit, queen, and fairy. It seems that gay male jokes are always good for a laugh, and any reference to lesbians tends to pander to the prurient (Vida, 1978).

On the other hand, more recently, in 1992 and 1993, k.d. lang was suddenly a celebrity lesbian. Glossy gay magazines began to flourish in the 1990s. In 1996, Melissa Etheridge was on *Newsweek*'s cover with her female partner. A lesbian woman kissed Roseanne on her television show. Films were made with positive gay/lesbian characters (*Longtime Companion* [1990]; *Philadelphia* [1993]; *Antonia's Line* [1996]). Feminist publishing burgeoned, and serious books, particularly nonfiction and mystery titles, were written about lesbians and with lesbian characters. However, this proliferation of material was not the result of advertisers' and political leaders' belief in the rightness of it all. It seems that members of the country's business and political establishment were gambling on claims made by gay groups about impressive demographics and high levels of discretionary income (Gluckman and Reed, 1997, Introduction). Ironically, the religious right used the information on the prosperity of many gay/lesbian/bisexual households to support lack of necessity for civil rights for gays.

At any rate, these changes toward the positive have occurred only in the past seven years or so. Even the youngest of our research respondents grew up and lived as adults without any positive lesbian images with which to identify. When there are so few lesbian images, those which appear, even the negative ones, are latched onto by women as a validation of their feelings. In her article about lesbian images in the media, Ginny Vida (1978) discussed a 1970s film, *The Fox* (1975), as one that portrays lesbians in an undesirable way. However, respondent #13, age fifty-three, describes her response to seeing lesbian references in public for the first time. She was apparently so gratified that a lesbian image existed in a film that she didn't evaluate whether it was a positive or negative image:

> I don't remember seeing a film about lesbians until I was in that graduate school experience, and I think we saw a film called *The Fox*. There was a movie I do remember that I went to with LuAnn, and it had lesbians in it; there were references, and I was amazed, you know, because it wasn't something that was talked about or that I'd read about.

[Maybe that was the first time you ever saw it represented around you anywhere.]

I think so. And *The Fox* sounds right to me. I remember there was a book, and then I saw the film.

These public images, models in the media, film, and book characters are what we might call *distant models.*

Another source of role models is colleagues, neighbors, co-workers, and so forth, people who surround women in their lives: these are the *close-up models.* According to a 1992 study, billed as the most comprehensive survey of American sexuality ever conducted, 0.9 percent of the women surveyed identified themselves as homosexual and 0.5, as bisexual. The survey was conducted among 3,432 randomly selected men and women ages eighteen to fifty-nine (Laumann et al., 1994).

This survey gives definite evidence that lesbians do exist; however, because of legal and institutional oppression, many feel unsafe revealing themselves to one another. Many lesbians who could identify with one another in the workplace, church, neighborhood, and so on, remain hidden from one another. This invisibility reinforces lesbian stereotypes because there are so few public role models to combat the stereotyped images. As a result, society maintains its attitudes. The individual lesbian may believe she's the only one who feels she doesn't fit because of the discrepancy between the distortions associated with lesbianism and her own more positive self-concept (Browning, 1984). She may say to herself, "I'm not like that. I must not be lesbian." This sense of isolation that she feels, in turn, reinforces her reluctance to seek information to counteract the contradictions. And so, the cycle continues.

If people become, in large part, what they perceive they *can* become, and that perception of what they can become depends on their knowledge of what others like them *have* become, gay/lesbian/bisexual people are just on the leading edge of learning about the possibilities. With a pervasive, negative social view of lesbians, those who are struggling with their own self-definition (could I be lesbian?) are also struggling with the social perception; they are trying to figure out if they fit, and where. If women are faced with images and stereotypes that present lesbians as very different from themselves, the belief persists that lesbians are so foreign that there could be no possible connection between themselves and anyone with same-gender impulses. When a woman recognizes a lesbian as less alien to her own self-concept, it is a significant moment for her (Charbonneau and Lander, 1991). Respondent #5, age forty-one, describes meeting the first lesbian with whom she could identify:

[And how did you meet Peg?]

I met her through a friend of mine. . . . I met Peg for coffee one morning after we talked on the phone. I met her for coffee and I was struck. I was stricken. I took one look at her and thought, I've had all these stereotypes of who I'd see come through the door, and she was not the stereotype. I'm embarrassed to say that I had those stereotypes, but I did. She just . . .

[What did you think lesbians . . . what was the stereotype you had in your mind?]

Just very heavy, totally cropped black hair, tough. But yeah, I did know other lesbians who . . . but not a lot of them. I thought they were like one in a zillion.

To know that she may be lesbian or bisexual, a woman needs to see positive, healthy images of ordinary lesbian or bisexual women with whom she can identify. Once a woman begins to see the possibility of her same-gender orientation, as Nichols and Leiblum suggest, two factors will most heavily influence her comfort in managing the incorporation of that possibility into her self-image. These two factors are:

1. how committed she is to the traditional female role identity, that is, her level of desire to escape the traditional role, and
2. how much support she finds in her life for assuming a lesbian identity. (Nichols and Leiblum, 1986)

To incorporate lesbian or bisexual into her concept of herself, she needs to alter the homophobic attitudes she has internalized from society. Association with supportive gay/lesbian and bisexual women who model comfort with their identities will encourage the cognitive restructuring or changes in thinking needed to alter her internalized homophobia and to support her changing identity. In this heterosexist, misogynist, and homophobic society, lesbian and bisexual women are seriously challenged in finding such public examples of healthy, self-accepting women. The models may be there, but even now, it is very difficult to see them undistorted.

Chapter 6

Now That She Knows . . .

At this point in the process of becoming aware of her own same-gender longings, the woman's process, similar to that of the women in this research, can take one of several different turns. She has evolved in her awareness so that she has thought she might be lesbian or bisexual, but so far, she hasn't made the major shift in gender orientation. Up to now, the barriers to her knowing have been primarily barriers she shares with others. As previously discussed, no woman—homo-, hetero-, or bisexual—has been given enough sexual information or permission to learn it in an atmosphere of safety and mutual respect. In the United States, the injunction that sex is base and shameful is "a direct residue of a Puritan past" (Kaufman and Raphael, 1996, p. 139). Whether she has married or not, no woman has completely escaped the pressure or the expectation that she will marry. Every gay, lesbian, or bisexual individual has experienced the confusing process of coming to terms with an identity denigrated and misunderstood by our hetero-centrist, heterosexist society. All women are bound by the idea or the enactment of what it means to be a woman under patriarchy. All the respondents needed women they could model themselves after, whose same-gender behavior they could emulate. At this point, if the woman has gotten past these external barriers and is finding her way through her own internal maze, what are the conditions for her making a move, making a declaration, making a change in her life that incorporates her same-gender orientation?

Troiden (1988) has said that lesbians and gay males typically begin to personalize homosexuality during adolescence. He refers to a quote from Vivienne Cass (1984) that describes the early phase of identity confusion, as follows:

> You are not sure who you are. You are confused about what
> sort of person you are and where your life is going. You ask
> yourself the questions "Who am I?" "Am I really a heterosex-
> ual?" (quoted in Troiden, 1988, p. 107)

This population of women who marry and come out later appears
to present a different picture. As adolescents and as adult women,
they felt and asked the usual questions about who they are, but the
respondents in this research did not tend to ask themselves if they
were lesbian when they were adolescents. The question "Am I
really heterosexual?" did not come into their minds in a direct way.
For reasons already discussed, if they had any awareness of their
same-gender feelings as teenagers and before their marriages, they
tended to be confused by them and didn't know how to accommodate such thoughts. Indeed, of twenty-four respondents, seventeen
had no conscious awareness of their same-gender orientation. The
other seven may have recognized the feelings as different from
those others were apparently feeling; however, only three of the
younger respondents (ages twenty-nine, thirty, and thirty-two) had a
word or label to describe what these feelings might be. The other
women did not know because their experiences, their role models,
and the "available social constructs" (Rust, 1993, p. 68) had not
allowed them to know. The greater awareness by younger women
appears to be a reflection of the gradually heightening social awareness of the presence of gays/lesbians/bisexuals over the last ten
years and the concomitant increase in role models and available
social constructs.

As stated previously, at this point, a woman may have thoughts
that she may be lesbian or bisexual, but she could also be having
thoughts that are more diffuse, relating to her life process in general. Fed by the confusion regarding gender orientation, which may
be unconscious, she might feel a general dissatisfaction with her life
and her marriage and be at a loss to explain it to herself.

Respondent #16, age fifty-one, describes this feeling:

> The thing that's hard about this, during this whole breakup—it
> would have been so simple to say [he was] unfaithful, there
> was abuse, there was an alcohol problem, but there wasn't. It
> was that, I guess, I had changed and needed more—I was

thinking and writing down. People to see and places to go, and I didn't want to be with him for some reason, and I didn't know why. . . . I didn't want him in my life. . . . I just knew there was something inside me that was, that was. . . . I just wasn't satisfied with being with Joe anymore. There was no other person or things going on. I realized that, again, he wasn't—I wanted to do more. I wanted to grow more.

Respondent #19, age fifty-two, describes similar feelings, but with more of a sense of emotional panic:

I've got four children and a husband who didn't do anything [to help me], and I started feeling very desperate, very trapped, because I didn't have any help. At that time I was about twenty-four, [and] I was very, very thin and tired. I loved my kids, but it's like God, [I] have babies—two babies and two older ones—and Jim's answer to everything was the bedroom. We did not communicate. And I didn't feel I had a choice to talk to my family. So I didn't, because I felt that my mother [was] not going to support me. . . . I felt like I was drowning in this relationship. He was gone all the time; he would work nights, and if for any reason I would indicate . . . smile at him in the morning . . . he would carry that all day long. It was very oppressive to me. Besides that, everyone else thought he was this really nice person and how could [I] ever not want to be in this relationship? And he was, now that I think on it. I really think he was obsessed with me. It's like I had a rope around me. I couldn't go anywhere, do anything. He was very controlling. Never hit me, of course not; he wasn't physical. . . . I contemplated killing myself because I wanted to get out of this. I simply could not deal with the pressure, and I just thought about how I was going to do it, and then I thought, "Well, maybe I'll just take some pills." I took a bottle of aspirin. Got very, very sick, and I still had to cook dinner. Take care of the kids. I still had to do what I was doing.

Respondent #4, age thirty-three, compares her marriage to her first relationship with a woman:

... I just realized. I mean, it just solidified my feelings that this is, I thought, ... what it's all about. Of course, I really didn't even want to meet a life partner at that point. I had been through what I considered forty-nine years in dog years of being married and in no way, shape, or form wanted to get into that again. But at the least, it just felt comfortable in the relationship and have that companionship and all of the things that I thought a marriage was going to be and never was for me, and I couldn't figure out why. I mean, we had the money, we had the house, we had the one kid, we had everything that looked good on paper, as far as marriage was concerned, but there was nothing there. So it was great to finally have that with a woman and go, "This is it. I get it now. Now I know."

At this point, some women found their process clarifying as the result of a definite attraction they felt for a woman. However, the attraction these respondents felt toward women was generally not so clearly sexual, for example respondent #22, age forty-five:

I was trying to picture—I met her in October; in January, she went to Hawaii, and it was April that I first spoke to her about it, so I don't think when I first met her I had stirrings in my groin—I didn't—it took a while until we spent time together and knew each other and laughed a lot.

As a matter of fact, it would appear that a number of these women tended not to use their sexual arousal or desire to inform their relationship lives with men either. Respondent #18, age fifty-one, discusses her decision process when she was getting ready to marry:

It was very interesting to me when I think back now though; the person I felt the most physical excitement with was the person I did not marry. And I don't know whether he had more wisdom about how to touch me or—he was also first and some of that is excitement about first. I don't know.

[That physical excitement wasn't part of your decision?]

It really wasn't. I don't think so. I think at the time I thought of myself as being pretty excited and expecting to enjoy a mar-

ried sexual relationship. Especially one that wasn't in cars and
in stolen moments, and . . . it was a shock to me that I didn't
enjoy it. . . . I was expecting that the freedom part of being
married . . . was going to make it wonderful, and it didn't. . . .
He was always trying to coax or cajole me into having sex, and
I was often trying to avoid it . . .

The majority of these women were not sexually experienced
before they married. Fifteen of the twenty-four women had no
sexual experience before marriage. Six had sexual intercourse before they married with the man they later married. One had sexual
intercourse with two men, both of whom had asked her to marry
them. Two women (ages twenty-eight and twenty-nine) began to be
sexually active with males as teenagers and had had a good number
of sexual partners prior to marriage. In 1980, the U.S. census began
registering households as POSSLQ (people of opposite sex sharing
living quarters) for the first time. The experience of this group of
women reflects the relaxation of sexual mores over the past twenty
years, in that the two youngest were the only women sexually active
before they married.

Respondent #3, age fifty-eight, has had some significant realizations about her early lack of sexual experience:

[Were you interested in sex (as a young, premarriage woman)?]

Oh God, no. I always said for the reasons that good girls don't,
and you just don't break this barrier because then what do you
do [afterward?] And then, of course, the fear of getting pregnant and all those kinds of fears we had back in those days.
I'm certainly sexual enough now, but if I was interested I
would have gone for it. Good girls were not [interested in sex].
It was just a good way of saying, "I'm a good girl." And it
complicated life . . . with men. So, therefore, I could date all of
these guys and not go to bed with them, and therefore, I could
date, you know what I mean? Which was the fun part to me.
So I was a virgin when I got married. Yeah, good for me. I
don't know nowadays if I would say that. You know, it's like
my daughter; she was a virgin of course, because she'd met—
well, she was a virgin when she got married, but the only man

she'd ever been with was Peter. They met when they were freshmen in high school. But now I say, "Cindy, you need to learn more about yourself and what you like and where your pleasures are and all of those things my mother would never have told me. . . ." About a year ago, she said, "Mom, I don't think I've ever had an orgasm." And we were just chatting about it, which is real uncomfortable when you're talking to your daughter. And then I thought, "I need to tell her something that is going to be real hard." [To myself, I said] "OK, grow up. You can find the courage." And I said, "Cindy, you need to take some time to find out what feels good and what doesn't. And you have to find that out on your own." And I thought, "I can't believe I actually told her to do that because my mother would have died at the thought." And I had to tell my daughter that it was OK, that it was important, that if she doesn't, she could be floundering around forever, trying to be the "good girl."

Therefore, when these women began to relate closely to other women, or to consider such relationships seriously, most previously had not related sexually to many people. In addition, their sexual experience with men tended not to inform their process of relationships with women because it was so different. The connections they were finding with women were very different from those they had had with men. Respondent #1, age thirty-six, expresses this line of thinking:

I had never experienced how I could feel so comfortable being sexual before. And that was, and to this day is, amazing to me. That sex can be so comfortable and expressive.

[How is it different from sex with your husband?]

I feel much more . . . let's see, what is the word I wanted to say—like whole. I don't know if that's correct. It's like I feel more complete, more . . . it just feels like you can really put yourself into it, like the world . . . the world goes away, and this is what's happening with you and your lover. And it's great. Where my sexual experience before was chatter in my head constantly about stuff I couldn't shut off.

[What was the chatter about?]

Anything from the grocery list, so I don't know if I was trying to back off, to, "Oh my God, what would people think if they knew?" . . . I hope the kids don't walk in, . . . or was it like . . .

[Were you aroused when you had sex with your husband?]

Not very often. There were times when I did have an orgasm, but it wasn't very often. But sometimes . . . I don't mean to put him down, but I think that has to do with me. That I'm able to be very expressive with Joan and I wasn't with him. There were times, I think; again, I don't want to speak for him, but in my mind, how it works for him is that this is not something you had to work at; you just do it this way, and this is the way it goes. And he wasn't real in tune to taking care of me as a sexual partner.

Although the draw, the pull, to relationships with women had a sexual aspect, this pull was not necessarily sexual or recognized as sexual. For example, respondent #25, age fifty-three, tries to describe what is different for her in her sexual relationship with her female partner:

You know, I wish I could identify that because it's something we talked about yesterday in that group, but one woman who had been married said she just couldn't stand sex with her husband and it was just torture. And for me, I loved it. So I had no problem with heterosexual sex. I mean, I loved sex with Paul; sometimes we had trouble and even had to get counseling, but he was a wonderful lover, and I had suppressed my sexuality for so long before I was married that once I got into sex, I was really into it.

[What was different about it, then, with women?]

When I had my first sexual experience with her, I knew this was something different and this is what I've been waiting for, and then, I mean I knew. I knew.

Respondent #8, age forty-three, talks about explaining to her husband and children what her coming out to be with women meant to her:

> And like I told Bernie, I really wanted to love him. I said, "I love you in a way I'll never love any other man." And I said, "I really tried hard not to be this, but it's destroying me." And I said, "I can't give it up anymore." And I told the kids that too. I said, "It's not about your mom going out and trying to find women and, this picture of sex in your mind—because that's not what I'm about and that's not what I'm looking for". . . . I said, "This is really scary for me at forty, to have to wonder where I'm going and what's down the road for me."

When women reach the point at which they are questioning their gender orientation, they may be at a disadvantage because they are missing complete access to all the information they need to draw conclusions. If a woman's sexual learning has been limited by what she was allowed to know, she may be at the "received knowledge" stage in her sexual development. At this stage, her experience will have made her what "they" wanted her to become (Belenky et al., 1986), which is, or can be, ignorant of her sexuality. In Chapter 1, we discussed how if Americans are taught about sex at all, it is taught as a mechanical process. Discussion of desire is absent from American education about sex. Fine (1988) has said also that female socialization tends to deny young women permission to feel desire, that they feel split off from their feelings of sexual arousal. This tends to be true for all women, hetero-, homo-, and bisexual. As Jean Baker Miller (1991) notes, at maturity, a woman is supposed to be fully intimate, when all her life she has been trained to be something else.

Respondent #13, age fifty-three, describes the feelings she had about women, as well as the paradoxical conditioning she got (women get) regarding her (their) sexuality:

> [You're saying that you felt this intensity and felt drawn to women sexually?]

> Sure.

[But you didn't really feel that for Larry?]

No, I didn't. No, not at all. And the feelings for women [were] more than I just wanted to hold them, wanted to touch them. I mean, I don't think I thought about genital sex at the time with women . . . maybe it's like the accelerator/brake motion. It felt really good, BUT . . .

[Put the brakes on?]

Yeah, right.

Therefore, a woman may be ignorant of her body and its arousal patterns. She may then feel sexual arousal around a woman but fail to recognize it as sexual because she has been taught that she's not supposed to feel it, that sex is mechanical, or that the only sex that qualifies as real is vaginal penetration with a penis (Ussher, 1992).

How did the women in the research group describe their feelings for women that were sexual—but not sexual? Consider the following comments made by three respondents. Respondent #8, age forty-three:

> . . . fell in love with Beth and couldn't tell her. Was afraid to tell her . . . finally told her the way I felt. . . . She said she shared some of the same feelings I had but she had a problem with it. You know, if God meant women to be with women, then, where would reproduction be? . . . I said, "A few nuns I know are lesbian . . . and if you take everything in the Bible literally" . . . like I don't believe that there's any living God up there that's going to condemn or send anybody to hell. I said, "For me, it's not about sex anyway."

[What is it about?]

I think, for me, it was more about feeling more connected with a woman inside emotionally. You know, I've been with a woman three times—different women—and it feels comfortable to me. I feel comfortable taking my clothes off. I never felt comfortable with guys in that area at all.

[It sounds like you feel comfortable taking your clothes off literally and you feel comfortable taking your emotional clothes off, opening up.]

Exactly. Myself.

Respondent #12, age fifty-three:

I was drawn and always felt more women-attracted physically than I ever did men. And that means in every way. Not only physically, but I just enjoyed their company. I have more to say to them.

Respondent #14, age forty-eight:

My first clues . . . that I had sexual feelings for women or that I trusted them, that there was an emotional closeness that I didn't find at all with men [were] that I could communicate with them, that I didn't have to explain myself the whole time. . . . there isn't as much of the power kinds of things. . . . I like not having the roles . . . and the emotional closeness is probably key. Sex still isn't top of my list, especially since I had breast cancer about— it's been five years now, and I went on tamoxifen for a couple of years. . . . I gained sixty pounds. I had a lot of side effects. Started having hot flashes, and I could really feel sex just dried, just going away. . . . Took me about a year and a half to regain my energy level, but I'm still not real interested in sex. It's not a big part of our life right now, so Rita could probably give you the date of when we had sex last but—there's part of me that's been such a healing thing, to be in a committed relationship with a woman and having one breast and . . . and . . . because I've had friends who lost breasts and couldn't get through dating, had trouble with men leaving them. . . . The men I was married to would not. . . . I'm not sure they would have stuck around. . . . Especially, I know none of them would have stuck around after six months of no sex. They'd have been gone.

Troiden (1988) made the point that self-labeling as homosexual was made more difficult in the past because men and women were unable to identify with the bizarre characterizations of homosexuals reflected in prevailing stereotypes. This assumption implies that accurate information about homosexuals and homosexuality is now circulated and widely distributed throughout society, making it easier for people to identify homosexual elements within themselves. However, the experiences of the respondents in this research do not confirm Troiden's assertion. In 2025, perhaps it may be easy. But in the 1980s and 1990s, internalized homophobia and lack of societal sanctions remain serious problems for many women, depending on where they live and work and their available social constructs. Respondent #21, age thirty, describes her experience of only twelve years ago, that is, 1987:

> [Did you understand what the relationship with Sue was, for you, at the time?]
>
> Did I understand? I don't know. If I think back then, I was so young and so drunk; I don't know. Yeah, there were times when I thought I was in love with her. A lot of times. I remember there was the song by Chicago at the time being played over and over called *Will You Still Love Me for the Rest of Your Life?* and that song reminded me of her. . . . And, you know, we were best friends, buddies; we were inseparable. . . . John and I decided to get married, and a few months before the wedding, I was taking this German class and found myself attracted to the German professor. . . . I had sexual dreams about her and I thought it was a case of cold feet. I remember thinking that the minister who married us was pretty incredible, and I could see myself crushing out on her . . . and then I thought, "Cold feet. I'm just having cold feet." And I pushed all that stuff out. I'm going to marry the man of my dreams . . .

In these previous quotes, the women's struggle with the meaning of their connections makes itself clear. Reiterating the paradox, they may feel sexual arousal, but sexual arousal is not the center of the connection, and yet the connection clearly includes a sexual aspect. As Ross has said, homosexuality (like heterosexuality) is "normal in terms of a human desire for a mutually loving and supportive relationship in which sex plays some part, rather than a relationship being seen as an appendage to sex" (Ross, Rogers, and McCulloch, 1978, p. 326).

The load of sexual responsibility carried by a woman in this society is enormous. Ever paradoxical, in addition to denying her the right to her own arousal, it is also normal for society to give women less sexual freedom and more blame for what does or does not happen sexually between adults. As long as a woman believes that her desire, arousal, and body responses do not belong to her, that they need to be unlocked by a man, she will have great difficulty defining her gender orientation. Most important for her, however, she may miss sexual arousal and orgasm—one of the profound pleasures of being human—which may be experienced privately as well as with a partner.

Respondent #24, age fifty-four, talks about her personal sexual development:

> [In my marriage], I didn't have really fulfilling sex, but to me, sex was interesting. And I needed so to be loved, and I needed to feel loved, that by being sexual I thought that's what it was. So—and sex was not real frequent—I had a far bigger threshold than he did. . . . [I had orgasms], but only if I was in one position; if I was on top and really moving hard, I could have one; otherwise I didn't. And so I thought just, you know, after he laid exhausted and I was exhausted, so therefore that must have been good. . . . [One day] I was watching Dr. Ruth. . . . She was talking about a book written by a woman—Barbara or something [Lonnie Barbach]—called *For Yourself* . . . and so I went and got it because she basically said women do not always know how to have an orgasm and know their own body. So I think I [need to] teach my body. It must be my fault. I'm obviously not as good at this as I could be. . . . And she is talking about having an orgasm with running water. Ok, well, I have a shower that doesn't have a showerhead, so here I am in this little apartment drowning myself in the kitchen sink. And what I discovered was that I was having an orgasm with the kitchen faucet that I'd never had in my life.

Our society's prescription that a woman's arousal must be controlled, that it doesn't belong to her, was reflected in the experiences of several respondents. The creation of the term frigid to describe women who failed to respond with enthusiasm to sexual intercourse allowed the threat to be dismissed by pathologizing it. Such women "threaten male dominance and civilization," and therefore, the label frigid could be used to control women (Ussher, 1992, p. 83). Respondent #18, age fifty-one, describes her feelings of responsibility for her low sexual response in her marriage and her willingness to blame herself completely—and the surprise and delight she felt when she realized she did indeed have her own sexual response:

> . . . felt inadequate in that marriage. Never was there an awareness that there was something else sexually that could be good for me. It was more that there was something really wrong with me. So I became . . . I got a job at that hospital [and met this] really interesting woman about the same age as me. She was divorced and a single mom with a couple of kids. She was the chaplain. I started going to therapy, and I remember telling the therapist this is the most compelling friendship I have ever had . . . . I was enormously drawn to her. First, in the sense of being so disappointed whenever she couldn't have lunch with me or whatever . . . and [at that conference], I ran into my new friend and her partner. . . . "Oh, you're here," and I gave her a big hug and she was stiff as a board, stiff as a board, and it was shocking to me because we were spending so much time, by that time, at work talking about so many important things . . . and later they were going through a door together and there was a wonderful, tender—the jealous partner just caught her elbow or something as she went through the door—where these light bulbs just went off enormously. I thought, "Oh my gosh," with that awareness of how drawn I am. . . . I was starting to recognize that I was attracted to her; I wasn't just friends and now—somebody who has a partner, how awful. . . . And about the first of December [I] had a Christmas party with this other nonprofit group and had my first moment of gut sexual response to a woman. She was younger than me, and I was very aware that she was a lesbian—and actually my husband was there . . . at the party; we were across the room from each other and for what reason, I don't know, we caught each other's gaze

. . . and my—I did an absolute flip-flop. . . . It felt like when a baby just flip-flops. I mean, I couldn't even think of her—I had a real sexual response . . . so it was pretty defining. . . . It was very powerful. . . . About a month after that response, [I told my husband] that I wanted a divorce. . . . I joined a group for women, which was very powerful . . . so all that happened in a six-month period. I would kind of let information in, and I opened up a lot of things that I had not let in before, and I wrote a poem, which I wish I still had. I was so scared that somebody would find it. I'd get hit by a bus or something . . . a poem about that moment of *that look* and what it meant.

Although taking back her sexual power can be satisfying and exhilarating, it can also be frightening. Women carry the shame of so many double binds. She is denied arousal because she is a slut and a whore if she acknowledges her desire; she is supposed to be alluring for a man but she is not supposed to plan it because if she plans it, she is full of carnal lust and insatiable; she is denied information and education about her own body, her sexuality, and so she must learn as she goes, inadvertently. Her challenge, however, is to pull all this off while looking innocent and totally unaware of it all. All women have internalized shame concerning sex to some degree, which makes it very difficult to address the sexual aspect of adult life and relationships directly. Any woman who achieves a level of comfort about her sexuality in this society has gained no small triumph. Thus, it's not at all surprising that sixteen of the twenty-four respondents said that after they began to have an idea of what was happening, and that it had something to do with their sexuality, they found coming out to themselves slow, difficult, and, at times, shameful.

Every lesbian and bisexual woman knows the important—but not central—place of sexual activity in her own gender orientation. However, the larger society believes that the center point of same-gender attractions is the total preoccupation with particularly salacious sex. Thus, a woman's internalized homonegative attitudes suggest that if she is to acknowledge her same-gender attractions, she will fight feelings of shame in addition to the sexual shame all women who are raised in this culture learn.

Respondent #23, age forty-seven, describes the process of taking back the right to her own sexual feelings, desires, and path:

I just didn't have any intimate friends for quite a long period of time.

[Do you know what that was about?]

It was about difficulty with intimacy, period. . . . There was a lot of verbal and emotional abuse that went on in my marriage and this whole terrible price of having secrets and shame brings to you. . . . Anyway, we agreed to separate and subsequently divorced. But after we separated, it took me a little while. . . . For a number of months there, I think what I was doing was grieving, but I don't think I was really grieving him . . . . Part of me was very aware that I was leaving a façade that I'd maintained for many years that had been an important façade for me, and then finally . . . if I was going to live and have a life, I was going to need to have a sexual life, and it was clear to me that I didn't want to date men. It was very clear. Actually, it might be interesting for you to know that the real bailout time in the marriage counseling had been when sexual issues started getting addressed too. . . . I didn't want to talk about it. . . . I went out to eat with a friend, and she had invited another friend to eat with us . . . in the middle of the dinner, the woman I didn't know very well just sort of dropped into the conversation that it wasn't unusual for lesbians to come out in midlife. . . . I don't think I heard a single solitary word the whole rest of the dinner after she said that sentence. It was like "Boing!" . . . so it was a tiny little hint or clue or something. I need to pursue this. How can I do this? . . . I was very frightened to do this.

[What frightened you?]

The shame of it, that somehow I would be shamed.

[By your counselor?]

Yeah, it's just very hard to—at this point in my life, it's hard for me to understand even the magnitude of that . . . even

> though I had a deep trust of my counselor at that time, and even though I'd been in counseling for that many years and I had heard other people share things about themselves that were very intimate. . . . It was still a scary thing to me, and I was aware that I didn't know much about my counselor . . . and she wasn't supposed to be judgmental, you know, but it still was a big step to even try to do this in that incredibly sort of safe space—but I did. I told myself, "OK, I am going to do this. I will do this." It was so funny. It was like jumping off a mountain and landing on a feather bed. . . . It was amazing. Basically what she said was to give me permission to explore this.

It was a significant moment when these women achieved the insight that their desire to be with women was a *sexual* desire as well as an emotional one. At that point, they were ready to take their own feelings seriously. They were claiming their own sexual power, as well as the personal power, to make relationship decisions for their lives. Through this process, they could allow themselves to feel their own desire with the object (person) of their choice. As Belenky and colleagues have noted, the identity achievement of hearing her own voice comes later for women (Belenky et al., 1986). Claiming her own sexual energy and power is obviously crucial to the development of her awareness that she is lesbian or bisexual.

During the period of time between realizing they had significant same-gender attractions and acting definitively on those feelings, these women were faced with many questions and challenges that needed to be addressed or solved. Any life transition will present such challenges.

For example, respondent #2, age twenty-nine, describes her evolution as a bisexual woman who is now closely bonded with a man:

> The work environment I was in at [job] is very open to looking at lots of different ways of doing things, and so I had a chance to . . . [use] great creative leeway to try things. Ways of thinking and . . . my relationship with Mary was a big part of that and learning to understand why I got married in the first place, what that was about for me and what . . .

[What was it about?]

At that point, it was about really enjoying getting the positive attention from society that I was getting about being involved with a man. What's different this time about being involved with a man is I am still out about being bisexual. I am still doing work that is important to me. He understands and is supportive and thinks that's great about who I am. That was missing before. I didn't have that. . . . I mean, I went from being gay to straight. Neither was working . . . and so I wasn't able to weave any of it together at all. Which is, for me, what being bisexual is really about. It's really a weaving of lots of different communities and ideas, and I will never be straight. I don't care who I am sleeping with at the time. It's not who I am.

During their transition process, two respondents were questioned by other women about whether they could claim a lesbian identity:

One woman with whom I briefly got involved told me I wasn't really a lesbian if I'd never slept with a woman. . . . Did she really help me to come out as a lesbian? . . . I didn't feel any more or less a lesbian after we slept together. It confirmed what I already knew . . . (Respondent #14, age forty-eight)

I remember a point in group when I said, "Well, I have to know. Did you need to make love to a woman to know you are gay, you are lesbian?" . . . I had had a number of what I would call lesbian relationships with women but never totally sexual. Mostly holding and emotionally attaching. She said, "Well no, I don't think that's necessary." And I said, "Well, I just feel like I'm on the fence." And then this woman said, "Are you? Are you on the fence?" . . . I said, "No. No, I'm not. I know where I am." (Respondent #5, age forty-one)

All members of this society are likely to have internalized the belief that there is greater value to a man, lesser value to a woman. Two respondents—#1, age thirty-six, and #10, age fifty-one—commented about how they had wondered as they became involved with women how they could have a family, be a family, if there was no man present. Another aspect of this is described by respondent #24, age fifty-four, as she discusses how the cultural devaluation affected her decision process while learning to love her new partner and making a decision about her marriage:

> And really . . . the whole world was upside down. I knew in my mind that I had left that marriage years ago. But my belief system was that I'd made a promise in God's house and so therefore I was married forever. . . . Better or worse, and knew that line very well. So I think, first, it was just fun, and I was just playing. . . . Yeah, I'm not fooling around with a man so therefore it's no big deal. Until I got the fact that it was a woman. And then—I'd better not be doing this; this is wrong.

When making the transition from heterosexual relationships to relationships with women, there is an entire culture change that can include an aspect of culture shock. Respondent #15, age twenty-eight, recalls that she felt somewhat daunted in the beginning, because she didn't know the rules of the new culture:

> I moved right from Jeff's to a relationship with another man. Kevin had been hanging around then too . . . and I went to [counseling] . . . because there was something else going on . . . talking about the sexuality piece, but jumped right into this relationship with this man.
>
> [What prompted going into a relationship with Kevin?]
>
> Ah, easier. . . . I knew what to do. I knew what it meant to be courted. I knew when he was flirting with me. I couldn't figure it out with women. You know through all this time I had been going to [gay club] and [lesbian club] or spending time with the women in my coming-out group, but I never—it was so confusing to me. I didn't know when somebody was flirting. There were no rules. I didn't know if they [women] really liked me. I knew Kevin liked me. He started it.

Dealing with the reactions of family, parents, children, and friends presents a major challenge for women who have realized they are on the path toward same-gender relationships. The sequence of events through which women come to recognize their same-gender orientation and disclose it to others is called coming out. (It is interesting to note that since heterosexuality is taken for granted and there is usually no process of discovery or disclosure for heterosexuals, the term coming out is applied only to homosexuals [Bohan, 1996]). Faced with the stereotypic myths and bizarre images of lesbian/bisexual life that are widely available, families and friends are usually appalled that their loved one would be/could be part of such a group. They may be sad, even feel deeply grieved, that she is rejecting the traditional female role. This is further complicated for married lesbians because their family/friends may be mourning the loss of her husband and her traditional family unit as well.

Respondent #1, age thirty-six, describes the result of her coming out to her parents:

> My parents have never even met Joan and are not willing to; they won't come to the house; they won't. . . . Joan is not welcome on their property. . . . They are . . . very "We do not support the gay and homosexual community; any type of communication with your so-called family would be in support of that, and we can't go against the way we feel" and so . . . they are very distant . . .

> [That must be very painful for you.]

> It has been in the past. And sometimes it still creates a big [large sigh] . . . but you just deal with it one day at a time. . . . I see in the future there will be a time when we have more comfort with each other, but I don't know how that is going to be created.

Respondent #5, age forty-one, describes a family's homophobic response to new relationships, even when the family has known and cared about the person they believed was a friend. When they learn she is a lesbian partner, they may withdraw:

[So your mother has a hard time accepting the changes in your life?]

Yeah. Initially she was great. She knew Peg when she didn't know we were a couple and thought Peg was wonderful, great. "Peg, she's just incredible; what a wonderful friend you have." Now Peg is nothing to my mother. She's the bad influence. My mom is still not there, and I don't know if she ever will be. She gave all the signs of being accepting . . . but when it came right down to her own daughter, it wasn't . . . there.

[How about your siblings?]

My sister doesn't approve, but she still—how do I describe it—it's a judgmental statement that she made to me, but yet she still cares about me. She says, "But you're a person and Peg is a person." . . . The two men in my family feel bad for Hank. And my brother said, too, "I don't judge you. That's fine. Whatever you want to do." So they're OK about it, which just blows me away. I thought the women would be understanding and the men would be . . . the men are the accepting ones and the women are like . . .

[What do you think happened to change your mother?]

It might have been the pastor at the church.

Four of the twenty-four women experienced acceptance from family members about their life transition soon after coming out to them. Several others worked on the connections with family members and gained acceptance after a period of time. When a change of this magnitude occurs in a family member, others in the family are forced to look at their own belief systems and make adjustments as well (Coleman, 1990).

The father of respondent #15, age twenty-eight, was accepting fairly quickly, but also expressed his reservations:

My dad said, "There's no way I wouldn't love you for being where you're at because you know, look it, Nicky is one of my best friends. This is not anything to me. I've always been open to this. It's hard because you're my daughter and I have . . . and I don't want you to be in . . . I don't like it to be hard for you, and being gay is going to put you in risky places and it's going to make you a vulnerable person."

These women expressed concern about how their lesbian or bisexual identity would affect their children. Patterson has conducted an extensive survey of the literature on lesbian mothers, gay fathers, and their children. She concludes that although much remains to be done to understand the conditions that foster positive mental health among lesbian mothers and gay fathers and their children, the results of early research, "provide no reason, under the prevailing best interests of the child standard, to deny or curtail parental rights of lesbian or gay parents on the basis of their sexual orientation" (Patterson, 1995, p. 284). In addition, the evidence has been clear in lesbian mother studies that no damaging consequences to a child's development come from a lesbian mother's sexual orientation (Kirkpatrick, Smith, and Roy, 1981).

A life change of this magnitude will, however, inevitably affect the children of a woman in such a transition. Lesbian/bisexual women who come out after marriage or anytime after adolescence have experienced a developmental delay. They will commonly find themselves feeling the high energy excitement of exploration for a period of time as they learn about their "new" selves. Since many women in this position did not have the same high energy fun that their heterosexual peers did at chronological adolescence, "adolescence" is usually delayed until after coming out and must be experienced then. For example, respondent #18, age fifty-one, talks about the concern for her daughter that derives from their both being "adolescent" at the same time.

> . . . there was just enormous support and identification with each other and we were running off to [lesbian bar] together on the weekend to see what that was like. We were just being totally adolescent. I think that my adolescent daughter suffered a little from my being adolescent at the same time as she was.

Coleman states that, in his clinical experience, negative effects on the children of gay and lesbian parents result more from discord between the parents' neglect of children's needs because of this conflict and the fears of the parents' separation. "When talking to children of homosexual parents, one quickly realized that the main trauma of growing up with a homosexual parent lies not with the parent's homosexuality but rather with the threat of dissolution of the marital relationship" (990, p. 126).

Respondent #6, age thirty-five, had concerns about what effect her gender orientation would have on her children:

> I still felt afraid to leave my marriage because, number one, I had a lot invested. I was in love when I got married to Barry, and I didn't want to give it up so easily. Plus, we had two children together and didn't know what kind of an effect this was going to have on their lives. And I was afraid that he would try to take my kids from me. It still took me three years before I gave him a definitive answer. I did move out of the house. . . . But I couldn't give him an answer that I was done. . . . It took me years to have enough nerve.
>
> [What did you need confidence about?]
>
> . . . that I wasn't going to be a bad influence on them. That was how I was wanting my life to change, as being lesbian was still going to be healthy for them. That I had then become healthy or had healthy thoughts, felt good about being a lesbian.

The children of respondent #10, age fifty-one, had a fairly typical response to their mother's coming out to them:

> We had a duplex. . . . We lived upstairs, downstairs. I mean, I would still. It was when my kids were in high school, I would sleep at Kris's and say, "Well, you know, you guys have to get up early and go to school so I'm just going to sleep at Kris's." I knew they'd see through that . . . but I still bothered to, and I didn't say the words to them until they each were about eighteen or nineteen.
>
> [What was their response?]
>
> Yeah, and so? It was sort of like they had always; they had always known that. My youngest son did not want to hear

much about it. But I don't think anybody wants to think of that in sexual terms. They don't want their mother to be different.

The experience of respondent #1, age thirty-six, illustrates Coleman's (1990) assertion that children of homosexual parents have the most difficulty with the separation of their parents and the changes that are foisted on them:

> The kids knew before we had gotten knew that I was becoming involved with Joan. . . . I don't know how much they knew in their minds. . . . My daughter has always had a pretty comfortable, "OK, well, this is what Mom's going to do, and this is how it's going to go then." And [my son] has been more resistant right along. The little boys were confused, hurt about the divorce, which I'm sure the bigger kids were too, but it took a rough year at school. . . . My youngest one who was always a very cuddly, very emotional child, kind of shut down his emotions completely and didn't want to hug [me], didn't want to touch [me]. And now you can't stop the kid from coming up and hugging you . . . his expression is there again. But I'm sure the whole event, whether it be the divorce or me falling in love with a woman and all the different roles the kids have to play with . . . it was tough on them. But they're happy, shiny children at this point now, so . . .

Homophobia and negative perceptions of lesbian/bisexual life may not be the only reason for potential changes in relations with family and friends. Several respondents in this research talked of lost friends or fear of losing friends and family support as they made the transition. Although no evidence supports the myth that lesbians reject all feminine interests and activities (Kirkpatrick, 1988), significant others may believe that a change in her gender orientation means that a woman will completely change her personality and not be the same person. These fears that their friend (daughter, mother) will become someone else are likely connected to the bizarre stereotypes to which the entire society is exposed. However, the fears may also be an expression of grief over the anticipated loss of the familiar person they know. Friends or family members may experience the change as a personal rejection of them and their life choices (Sales,

1978; Gartrell, 1981). Coming out as a lesbian/bisexual woman will definitely change her life circumstances, but the core of the woman can be sustained. Only time and experience will reveal that to the people in her life.

When respondent #16, age fifty-one, left her husband, her closest friend had great difficulty accepting the change:

> I didn't want Joe, and I was the one who asked for the divorce and some had a hard time. My very dear friend Sally, she and her husband were best friends to both of us. We were best buddies, and it affected her very deeply and hard, and for about a year, she hardly talked to me. And some of my friends said, "Why don't you just write her off," and I said, "No, I can't. She's worth too much to me." And that took about a year, and we sat down and we talked and were very gentle with each other . . . and finally about a year, year and a half later, Sally and I are back on track, but she had a hard time.

The core personality of the woman may stay essentially the same, but a woman who comes out is, indeed, changing her life in fundamental ways. As she embraces a lesbian or bisexual social role and identity, she is leaving behind the traditional female identity and social role. First of all, she is escaping much of the sexism, deferential behavior, and caretaking inherent in many heterosexual relationships. She is forced to develop autonomy and independence not automatically required of heterosexual women. She is likely to participate in an all-female community—that community being an alternative to the traditional structures she needs to give up when she comes out (Nichols and Leiblum, 1986). That the woman becomes more independent and assertive may be alarming to her family and friends. That she appears to need them less may be a threat.

Respondent #14, age forty-eight, describes her brother's reaction to her leaving a marriage:

> [Did you have a sense of leaving for a reason other than that the marriage wasn't right?]
>
> Other than it didn't fit, other than I felt like I wasn't—like I just never would be a good wife? I wasn't subservient, and I

had a brother tell me that if you just learned to be subservient, you could stay married, you know.

Respondent #16, age fifty-one, talks about her changes and the responses and reactions of those she cared about while she was becoming more aware of herself and her own needs:

I was discovering—I want to use the word powerful in a couple of different ways here—I was noticing I was [powerful]. My profession was as a director who was among the leadership of women in the same business. . . . I just said, "It's women, OK." I was meeting some very powerful, influential, strong, fun women, and I really enjoyed being with all of them. We were doing stuff professionally, as well as just some fun things. That was another thing that threatened Joe. He called them "yay-hoos." He said, "I don't know why you want to get together after work once a month on this professional meeting day." There would be about ten of us who would get together after a professional meeting and go to [hotel] or some place for happy hour and still be home by 5:30 or 6:00, and usually we talked business anyway, but it was such fun and so stimulating, and I so enjoyed that. He did not like that at all . . . and so it was difficult. I remember somebody saying to me—I think it was my mother—she said, "Think of poor Joe." . . . She still doesn't understand, but as best she could [she tried to say] . . . divorce isn't the end of the world.

Psychotherapists know that when a major change takes place in a client's life, the change will bring both losses and gains. The women in this research group talked about the losses, but they described the embracing of their lesbian or bisexual identity as a primarily positive life change. Although coming out involved incorporating a stigmatized identity, the loss of entitlement to marry or to carry joint health insurance with partners, the loss of the right to publish pictures of their relationships in local newspapers, as well as likely censure for public displays of affection, these women did not mention any of these issues. They may have felt some sadness and some grief at the endings of their marriages, their heterosexual lives, their homes, and so forth, but only one respondent raised this issue spontaneously. Only two major fears about the transition did come up again and again: they feared that they might not be able to take care of themselves and their children alone, and they feared that their lesbian or bisexual identity could cause them to lose custody of their children.

Respondent #20, age fifty-four, describes her early desire to leave her marriage, without knowing why, and her fears about leaving and not being able to take care of herself and her children:

> I had affairs with men . . . and sometimes I—I'd say I was looking for something, and I didn't know what it was until I met Laraine, you know?
>
> [Before you met her, you were searching?]
>
> Yeah, you know. That's what I was doing. But I know that the men that I . . . why would I leave Eddie for that one? I mean it wasn't that I wanted [a man], so then I stayed with Eddie and some of it, you know. I thought about it and thought, "I'm not going to lose Eddie and go off with someone else and not be able to support myself and not be able to support my kids." I just wouldn't do it.

Three respondents talked about their serious problems with alcohol and one with drugs, all of which appeared to subside as the women clarified their same-gender attractions. For example, in the case of respondent #8, age forty-three, her fears of being unable to take care of her children were complicated by her dependence on alcohol:

> We had separated again, and all the separations when I moved up here were about basically because I don't know. I wanted him, but I didn't want him. I wanted to be with my woman friend. I didn't want to be with him. And then I'd get scared and run back to him.
>
> [What were you scared of?]
>
> Financially not making it . . . [the kids were teenagers] and I needed to, you know; I needed to be sober for them.

Twelve of the twenty-four respondents talked about their coming out under a cloud of fear that somehow their lesbian and bisexual identity might cause a custody fight. They feared losing custody of their children. It should be noted that two respondents, in addition to the twelve, had adult children at the time of their coming out, and several of the twelve had to delay their coming out until their children got older to reduce the likelihood of a custody issue.

Respondent #5, age forty-one, talks about her concern regarding custody:

> So I came home, and when Hank asked me, I just said, "I want to go. I don't want to be married anymore." And I really couldn't tell him the whole reason why because I was afraid and my lawyer said not to. I had talked to a lawyer, just to ask. A lesbian lawyer. So I really couldn't tell him the whole time. I did come out to him and say, "I feel like I'm bisexual." But that was all I really said to him, just because of fearing he would take custody.

Being a lesbian in the 1990s in the United States means being a member of a stigmatized group. For evidence of this, we need only follow the stories appearing in the media over the past few years, for example, the trials of Methodist, Episcopalian, and Lutheran ministers who have been expelled or admonished by their denominations for performing marriages for gay/lesbian couples, or for being gay or lesbian themselves. Similar evidence can be found on the computer, for example, Web sites, such as the one maintained by Reverend Fred Phelps, whose ministry is located in Topeka, Kansas, that disseminate misinformation and hate messages about gays and lesbians. If one were to perform a computer search on the Internet using the key word lesbian, the result would be a list of over two million Web sites, the vast majority being lesbian pornography or offers to "peek" at the supposedly salacious lesbian "lifestyle." Few opportunities are given for dissent to such evidence of contempt. The misunderstanding is profound. Homosexuality is no more a *lifestyle* than heterosexuality is. "The lesbian or gay experience is a way of being, not a 'style'" (Kaufman and Raphael, 1996, p. 123).

Because of this stigma, this homophobia, this heterosexism (that is, sex role rigidity and degree of conservatism) in the United

States, a woman is likely to experience a homonegative response to her announcement to her world that she has begun seeking intimate relationships with women. When she states that she is coming out, she is at high risk for psychological distress (Ross, 1996). Ross has stated that generalizability of the following research from gay men to lesbians is unclear. However, given the likelihood that at least some generalization will be possible, some of his ideas seem appropriate in this context.

According to Ross (1996), no matter how well a gay person's life is going elsewhere, for example, success at work, thriving extended family, beautiful home, healthy achieving children, and so forth, if she experiences homonegative events—for example, a punishing response from her parents and siblings to her coming out—she will experience significant psychological distress. The other positive life events will not easily mediate the stress impact of this blow from her family. Ross suggests that the highest levels of distress, potentially the most negative psychological functioning for gays, are correlated with the impact of gay-associated life stressors such as trouble in the relationship with a same-sex partner and coming-out issues. Thus, it is safe to assume that the woman who has made a declaration stating her intention to pursue her same-gender orientation is at high risk for severe psychological distress.

Ross has further stated that psychological well-being is highly correlated with social support and that the stresses of homonegativity may be mitigated by social supports. Social support may be defined as "the number and strength of connections of individuals to significant others in their social environments" (Ross, 1996, p. 213).

To cope with the stigma of lesbian identification, the woman seeking same-gender relationships is highly encouraged to become involved in an all-female community. Contact with the lesbian, bisexual, gay subculture provides healing norms. For example, hearing from others, "This is OK here; it's normal to love a woman" will validate and normalize homosexuality as a way of being. This comfort and safety will also encourage her progress in general identity development—for example, from the foreclosure identity status of assuming the values and beliefs of her parents without thinking them through for herself to moratorium status of beginning to determine her own values and beliefs (see Chapter 3 on general identity formation). Of course, the ideal is that she discloses herself publicly, as well as privately, in a safe community so that she can experience congruence and her lesbian identity can be integrated as only one aspect of herself, not as "the" identity that defines her (Cass, 1979).

For the short term, interactions with a lesbian community that models comfort with that identity will help encourage the new ways of thinking she needs to counteract internalized homonegative attitudes (Cass, 1979). Respondent #5, age forty-one, states that finding a community of supportive women is not necessarily so easy:

> [What community did you have? Have you found a community together or on your own?]

> Well, my community was my friends, the one at work and another that I met through her, another woman I knew who I guessed was lesbian. I turned out to be right. So then I had breakfast with her. It was just a few unconnected women and that was my community. . . . So when Peg and I came together, and Peg didn't really have much community either that she had built and so . . . these women we met now, we feel like we have this group of friends who we can call and [it's] sort of nice because it feels very lonely for us. We feel isolated. When we first met, it was very isolating. We had each other.

Evidence also suggests that lesbian and bisexual women may not necessarily welcome a formerly married woman with open arms (Nichols and Leiblum, 1986) The woman may be viewed with suspicion or, at least, reluctance because lifelong lesbian women have suffered through years of prejudice and could resent that a woman had a marriage and family and then wants to experience the benefits of a woman's community now that there is relatively more lesbian acceptance. Another possible reason for their reluctance could be that a woman does not want to fall in love with a new member of her community and then find that the woman goes back to her husband.

Respondent #9, age fifty-seven, came out sixteen years ago, in a community where her husband was a public figure, and therefore, her coming out drew attention:

> At first, I was terribly excited to go to women's events and seek the company of other lesbians. I had idealized the women's community and thought I would find wonderful new friends and great support. I was shocked that I was treated politely but coldly. Nobody wanted to get together. I was so hurt and felt utterly alone. Oh, I had friends from before, but none of them were lesbian, and they didn't and couldn't get what I was feeling and going through, particularly around the hurt I knew my children felt about the changes. I wanted someone to talk to about that. I needed support. I stayed in that community for two years after I came out so it was a long haul. Eventually I found good support—one friend who was formerly married was a good friend, but pretty unavailable because she was deeply in love with her new partner at the time, so I could never be alone with her. The other one was a straight woman whom I had known a long time who just seemed to understand in all the right ways. It was complicated, though, because she was a good friend of my ex-husband, and after I left that community, I think he got custody of the friends. Or, at least, it was hard to trust that she wasn't talking to him about everything I was telling her. . . . I got the best support in the new community where nobody knew me.

One very important source of social support can be the blood family. Support and acceptance by blood kin can be very sweet. However, blood families often reject or withhold recognition and acceptance from lesbian/gay/bisexual family members. Kath Weston's book, *Families We Choose*, includes a sensitive, comprehensive chapter titled "Coming Out to 'Blood' Relatives. Weston (1992) writes,

> Aside from AIDS, no other topic encountered during my fieldwork generated an emotional response comparable to coming out to blood (or adoptive) relatives. . . . Claiming a gay identity in the presence of parents or siblings frequently involved an

anxiety-filled struggle to bring speech about sexual identity (if not sex) into the cultural domain of the family. . . . Coming out to relatives put to the test the unconditional love and enduring solidarity commonly understood in the United States to characterize blood ties. . . . "When I tell you who I (really) am, I find out who you (really) are to me." . . . Not everyone was willing to put kinship relations to this test. (pp. 43, 44, 51)

Contact and socializing with blood family may be awkward, perhaps even painful. Two respondents talk about their situations:

I can't see my granddaughter if my partner is with me. . . . I wished she was there . . . [so] we decided; we dressed her up as a six-foot purple bunny for—my daughter always has a big Easter egg hunt and I knew they couldn't throw the Easter bunny out. (Respondent #14, age forty-eight)

They think I am going to be judged when I get to heaven. (Respondent #4, age thirty-three)

In *Families We Choose*, Weston talks about another option, the "positive sense of choice and creativity associated with gay families" (Weston, 1992, p. 117). The option of forming relationships with gay/lesbian/bisexual people who are loved and chosen to be part of a "family" is one example of acculturation into the gay/lesbian subculture. Through social support from this subculture, the lesbian/bisexual woman can develop the structures for emotional support that create an alternative social system to counter heterosexism. As she finds significant others from whom she perceives she will get help and support if she needs it, she can be provided with a buffer to heterosexism and homonegative attitudes and is less likely to experience extremes of psychological distress during life changes and difficult events (Ross, 1996).

Although a "chosen" family may form eventually, that is likely to take some time. A circle of friends, probably all female, is most likely to offer social support initially. These friends, plus the larger community with its own structures, meeting places, and rituals, will provide a place where she "fits in." This community will help her to grieve, rage about, and celebrate all the changes she experiences as she "comes out" (Thompson, 1992).

Two respondents describe the process of beginning to find a community:

> [A therapist] pushed me to do something . . . like look into organizations, read the literature. Look into [local gay newspapers] . . . and their directory and find out what is going on, and I did start . . . going to different events, not knowing exactly what kind of event it was, but being very nervous to be going there alone. . . . I was in [a support] group for; I forget how long we were together, but I started doing things with one woman who was in the same situation. I mean we would go to these events and we would just giggle . . . and that's when I answered some ads. And I was petrified, and I remember picking up the phone, picking it up and putting it down. And that's how I met Lee. (Respondent #25, age fifty-three)

> [When you came out to yourself, who supported you?]

> I was very supported by a good friend at work. It wasn't complicated yet. It was more like I was—she was the first person I came out to other than myself. She was delighted. She really didn't let herself act or think about her feelings for me until I said something first. It was really after—we had parallel happenings—I told her I decided to pursue a group. And then in that group was my supporter! . . . Definitely that group supported me, and we did, in very adolescent fashion, and it's interesting; this group was mostly thirty-five- to forty-year-old women . . . (Respondent #18, age fifty-one)

In the excitement and drama of the coming-out moment, the formerly married lesbian/bisexual woman may not realize at first that she has lost privileges she wasn't consciously aware she had. Although our survey respondents did not specifically refer to all of these losses, Thompson (1992) suggests that losses precipitated by coming out are causes for grief for many women. They are privileges accepted as givens by heterosexuals in our society. Some of these lost privileges are explicit, and many are implicit, in the interviews. Bohan lists the following as "heterosexual privileges": public recognition and support for your intimate relationship; paid leave for spouse's death; as well as leave for her illness or for the death of spouse's family members; immediate access to and rights to make medical decisions with your loved one in case of emergency or illness; support and pride in your relationship from family of origin; social acceptance for your partner; social acceptance for your plans and activities; open support when a relationship ends; filing joint tax returns; automatic inheritance; sharing health, auto, and homeowners policies at reduced rates; open employment opportunity; validation from the religious community; and basic integrity and safety in who you are (Bohan, 1996).

Despite the difficulties, losses, and challenges of coming to terms with a lesbian or bisexual identity, these women did not express regret or sadness that they were a part of a stigmatized minority group. The excitement and positive attitude expressed by these twenty-four women are very likely connected to their willingness to participate in this study. It is also likely that some lesbian/bisexual women do regret their identity and wish they could change this part of themselves. Perhaps the fact that no women with such regrets volunteered is a limitation of the present research. The one regret that was expressed by a majority of the women was that they did not know about their same-gender attractions many years earlier.

Although some women wished that they could have known about their identity sooner, respondent #10, age fifty-one, considers herself fortunate to be in this social location at this time in her life:

> So I just feel incredibly lucky that I have an option. I don't feel damaged in any way by being a lesbian or being bisexual. I didn't have to grow up feeling different. I sort of feel very lucky that it could happen this way.

The thoughts and feelings of joy and resolution when they finally *knew* were repeated in a variety of ways by many respondents in the study, for example, respondent #16, age fifty-one:

> . . . it was like the first time we were together physically there was no question in my mind how I wanted things to go or what I liked or what I desired. It didn't scare me or anything. . . . It's like, this is what I've been waiting for all of my life; now things make sense. This is why I had a crush on my son's

second grade teacher; this is why I kind of liked to stay after school after I worked in the library for awhile at my son's elementary school. I would find excuses to go into the teacher's room and visit with her after school. . . . I just always wanted to be with my girlfriends in high school . . . things just started to make sense, and, as I say, physically, when I started being involved, it was the most natural thing in the world.

DISCUSSION

A few years ago, I was sitting at a professional meeting with a colleague who asked me what I was currently researching. I told him that the project was investigating the process of women who come out after having been married to a man, and he said, "You know, I've always wondered about those women. How could they not know something that is so central to their lives?" Good question. How could they not know? And so we come back to the beginning, back to the place where we started, and as T. S. Eliot said, "We know the place for the first time" (1971, p. 145). As a result of this research, we know, for example, that sexual attraction plays a significant part in same-gender attractions for women. However, we know as well that the attraction encompasses the total person and is emotional as well as sexual, with sexual attraction being the glue that holds it together.

This research reveals that all the influences considered in this. study that go into making an American woman also work against her knowing that she may have same-gender attractions, that she may be lesbian or bisexual. From the day she begins to learn about her reality, her sexuality, as she begins to get to know the body "container" within which she navigates through the world, she is discouraged from enjoying and understanding that container, shamed if she wants to learn about it, and split off from consulting with the self that lives inside that container. She is told that the feelings generated from within that container—plus the container itself—are not hers; they belong to the men with whom she relates. She is told there are feelings she is incapable of creating without him, and what's more, she is not supposed to be in charge of those feelings because if she tries, she will not be respected and loved by the other beings in her circle. She is told she doesn't know enough to make decisions, and when she tries to learn so she will know enough, she is told she is overstepping her bounds and that she can't know. She is told that marriage is expected of her, will satisfy her. In the past (this is changing), she has been told that only in marriage to a man may she fill the empty space inside the container. She is told that filling that empty space will complete her, fulfill her identity. Of course, all this "telling" is done either through innuendo, shaming, and inference or through the telling of normative stories. For example, all women have heard the following and similar comments, over and over:

> Did you hear, Mary Jane is getting married? Isn't that wonderful? We thought she'd never find a man. When is the wedding? . . . OR . . . Have you heard? Irene is working down at the bank. Well, I don't want to be critical, but you know, since they made her the head teller, she doesn't think about anything but her work. She doesn't call her mother anymore. . . . OR . . . Did you know that Lois is going back to school? And she has those two teenaged girls who need her now more than ever. Isn't she satisfied? I've always thought that she seemed to like teaching those schoolkids more than she liked being with her own . . .

Soon this woman does not need to be silenced because she learns to censor and silence her ambition, original thought, and curiosity herself. She may have a sense of inauthenticity, of things not feeling quite right, but her prescience is not respected. She judges the relational cost of resisting all these prescriptions to be too high. Because she navigates the world by the compass of connection and relationship, because she wants to keep intact the relational networks of her life, her tendency is to obey most rules, follow most prescriptions, and remain ignorant of her container or, in any case, keep quiet about what she knows and cooperate with the system. She is now a well-socialized and mature American woman.

How does she move from there to here? As we have seen through the process of change navigated by the twenty-four respondents to this study, well-socialized American women do learn and grow and change. They move from fulfilling expectations (a key part of their identity) to making choices based on their own assessments and judgment. They move from not knowing and not acknowledging their experience to consciously living it.

One method of mapping out this process of change is through the Precede Model developed by health educator Lawrence Green (1991). This model was developed to organize the information and process learning to any health outcome; in this case, a psychological health outcome. A significant piece of psychological health is found in embracing one's gender orientation and living one's life accordingly. When one is living one's life according to one's own values, attitudes, and beliefs, one is approaching the status of identity achievement. Bohan (1996) and Kaufman and Raphael (1996) have written comprehensive assessments of the damaging psychological effects of denying one's gender orientation. This study has shown the major sociological and psychological effects of not living out one's gender orientation.

Green and Kreuter's (1991) model lends organization and clarification to a complex process. The Precede Model organizes the change process into factors in the situation that *predispose* toward the accomplishment of the outcome of becoming aware and coming out, factors that *enable* the process, *cues to* taking *action* toward the accomplishment of the outcome, and factors that *reinforce* the path leading to the outcome. This model helps organize the experience, but it doesn't suggest that the events happen in this sequence. Living a life, with all its serendipity, is not an orderly process. A person may go back and forth many times among the factors, much in the same way a person experiences the stages of grief, before the outcome may be reached. She may even realize an outcome and recede from it without resolution if she isn't ready or has too little social or psychological support. Looking back over this research, it is clear that these twenty-four respondents illustrate all the factors in this process.

Predisposing Factors

The woman who may ultimately realize her same-gender attractions brings, first of all, the potential or characteristic of feeling attracted to and drawn to same-gender partners. Predisposing factors include knowledge, attitudes, beliefs, values, predilections, and perceptions that predispose her to sense the need for this change and to pursue this change. For instance, she could bring knowledge in all the thematic areas covered in this study, such as knowledge of her body and its arousal patterns; attitudes that same-gender relationships are acceptable; beliefs that she has a right to, and that she must experience her own life, follow her own path; values that place her own rights on an equal par with the rights of others; and perceptions that lesbian/bisexual women are, for example, independent women who tend to speak for themselves. To the degree that she has attitudes different from these, such as the belief that same-gender relationships are unacceptable, or different values, such as the value that places her rights as second to men or second to her husband, she will have a more difficult time traversing this path. In that case, even though she has the predilection for same-gender relationships, she may not reach awareness of her gender orientation easily, or at all.

The previous chapters contain many other examples, but here are two more illustrating the predisposing factors. Note that these are two very different roads to a similar realization, or epiphany. Respondent #19, age fifty-two, realizes here that although she has fallen in love with a woman, that woman is only part of the process. She has to make decisions about her own life for herself:

> So I wrote a note and I left and we took a bus. We got as far as Chicago. She called back to Pittsburgh to a friend, and the friend said, "You have to come back. Everybody knows; you have to come back." And I can remember we were down in the Greyhound station in Chicago and it was on a lower level— there were all these pay phones—and she turned to me and said, "You've got to go back." Then she turned back to talk some more, and it was at that moment in my life that I realized that the only person that could take care of me was me. I can't depend on this person. So I walked out of the terminal, bus station, got a cab, got to the airport because I had some money, and found out where I could fly to that would be possible with that money, and I flew to Denver.

Respondent #12, age fifty-three, also talks about early learning and how she evolved to living her own life and the satisfaction of making her own discoveries:

> I don't even know when I first knew about gay and lesbian. I know that I did, probably in high school, but I just, I thought it was someone else. Of course, I was going to marry and I was going to have two children and I was going to live with my husband. I had all that drawn out . . . [I did marry]. I tried to get a divorce when my son was two and a half or three, and my father stepped in and that didn't happen. So I waited until he [father] was dead and then I started to realize that I was having more fun with women, and I was in my early forties, and I wasn't going to wait until my son was out of high school so I didn't. . . . The moment that I came out to myself I think was when I was strongly attracted to Susan. My first true lesbian experience when something physical happened other than hugs was with Valerie. . . . But I knew by the time I was seeing Valerie, in a relationship sort of way—I don't use the word dating but I mean we saw each other—that I definitely was interested. And I didn't have a moment's hesitation. I didn't have guilt; it was like, "My gosh, this makes sense. What a wonderful option this is."

Enabling Factors

Enabling factors are skills and resources that allow the process toward her real orientation to begin and to continue. Among these are skills such as the confidence and social skills to find new groups of women and relate comfortably with them. Another aspect of this skill could be the security in herself that allows her to know about her same-gender attractions at some level and to believe her self-knowledge, even when the patriarchal social structure does not "allow" her to know what she knows. That is, self-awareness of the validity and clarity of her own feelings, regardless of feedback from others, is a skill. Another skill is the confidence leading to the willingness to reevaluate the decision to marry and to risk the social, economic, and personal consequences of leaving a marriage.

Some examples of resources are a positive lesbian or bisexual role model, that is, a friend or colleague who is lesbian or bisexual and willing or able to offer support; access to a potential community to support the declaration of her same-gender orientation; and a friend or family member who is not lesbian or bisexual, but who supports the woman's personal growth in whatever direction it may take her.

Three respondents talked about factors present that enabled—or missing factors that delayed—the process. Respondent #3, age fifty-eight, describes how she knew her marriage wasn't right, but she didn't feel ready to leave. She had the self-awareness of her feelings, but not the confidence that would lead to willingness to risk. At that time, she didn't *know* there might be a supportive community that could help her develop courage:

> [When you met Katherine, then did you get involved with her?]
>
> No.
>
> [What happened with your marriage?]
>
> Well, once I realized that I had more passionate feelings about this woman than I had ever had about a man, I realized that I was in the wrong relationship and things didn't go any better at home. Obviously, they started to go worse at home, and I wanted to spend less time with Michael. And so, I really eventually just separated emotionally more and more. And I finally told him, "I just can't stand this marriage any longer." I had a conversation with him about two weeks ago, . . . and I said, "You know, Michael, one of the things I was trying to tell you, but I knew you wouldn't understand, was I couldn't be the wife to you that you deserved. My emotions weren't there and I didn't know how to tell you without giving myself away because I didn't have the courage . . ."

Respondent #5, age forty-one, talks about having the realization that something needed to change, but pushing it away, over and over, and eventually feeling enough support to make the break.

Eventually, the support of a friend and a group of similar women, coupled with her own growing confidence, gave her the strength she needed to enable the process:

> But sex was never talked about [at home] . . . and I think, too, I never thought of sex as an emotional connection. . . . I can think of a couple of times when I felt close to Hank when we were making love, but not . . .

[What brought you to the decision to leave?]

> Knowing that there were other women, just talking to other women in that group who were alive and thriving, and it's OK; it's OK. And knowing my friend from work, and she had a partner and they have this house together and they had a committed relationship. Part of it was just, I just had to do it. I just had to have the faith that it's OK. I'm OK, and this is where I am. I started feeling more whole, too, just in the whole process. I started to feel like a whole person. I hadn't felt whole . . .

[It sounds like you identified the moment when you knew you had a long history of knowing, but you didn't allow yourself to take the information in. Push it away, push it away, and then, it just can't be pushed away anymore. Is that fairly accurate?]

> Right, exactly. I can't push it away anymore. And I can get out of this marriage and I can change my life. I mean, I figured if I just waited, maybe Hank, if Hank passes away before I do, then I'll experience this life. And then I got down to maybe when the kids move out of the house. It was always me putting off my life because I didn't want to hurt anybody. But now, I look around and I think we're all much better off—everybody.

When a very significant woman friend had ended a friendship and rejected her, respondent #16, age fifty-one, showed that she had the predisposing factors—she knew she was attracted to this woman—but her enabling factors were weak. She needed to develop the skill of certain knowledge of her own valid feelings to *enable* the process to continue. She expresses her thoughts as she began to validate those feelings herself:

It was terrible, especially when we were going to be still seeing each other from time to time in the building and when I would see her being friends and talking with people and she could barely give me the time of day. And of all the things we had shared and the closeness we had shared. Anyway, I didn't do very well. I went into—the therapist said it was a reactive depression. [I] saw a therapist for about six months and gradually pulled out of it because—it was interesting—because I remember I was feeling the two things [the divorce and the loss of this woman], but I've got to deal with the loss of this woman. It hit me real bad. Not having this person in my life is the toughest. . . . People thought I only shared it [depression] with a few people and they said, "Oh, it's the divorce. It's the aftermath of the divorce." And I thought, "God, the divorce was nothing; the divorce is a piece of cake compared to this." If I had any, even a fraction of the feeling for Joe that I had for this person . . .

[Did you tell people that you shared with that you loved her?]

Yeah, there were about four people.

[What do you think, that they didn't get the depth? I mean the lesbian part, they didn't get that?]

No, *I* didn't know it. It was me [who] didn't know what was going on. I didn't associate. . . . I mean truly. . . . I just know that I felt this way about this other woman and I thought, "Something is wrong here," and then I thought, "Wait a minute. I'm dealing with the loss of this relationship but there is something else here. These feelings are real; the feelings were valid and they were wonderful. Something is going on here. I've got to look into that part." While I was getting better in this loss of a relationship, I said, "I need to start thinking about my sexuality here."

Cues to Action

A cue to action is, for example, a realization that she has attraction for one particular woman or an insight that helps her see more clearly a need for change in some area of her life. Respondent #23, age forty-seven, talks about an insight that something has to change:

[Can you think of a moment when you knew something had to be different?]

Yeah. For reasons that I don't think I was ever very clear about at the time, or at least I didn't think through at the time. When I was ordering Christmas presents that year, I ordered a statue of the goddess Uma; I think it's a Nepalese bronze, very beautiful statue, and I ordered it for myself. I liked it. I looked at the catalogue I think; "I really like this. I'll get myself something. I'm getting this." . . . the day that it came I was alone in the house in the afternoon. I got home from work; my children weren't home from school yet, and that package was there, and I took it up to my room and I unwrapped the package and I started to cry. It was a very beautiful woman, and just to be able to hold that and touch that made things more emotionally concrete to me. I guess at that point, I really decided I am going to have to do something about this. Without even understanding what it was that I needed to do or anything, but it was very definite to me that I was going to need to do something about that.

The cue to action can be a specific insight that she is generally attracted to women, for example, respondent #9, age fifty-seven:

I was at a weekend therapy retreat with seventeen other women and two therapists. It was held at a Girl Scout camp, very rustic and comfortable. It was a "get to know yourself and open up to your own process" weekend. I had come because I was in another marriage and feeling very lost and empty and lonely. I wasn't lonely for people. I was longing for something—I think it was a part of myself. I met a woman on Friday evening whom I liked, and she was a poet and taught English at [university]. I was impressed with her sensibility and knowledge. After talking, we all went off to bed in our little bunks and sleeping bags, and the next morning I got up early to go to the bathroom. As I walked by the central room, I saw her sitting at a table having coffee and smoking a ciga- rette. Suddenly, like a shock to my body, I was filled with the most incredible sexual rush. My whole body was suffused with it. I ran back to my sleeping bag and hunkered down and said to myself, "What is happening here? Oh my gosh, this is like Jane!"—a girl I'd loved when I was eleven. I hadn't felt sexual like that since I was eleven years old. And after an hour or so of thinking, I knew, I just knew. Oooh, this is what the emptiness has been about. This is the missing piece. This is why I haven't felt close to the men I married. I don't have a sexual problem. It's women. It's women I've wanted to be with all the time . . .

The cue to action can be specific to one particular woman. A woman may realize that she has a new relationship that connects her to deep needs she didn't know she had. For example, respondent #24, age fifty-four, describes how she realized for the first time that the woman she loved touched her with a kindness that she didn't get from her husband:

So I decided that I would bear with this [continue the mar- riage] for four years. Because I wanted to get my son through college. That's what I promised, and that's what I needed to do. So four years down the road, we could be living together. And Laura, I'm thinking it's important, she's going to be a part of my world, she must meet my family. Get to know the kids slowly. And she came to spend a week with us. . . . Bob would work the store and then we would travel around. I would show her all of Montana because she is our guest, and one day we went to Glacier Park. . . . There are mountain goats there and they are climbing around, Bob taking all these pictures, and I'm climbing up these rocks and I slip and fall. And I have bike slacks on and I'm going down. Laura is concerned. "Are you OK?" she says. Down comes Bob, yelling at me about— "Look what you did to your slacks; they're all filthy and dirty" and whatever. Never an "Are you OK?" . . . or . . . it was so clear. So synonymous with aha!

Reinforcing Factors

Reinforcing factors are, obviously, those which reinforce and support a process that may have already begun. The reinforcing factors do not necessarily need to be about gender orientation to reinforce the process. Experiences such as taking her own power by making an important decision or asserting her needs, as well as paying attention to her own intuition and insight, can be great reinforcers along the way to discovering and uncovering personal identity and gender orientation. Examples could be, again, the developing ability to "know" what her society isn't helping her to know or a significant woman or lesbian friend or other lesbian or bisexual role model who offers her support for her declaration that she is, indeed, lesbian or bisexual. A friend or family member who sees her confusion and wants to support her right to find her own life can be a very significant reinforcer.

Learning to take their own judgment and ideas seriously, that is, getting past diffusion identity status to moratorium identity status (on their way to identity achievement—see Chapter 3 on identity formation) was a significant change for the interview respondents. Respondent #1, age thirty-six, describes a process of self-discovery that reinforced her self-confidence and self-assurance and encouraged her to continue to make her own decisions:

> I was very happy for many years as an at-home mom and taking care of the kids, but something had kind of completed itself, and I was ready to do something different with my life. For the most part, I was very happy for many years. I would say, for the last five years of my marriage, I wasn't happy. And as I look back, there are times I was probably, you know, would have profited from seeking psychiatric help or something that would make the blue go away. You know, make it not so gray. But I didn't know at the time that was a possibility. It was like I never had had any experience like my parents, my in-laws; nobody around me had ever even suggested that or experienced that . . . [counseling] was a possibility. It was just like, yeah, some people do that, but I didn't know anybody that did. And I thought I could do this by myself . . . "OK, it's kind of blue and gray, but I can do this." And I did, but I look

at a time where I just didn't want to get out of bed; I didn't want to. The robotic action of get up, make breakfast, clean the house, do the dishes, do the laundry, make lunch; it was just like very robotic and that the heart of keeping the home nurtured had gone out of it. . . . When I look back now, it's like, well, there was something; it wasn't being an at-home mom that was not OK, and the whole thing became robotic. . . . I had to take care of my kids, and I knew it wasn't them that was creating that; it was like I had something else going on, and once I made the big, explosive decision, "I don't care what anybody says; I'm going to school," a whole lot of stuff started falling. People started thinking, "What is she doing?" My parents were like, "What do you want to do that for?" My husband was very—a lot of reaction that was like this. And I said, "I'm going to do this." . . . That voice shocked them more than my wanting to go to school, I think.

When respondent #21, age thirty, was asked a direct question about herself, she had a realization that the process taking place inside of her could be valid, primarily because her friend saw it and opened up her thinking:

Well, the night before Take Back the Night at Ellie's apartment and we're getting set; we're making up signs for the march, we're painting the banner, and I'm looking at her books and see she has some books on bisexuality and stuff like that. And we're talking back and forth and she says, "Marian, are you straight?" And I say, "I'm a married woman; of course I'm straight." She says, "That doesn't mean anything; come on Marian, think about it. Are you straight?" And I'm having all these crushes, all those teachers, Sue, and I think, "I'm bisexual!" Oh my God, kinda laughed with that, feeling happy and scared at the same time. And [then] I thought I was bisexual because I was married to a man.

Paths to Learning

As she navigates the process of realizing her identity, her gender orientation, there are three paths by which a woman's learning occurs: the cognitive or thinking path, the affective or emotional path, and the behavioral path. A woman may learn about her gender orientation through just one or all three routes. In terms of the Precede Model (Green and Kreuter, 1991), an important assumption underlies our discussion. That is, to be going through this change process, the woman in question is predisposed (has the predisposing factor) to feel same-gender attractions and has within her the potential for wanting such relationships.

Consider first the cognitive path, for example, cognitive learning about sexuality. This study has reinforced the fact that most people in this culture do not receive accurate cognitions—thoughts and ideas—about sex because education and information is presented so inconsistently, inadequately, and indirectly and is often cloaked in shame and embarrassment. Women are shamed for wanting to know about sex. Thus, the factors that could have predisposed these women to know themselves—factors such as sexual information and beliefs—were usually prevented from entering their consciousness. This prevention took place, for example, because they didn't want to feel the shame or guilt they would have felt if they let the sexual thoughts in. They were not supposed to think about sex. Therefore, since sex is one of the central factors of human existence and they needed this information to navigate their lives, these women were forced to quietly find the information for themselves, usually under the cloak of secrecy and shame. They didn't tend to find accurate sex information because of the paradoxical cultural message they faced: they were "supposed to know," so they were embarrassed to ask questions of those who really did know, and they were not supposed to know because if they knew, they weren't feminine, were not "good" women. Sex was often presented as violent or only for men. Misinformation and inadequate information were inevitably learned and taught. Misinformation became distorted as it was passed around. The shame and forced secrecy further distorted the information. Thus, the cognitive path offered these women either inaccurate or distorted cognitive messages. Therefore, the *cognitive* path to learning was *blocked*.

In terms of the Precede Model (Green, 1991), even though she may have had predisposing factors, the cognitive distortions and misinformation were *disenabling* and negatively reinforcing, thereby offering no support at all for her to move toward the goal of reaching awareness of her identity and enhancing her psychological health.

The affective or emotional path teaches a woman about sexuality through the feelings she has concerning her sexual and other emotional responses. Once again, this study showed the lack of permission for women to feel their own arousal or to experience their own sexual pleasure. If a woman felt her own arousal despite the negative sanctions around it, she was likely to feel guilt because she should be repressing her interest and shame because she was not repressing it. These conditions are true for all women in this culture, regardless of orientation. If one of these women felt aroused in relation to another woman, however, she was likely to feel an additional layer of affect. She might have experienced the interest as "falling in love," but it was more likely that she caught herself thinking that the feelings were weird, different, true only for her, and unlike what anyone else was feeling, which then added an additional layer of shame because she felt alone and strange and had to keep all of this a secret. In terms of the Precede Model (Green, 1991), this shame, distortion, and detachment *disenabled* and negatively reinforced behaviors that might have generated the emotions that would have helped her to learn about her gender orientation. She was then likely to further repress her interest, which added another layer of guilt and shame around the secret or possibly detached her from her sexual feelings entirely. The *affective* path of learning about her gender orientation was therefore *blocked.*

The third path of learning, the behavioral, is somewhat less likely to be activated without support of the cognitive and affective pathways, but it is possible that the woman will learn something through the behavioral path inadvertently. The women in this study found themselves acting out behaviors such as repeatedly putting themselves in the presence of one particular woman or going to a women's music concert or to a woman's social club or bar to dance. This study has shown that those behaviors were identified in their minds only with groups they had learned to revile—such as lesbian women and the stereotypes that surround them. These women, therefore, were likely to deny themselves that behavior by saying, "I can't do that. I'm not that way." They tended to delay experiencing the reinforcing aspect of the supportive community and positive role models they might have found at that social club or with that particular woman. They delayed, therefore, allowing themselves to feel the joy they might have known at holding a woman as they danced or the pleasure they may have felt in a particular woman's presence. By not experiencing the behavior, the process of moving toward a lesbian/bisexual identity was *disenabled*. The process was not positively reinforced. The *behavioral* path to learning was, therefore, *blocked*.

All three paths of her learning about her sexuality and her gender orientation—cognitive, affective, and behavioral—were thereby blocked. Knowledge and awareness were then effectively blocked. This study has looked at the process women must go through to unblock those paths. Women cannot make decisions based on knowledge (thinking, emotional, or behavioral knowledge) that they don't have.

This study has shown that a woman may be aware for many years that she has a strong desire to be in the presence of women or to spend a great deal of time with one particular woman, but she may interpret that as a desire for a close friendship. Indeed, these women tended to place close friendships with other women at a priority, whether or not they were ultimately drawn to them as primary partners. Most women had one or two "best friends" with whom they shared inner struggles and joys. When these women realized that they were not only drawn to a woman or to women but that they had sexual feelings for these women, it was a significant moment of personal empowerment for them. When we consider that women tend to grow and flourish within their connections to others, and that social constructions, institutions, representatives of the society, and family members may have been on the side of keeping these women from this information, this sexual awareness, such a realization was a triumph.

Drawing from psychophysics, this experience can be compared to the figure/ground awareness. The picture containing a mass of tiny dots of color that, at first, looks like a total sea of pink, will—after one has looked at it long enough—begin to present a shape of another color, perhaps lavender, that appears out of the background. This figure/ground dimension illustrates that the human eye is not capable of picking out the second picture embedded in the first until a few seconds has passed. Gradually, the second picture rises out of the first. The figure appears, rises out of the background, and becomes obvious where at first it could not be discerned.

In this way, sexual attraction as a part of a relationship became gradually clear and separate from the affectionate friendship part for these women. At that point, sexual and emotional attraction—enhanced by cognitive clarity and recurring behaviors—rose to cause an emotional realization, or an epiphany. That is, we have seen that these women grew and identified within relationships, within connections. Because they were accustomed to placing a high value on their connections with people, these women did not see their connections to significant women as more than simple friendships. As they moved through the process of becoming aware of their same-gender orientation, the figure (sexual feelings) began to be discernible from the ground (friendship connections). They began to see clearly what they had been unable to see before.

This figure/ground process appeared to occur at many levels in the lives of these women. Because these women had no support in this society for their sexual learning, the establishment of their own personal identity, and the allowance to "know" what it is they knew, they were effectively disempowered in many areas of their lives. They were likely to find themselves having figure/ground experiences, that is, having the truth slowly appear, or even leap out at them, on many levels, if they were allowed the opportunity for personal reflection and independent experience. The women in this study experienced these moments of truth in a variety of situations, sometimes when they had taken a chance, when they had risked behavior that was not supported or sanctioned by their social milieu, and sometimes when the pressure lifted, when their accumulating information and knowledge, their self-confidence and self-awareness had reached a critical mass and the resulting burst of energy caused an explosion of change.

The figure/ground shift representing a moment of truth sometimes rose out of the background quietly and gradually, as it did for respondent #6, age thirty-five:

I still didn't have emotional needs met. Barry was more emotional, but I still felt it didn't go very deep. He could talk to a certain point, and once I got past a certain point, he didn't get it. I don't know how to say what he didn't get, but I didn't feel emotionally full. That became the turning point, I guess, that I felt really alone and unfulfilled emotionally. I still enjoyed being sexual with Barry and that wasn't ever a problem. He was always good in the sexual sense, but not emotionally fulfilling. And I think for a long time, I thought of him as being emotional, and I probably gave him credit for being more emotional than he was. I think I was putting it all together how I wanted to put it together, but he wasn't really there. And I didn't really . . .

[You made him up, partly?]

I think I made him into something he wasn't really. He was a tender, nice person, and for some reason, I think I fantasized him to be more than what he was in that sense.

[So your leaving the marriage was not about—I mean, finally getting the divorce was not about meeting someone specific; it was about knowing what there is to life that you wanted?]

Right.

On the other hand, the figure/ground realization could have presented itself in a more dramatic way, as it did for respondent #16, age fifty-one. She went to a weekend encounter group with her husband, believing her marriage was OK. Two days later, the cognitive and affective paths to her knowing had been unblocked. She knew something had to change:

It said in the pamphlet [that] this is not a therapeutic marriage counseling thing. You really have to be in fairly good shape with your marriage. It's pretty intense to go to this, and I said to Joe, "Let's go to this. I've heard good things about it, and we're not in trouble. I think what we need to do is learn how to communicate a little bit more. We've been in counseling off in our own direction and we just need to learn how to communicate more." And he wasn't too gung ho but he said, "OK; OK, I'll go to this." So we went to the Lutheran Marriage Encounter in December of '82, and as I say, it was one of the worst weekends because we communicated all right, and I found that by communicating my thoughts to him and being with him for almost forty-eight hours continuously and sharing thoughts, that I didn't want to be with him. . . . They'd ask us questions as a couple and then we'd separate and go to a separate place for an hour, write down [your] thoughts, come together and share them. Oh, God, it was awful. Just awful. Anyway, we had to come back and share thoughts about where [we] want to be in a few years and what [we] want to be doing together or what such and such means to you. . . . What came out was I really didn't want to be with him. That Sunday night when we left . . . before we left, they had a little church service, communion or something, and during the service, we all had to repeat our marriage vows, and I couldn't do it. It was one of the worst things I had ever been through. Total mind/body experience. I almost left the room. I thought, "I'm going to die here," because I'm looking at him—we are supposed to be looking lovingly at each other's face, like all the other couples are doing here, repeating our marriage vows. I couldn't do it. Anyway, I was never so happy to get out. I felt that I had been in jail for the weekend. I remember walking out of this place and into the fresh air—Christmas-like—breathing this air and thinking. . . . I guess I had changed. . . . I didn't want him in my life. . . . But there wasn't anyone or any one thing. I just knew there was something inside me that was; I wasn't satisfied with being with him anymore. . . . I wanted to be on my own.

An epiphany is an emotional realization, when the essence of something is revealed in a sudden flash of recognition. As I have outlined in detail, women's learning can be blocked on all three paths, the cognitive, the affective, and the behavioral. As this study has illustrated, these women grew in experience as they moved through the varied social landscape. Because they had a predisposition for same-gender attractions, they saw and heard accurate information as it came in over the barriers that they consciously rejected—but unconsciously took in. They found themselves comfortably performing new behaviors that formerly would have been unacceptable to them. Over time, they began to feel an accumulation of affect, of emotional responses, a buildup of emotional tension that they stored away without being fully conscious of it. This accumulated affect appears to be what finally pointed them in the direction of the outcome.

It is as though each of these women was traveling in a canoe down the river toward Niagara Falls. She was being carried along by the current. There was a point in the river, in the approach to the falls, beyond which she couldn't turn back because the current was too strong for her to turn around and go upstream again. She was compelled to continue toward the falls. If she had accumulated enough self-knowledge and information, if the internal or external pressure against her knowing had lifted somewhat, whether or not she had found new role models or a community, if the accumulated affect or feelings were strong enough, she was pulled inevitably toward what she felt was her more true gender orientation. She could no longer turn around. Her emotions swamped—overwhelmed—all the conflicting and limiting cognitive messages and expectations. She began to reconstruct her identity. She was lesbian. She was bisexual. She was herself.

CONCLUSIONS

I could find no previous research that examines what happens to a woman before she begins to question her identity as a lesbian/bisexual woman. Major theories of sexuality development that address lesbians have begun with the awareness of difference and made the assumption that women know how they are different from others and must learn to accept the differences. This research does not support that knowing.

Although they now identify as lesbian or bisexual, fifteen of the women studied here had no same-gender attractions before they married, and two more were totally unaware that same-gender relationships existed as a possibility for them. These seventeen women did not struggle with their orientation and marry to hide it or overcome it. They didn't ask themselves if they were lesbian before they were married. The idea that they were lesbian or bisexual didn't occur to these seventeen women until they had married.

All twenty-four of these women had the predilection for same-gender attraction that was effectively kept from them. The purpose of this study has been to find reasons why this occurs. Following are chapter headings and summaries of each chapter, outlining some reasons why women don't know sooner and describing other conclusions of this research.

Sex Education and Information: In the United States, She Must Find Her Way in the Dark

A general attitude of guilt/sin/danger regarding sexuality exists in this society, as well as the further implication that sexual experience and feelings are for men, not for women. If women discuss sex in public, particularly if they talk about their enjoyment of sex, they are usually considered unsavory and even salacious. Women grow up without a working knowledge of their bodies and their bodies' functioning. Women are shamed for seeking information about their bodies and their sexuality. This shaming may occur directly as the result of their questioning, or it can occur as parents and other adults—either in childhood or in adult life—recoil or withdraw from direct discussion of sexual issues. Myths and inaccurate information are the natural result of having sexual knowledge restricted. The most significant impression that most girls and women get about sex is that it is a secret, off limits, inappropriate, or bad for them to think or talk about. Therefore, the meaning and value of sex can remain a mystery, except as a mechanical process.

Women grow up largely unaware that sexual arousal is a part of normal human functioning. Therefore, they learn to feel guilty and ashamed about their feelings of sexual arousal. There is discouragement concerning girls' and women's general self-knowing in this society. This discouragement further complicates women's ignorance of their anatomy and sexuality. Further, since—if they are taught anything about sex—they are taught the mechanics only, they do not learn that sex is an emotional and relational process. The encouragement that women traditionally feel to remain subordinate and inexpressive—particularly about sex—teaches them that they have no sexual choices. Left with the impression that they have no choices, they often don't know what their arousal means or that they can say no to sexual experiences they don't want or for which they aren't ready. Without awareness of their options, they don't learn that there is a range of normal outcomes for their sexual and relational lives.

Sex and sexuality are paradoxical in this society. These sexual paradoxes—which are taboo for discussion—create major problems for girls and women. In this society, sex is treated as something dangerous and distasteful—and also very desirable and exciting. Sex is touted in popular culture as the central point of a relationship, but it is never to be discussed in polite company. The message to a woman is that her arousal is crucial for a man's enjoyment but that her arousal also renders her loose and vulgar. She is admonished to dress and paint for him, but is accused of inviting his attention when it comes. In the tightly woven tapestry of sexuality in this society, patriarchal attitudes about women are the warp and these paradoxes and double binds are the woof. Within this context, claiming her own sexual energy and power—whatever that means for the individual woman—and hearing her own voice are most crucial to her development of awareness that she is lesbian or bisexual.

Why Do These Women Marry Men?

Marriage for these women was not presented as an option. This society presents marriage as the inevitable act defining adulthood. Heterosexual marriage—that between a man and a woman—is part of social law, and there has been, and continues to be, major social censure for those women who do not marry. The power of the social force to marry creates a script for women's lives that is so powerful that their own internal messages can be, and sometimes are, overwhelmed.

How Do Women Establish Personal Identity and Gender Orientation in a Heterosexist Society?

With regard to identity development, traditional theorizing has been based on men's agentic developmental patterns and needs.

Women's development has been considered deviant because it differed from that of men. The experiences of the women in this study reflect what is now considered to be the normal pattern for women. That is, women's lives tend to develop with a balance between the agentic, totally self-determining self and the self as it connects and relates to others. Because this balance is normal for women, it is also normal for women to give major consideration to the needs and opinions of others and to commitments that do not threaten their network of life relationships. Because of the public censure of lesbianism and bisexuality, the scarcity of positive role models, and the absence of the right "social landscape," these women often did not see the range of choices available to them and/or did not act on the options they might have seen.

Regarding gender orientation, the experiences of the women in this study reflect the fluidity of women's sexuality. Their experiences demonstrate the social constructionist mode of identity formation: women are able to pursue their relationship goals from the perceived available outcomes.

How Do Women Know?

The results of this study confirm that the traditionally patriarchal culture in which we live constrains women's knowledge and self-knowledge in general. Specifically regarding gender orientation, if these women had thought of their attractions to women, they would have risked defying the dominant group that dictated the heterosexual model. Further, women are subject to ascriptions of temperament and role that are defined by social standards. Most of these women had been directed and controlled in their lives and were not accustomed to making decisions for themselves that they acknowledged to others. In addition, because of prejudice against lesbian and bisexual women, there was valid concern that revealing their gender orientation would put custody of their children at risk. In addition, and in conjunction to the reality that women make less money than men do and are often limited in their choice of careers, a central factor with regard to their knowing was that they had been taught to be afraid and not to know that they could be fully capable of taking care of themselves.

Where Are the Lesbian Role Models?

With regard to role models, the study reveals that these women were restricted in their knowing by (1) a dearth of positive lesbian and bisexual role models and (2) the certain exposure to homophobic myths and stereotypes. These women had been immersed in the beliefs that only women and men are paired and that women need men to care for them. They had learned that single women who live without men are ridiculed or evil—or they are ignored, which makes them invisible. If these women did know about the existence of lesbians, until very recently, lesbian women were represented only as sex crazy and/or as tough and masculine. Even in the greater openness that has developed in the 1990s, it is difficult for these women to find positive, undistorted lesbian and bisexual role models in the media and public life, as well as in their private lives.

Now That She Knows

Finally, I found that even after these women knew there was something special in their feelings for women and that a significant life change was brewing, they still had a difficult time acknowledging their feelings, accepting that a change was coming, that children could adjust, and that it was possible to follow the life path they chose for themselves. Social support concerning this issue was not readily available, even among other lesbian and bisexual women, but once it was found, it was crucial to their evolution as persons.

Along with all women in this society, the judgment and perceptions of these women had been both flagrantly and subtly denigrated so that independent thought and action were thoroughly discouraged. They were unaware that their essence, their identity, was being shaped by powerful heterosexist conditioning. To embrace all aspects of their identity, these women needed to accumulate the critical amount of experience, knowledge, self-awareness, confidence, and support. When they had accumulated this critical amount, they were drawn by the river current of their own realizations. They were well on their way to the falls. There was no turning back. Even if they could have turned around, they didn't want to.

Bibliography

Abbott, Deborah and Farmer, Ellen (1995). *From Wedded Wife to Lesbian Life: Stories of Transformation*. Freedom, CA: The Crossing Press.

Amussen, Susan (1997). Personal Communication.

Baetz, Ruth (1984). The coming-out process: Violence against lesbians. In Trudy Darty and Sandee Potter (Eds.), *Women-Identified Women*. Palo Alto, CA: Mayfield Publishers, 45-50.

Bandura, Arthur and Walters, R.H. (1969). *Social Learning and Personality Development*. New York: Holt, Rinehart and Winston.

Barbach, Lonnie (1973). *For Yourself: The Fulfillment of Female Sexuality*. New York: Doubleday.

Beauvoir de, Simone (1953). *The Second Sex*. London: Jonathan Cape.

Belenky, Mary Field, Clinchy, Blythe McVicker, Goldberger, Nancy Rule, and Tarule, Jill Mattuck (1986). *Women's Ways of Knowing*. New York: Basic Books.

Bell, Alan and Weinberg, Martin (1978). *Homosexualities: A Study of the Diversity Among Men and Women*. New York: Simon and Schuster.

Bell, Alan, Weinberg, Martin, and Hammersmith, Sue (1981). *Sexual Preference: Its Development in Men and Women*. Bloomington, IN: Indiana University Press.

Bell, Ruth (1987). *Changing Bodies, Changing Lives*. New York: Vintage Books.

Bjorklund, David and Bjorklund, Barbara (1988). Straight or gay? *Parents*, 98, 93-96.

Bohan, Janis (1996). *Psychology and Sexual Orientation: Coming to Terms*. New York and London: Routledge.

Bornstein, Kate (1994). *Gender Outlaw*. New York: Vintage Books.

Brehony, Kathleen (1983). Women and agoraphobia: A case for the etiological significance of the feminine sex-role stereotype. In Violet, Franks and Esther Rothblum (Eds.), *The Stereotyping of Women*. New York: Springer, 112-128.

Bridges, Karen and Croteau, James (1994). Once-married lesbians: Facilitating life patterns. *Journal of Counseling and Development*, 73, November/December, 134-140.

Brock, Linda and Jennings, Glen (1993). Sexuality Education: What daughters in their 30s wish their mothers had told them. *Family Relations*, 42(1) January, 61-65.

Brooks, Virginia (1981). *Minority Stress and Lesbian Women*. Lexington, MA: Lexington Press.

Broverman, Inge and Broverman, M. (1970). Sex role stereotypes and clinical judgments of mental health. *Journal of Counseling & Clinical Psychology*, 34, 1-7.

Brown, Harold (1976). *Familiar Faces, Hidden Lives*. San Diego, CA: Harcourt Brace Jovanovich.

Brown, Laura (1995). Lesbian identity: Concepts and issues. In Anthony D'augelli and Charlotte Patterson (Eds.), *Lesbian, Gay, Bisexual Identities over the Lifespan*. New York: Oxford University Press, 3-23.

Brown, Lyn Mikel and Gilligan, Carol (1992). *Meeting at the Crossroads*. Cambridge, MA: Harvard University Press.

Browning, Christine (1984). Changing theories of lesbianism: Challenging the stereotype. In Trudy Darty and Sandee Potter (Eds.), *Women-Identified Women*. Palo Alto, CA: Mayfield Publishers, 11-30.

Brownmiller, Susan (1975). *Against Our Will: Men, Women, and Rape*. New York: Simon and Schuster.

Brownmiller, Susan (1984). *Femininity*. New York: Fawcett Columbine.

Burch, Beverly (1993a). Gender identities, lesbianism, and potential space. *Psychoanalytic Psychology*, 10(3), 339-345.

Burch, Beverly (1993b). Heterosexuality, bisexuality and lesbianism: Rethinking psychoanalytic views of women's sexual object choice. *Psychoanalytic Review*, 80(1), Spring, 83-99.

Burch, Beverly (1997). *On Intimate Terms: Lesbian/Bisexual Experience and Psychoanalytic Views of Women*. New York: Columbia University Press.

Butler, Judith (1990). *Gender Trouble: Feminism and the Subversion of Identity*. New York, London: Routledge.

Calderone, Mary (1983). Fetal erection and its message to us. *Siecus Report*, 11(5/6), 9-10.

Cammermeyer, Margarethe with Fisher, Chris (1994). *Serving in Silence*. New York: Penguin Putnam, 78-83.

Cass, Vivienne (1979). Homosexual identity formation: A theoretical model. *Journal of Homosexuality*, 4, 219-236.

Cass, Vivienne (1984). Homosexual identity formation: A theoretical model. *Journal of Sex Research*, 20, 143-167.

Charbonneau, Claudette and Lander, Patricia Slade (1991). Redefining sexuality: Women becoming lesbian in midlife. In Barbara Sang, Joyce Warshow, and Adrienne Smith (Eds.), *Lesbians at Midlife: The Creative Transition*. San Francisco: Spinsters Book Company, 35-43.

Chesler, Phyllis (1972). *Women and Madness*. New York: Avon Books.

Chodorow, Nancy (1978). *Reproduction of Mothering: Psychoanalysis and the Sociology of Gender*. Berkeley, CA: University of California Press.

Clement, Ulrich, Schmidt, Gunter, and Kruse, Margaret (1984). Changing sex differences in sexual behavior: A replication of a study of W. German students, 1966-1980. *Archives of Sexual Behavior*, 13, 99-121.

Coleman, Eli (1982). Developmental stages of the coming out process. *American Behavioral Scientist*, 25, 31-43.

Coleman, Eli (1985). Bisexual women in marriages. In F. Klein and Tom Wolf (Eds.), *Bisexualities: Theory and Research*. Binghamton, NY: The Haworth Press, Inc., 87-98.

Coleman, Eli (1990). The married lesbian. In Franklin Dozette and Marvin Sussman (Eds.), *Homosexuality and Family Relations*. Binghamton, NY: The Haworth Press, Inc., 119-135.

Cook, K. (1983). The Playboy reader's sex survey. *Playboy*, May, 126.

Dank, Barry M. (1971). Coming out in the gay world. *Psychiatry*, 34, 180-197.

Davis, Murray (1983). *Smut: Erotic Realities and Obscene Ideology*. Chicago: University of Chicago Press.

Dinnerstein, Dorothy (1976). *The Mermaid and the Minotaur: Sexual Arrangements and Human Malaise*. New York: Harper.

Driver, Emily and Droisen, Audrey (1989). *Child Sexual Abuse: A Feminist Reader*. New York: New York University Press.

Eliot, T.S. (1971). The Four Quartets—Little Giddings. *The Complete Poems and Plays 1909-1950*. New York: Harcourt, Brace and World.

Elliott, Phyllis E. (1985). Theory and research on lesbian identity formation. *International Journal of Women's Studies*, 8, 64-75.

Enns, Carolyn (1991). The "new" relationship models of women's identity: A review and critique for counselors. *Journal of Counseling and Development*, 69, 209-217.

Enns, Carolyn and Hackett, Gail (1990). Comparison of feminist and nonfeminist reactions to variants of nonsexist and feminist counseling. *Journal of Counseling Psychology*, 37(1), 33-40.

Erikson, Erik (1950). *Childhood and Society*. New York: Norton.

Erikson, Erik (1968). *Identity, Youth and Crisis*. New York: Norton.

Evans, Nancy and Levine, Heidi (1990). *Perspectives on Sexual Orientation: New Directions for Student Services*. San Francisco: Jossey-Bass.

Faderman, Lillian (1981). *Surpassing the Love of Men*. New York: William Morrow and Company.

Faderman, Lillian (1991). *Odd Girls and Twilight Lovers: A History of Lesbian Life in 20th Century America*. New York: Penguin.

Falco, Kristine (1991). *Psychotherapy with Lesbian Clients: Theory into Practice*. New York: Brunner-Mazel.

Feinstein, Sherman, Looney, A., Schwartzberg, A., and Sarosky, A. (Eds.) (1982). *Adolescent Psychiatry: Developmental and Clinical Studies,* Volume 10, Chicago: University of Chicago Press, 52-65.

Fine, Michelle (1988). Sexuality, schooling, and adolescent females: The missing discourse of desire. *Harvard Education Review*, 58, 29-53.

Fine, Michelle (1993). Sexuality, schooling and adolescent females: The missing discourse of desire. In Lois Weis, and Michelle Fine (Eds.), *Beyond Silenced Voices: Class, Race and Gender in United States Schools*. Albany, NY: State University of New York Press, 62.

Fisher, William, Byrne, D., and White, L. (1983). Emotional barriers to contraception. In D. Byrne and William Fisher (Eds.), *Adolescents, Sex and Contraception*. Hillsdale, NJ: Lawrence Erlbaum, 207-239.

Francoeur, Robert (1991). *Becoming a Sexual Person*. New York: Macmillan.

Freire, Paulo (1971). *Pedagogy of the Oppressed*. New York: Harder and Harder.

Frieze, Irene, Parsons, Jacquelynne, Johnson, Paula, Ruble, Diane, and Zellman, Gail (1978). *Women and Sex Roles: A Social Psychological Perspective.* New York, London: W. W. Norton.

Fullinwider-Bush, Nell and Jacobvitz, Deborah (1993). The transition to young adulthood: Generational boundary dissolution and female identity development. *Family Process*, 32(1), 87-104.

Gagnon, John (1985). Attitudes and responses of parents to pre-adolescent masturbation. *Archives of Sex Behavior*, 14, 451-466.

Galenson, Eleanor and Roiphe, Herman (1976). Some suggested revisions concerning early female development. *Journal of the American Psychoanalytic Association*, 24(5), 29-57.

Gartrell, Nanette (1981). The lesbian as "single" woman. *American Journal of Psychotherapy*, 35(4), 502-516.

Gay, Peter (1988). *Freud.* New York: Norton.

Gilligan, Carol (1982). *In a Different Voice.* Cambridge, MA: Harvard University Press.

Gilligan, Carol (1986). Exit-voice dilemmas in adolescent development. In A. Foxley, M.S. McPherson, and G. O'Donnell (Eds.), *Development, Democracy and the Art of Trespassing: Essays in Honor of Albert O. Hirchman.* Notre Dame, IN: University of Notre Dame Press, 283-300.

Gilligan, Carol (1987). Adolescent development reconsidered. In C. Irwin (Ed.), *New Directions for Child Development: Adolescent Behavior and Health.* San Francisco: Jossey-Bass, 63-92.

Gilligan, Carol (1989). Preface, Teaching Shakespeare's sister. In Carol Gilligan, N. Lyons, and T. Hammer (Eds.), *Making Connections: The Relational World of Adolescent Girls at Emma Willard School.* Cambridge, MA: Harvard University Press, 6-29.

Glaser, Barney and Strauss, Anselm (1967). *The Discovery of Grounded Theory: Strategies for Qualitative Research.* New York: Aldine DeGruyter.

Glodis, Kimberly and Blasi, Augusto (1993). The sense of self and identity among adolescents and adults. *Journal of Adolescent Research*, 8(4), October, 356-380.

Gluckman, Amy and Reed, Betsy (Eds.) (1997). *HomoEconomics: Capitalism, Community and Lesbian and Gay Life.* New York, London: Routledge.

Goffman, Erving (1963). *Stigma: Notes on the Management of Spoiled Identity.* Englewood Cliffs, NJ: Prentice-Hall.

Golden, Carla (1987). Diversity and variability in women's sexual identities. In Boston Lesbian Psychologies Collective (Eds.), *Lesbian Psychologies.* Urbana, Chicago: University of Illinois Press, 19-34.

Gonnerman, Jennifer (1994). Who's afraid of Shere Hite? *Ms*, 5(2), 75.

Gonsiorek, John and Weinrich, J.D. (1991). *Homosexuality: Research Implications for Public Policy.* Newbury Park, CA: Sage Publications.

Goodman, M.E. (1983). Biology of sexuality: Inborn determinants of human sexual response. *British Journal of Psychiatry*, 143, 216-220.

Gramick, Jeannine (1984). Developing a lesbian identity. In Trudy Darty and Sandee Potter (Eds.), *Women-Identified Women*. Palo Alto, CA: Mayfield Publishers, 30-44.

Green, Lawrence W. and Kreuter, Marshall (1991). *Health Education Planning: An Educational and Environmental Approach*, Second Edition. Mountain View, CA: Mayfield Publishers.

Green, Richard (1978). Sexual identity of 37 children raised by homosexual or transsexual parents. *American Journal of Psychiatry*, 135, 692–697.

Greven, Philip. (1991). *Spare the Child*. New York: Knopf.

Haas, K. and Haas, A. (1993). *Understanding Sexuality*. St. Louis, MO: Mosby.

Hafner, D. (1992). From where I sit. *Family Life Educator*, 2(11), 14-15.

Hagee, Maggie (1994). A response to Weille's "Reworking of developmental theory: A case of lesbian identity." *Clinical Social Work*, 22(1), Spring, 113-117.

Heiman, Julia (1977). A psychophysiological exploration of sexual arousal patterns in females and males. *Psychophysiology*, 14, 266-274.

Hencken, J.D. and O'Dowd, W.T. (1977). Coming out as an aspect of identity formation. *GaiSaber*, 1, 18-22.

Hetrick, Emery and Martin, A. Damien (1984). Ego-dystonic homosexuality. In E. Hetrick and T. Stein (Eds.), *Innovations in Psychotherapy with Homosexuals*. Washington, DC: American Psychiatric Press, 3-21.

Hinchen, Keziah (1988). Gay and lesbian adolescence. Master's thesis. St. Mary's University Graduate School, Minneapolis, MN, April.

Hoare, Carol (1991). Psychosocial identity development and cultural others. *Journal of Counseling and Development*, 70, September/October, 45-53.

Hopkins, Linda (1980). Inner space and outer space identity in contemporary females. *Psychiatry*, 43, February, 1-12.

Ireland, Mardy (1993). *Reconceiving Women: Separating Motherhood from Female Identity*. New York: Guilford Press.

Jordan, Judith (1991). Empathy and self boundaries. In Jordan, Alexandra Kaplan, Jean Baker Miller, Irene Stiver, and Janet Surrey (Eds.), *Women's Growth in Connection*. New York, London: Guilford Press, 67-80.

Josselson, Ruthellen (1987). *Finding Herself: Pathways to Identity Development in Women*. San Francisco, CA: Jossey-Bass.

Josselson, Ruthellen (1996). *Revising Herself: The Story of Women's Identity from College to Midlife*. New York and Oxford: Oxford University Press.

Jung, Patricia and Smith, Ralph (1993). *Heterosexism: An Ethical Challenge*. Albany, NY: SUNY Press.

Kahn, Marla J. (1991). Factors affecting the coming out process for lesbians. *Journal of Homosexuality*, 21(3), 47-70.

Kaufman, Gershen (1982). *Shame: The Power of Caring*. Cambridge, MA: Shenkman.

Kaufman, Gershen and Raphael, Lev (1996). *Coming Out of Shame*. New York: Main Street by Doubleday.

Kinsey, Alfred, Pomeroy, Wardell, and Martin, Clyde (1948). *Sexual Behavior in the Human Male*. Philadelphia, PA: Saunders.

Kinsey, Alfred, Pomeroy, Wardell, and Martin, Clyde (1953). *Sexual Behavior in the Human Female.* Philadelphia, PA: Saunders.

Kirkpatrick, Martha (1988). Clinical implications of lesbian mother studies. In Eli Coleman (Ed.), *Psychotherapy with Homosexual Men and Women.* Binghamton, NY: The Haworth Press, Inc., 201-211.

Kirkpatrick, Martha (1990). Thoughts about the origins of femininity. *Journal of American Academy of Psychoanalysis,* 18(4), 554-565.

Kirkpatrick, Martha, Smith, Catherine, and Roy, Ron (1981). Lesbian mothers and their children: A comparative study. *American Journal of Orthopsychiatry,* 51, 545-551.

Kisker, Ellen Eliason (1986). Teenagers talk about sex, pregnancy and contraception. *Family Planning Perspectives,* 172, 83-89.

Laumann, Edward, Gagnon, John, Michael, R.T., and Michaels, S. (1994). *The Organization of Sexuality: Sexual Practices in the United States.* Chicago: University of Chicago Press.

Lee, John Alan (1977). Going public: A study in the sociology of homosexual liberation. *Journal of Homosexuality,* 3, 49-78.

Lehman, Lee (1978). What it means to love another woman. In Ginny Vida (Ed.), *Our Right to Love: A Lesbian Resource Book.* Englewood Cliffs, NJ: Prentice Hall.

Lerner, H.W. (1977). Parental mislabeling of female genitals as a determinant of penis envy and learning inhibitions in women. *Journal of the American Psychoanalytic Association,* 24, 269-283.

LeVay, Simon (1991). A difference in hypothalamic structure between heterosexual and homosexual men. *Science,* 253, August 30, 1034-1037.

Lewis, Sasha (1979). *Sunday's Women: Lesbian Life Today.* Boston, MA: Beacon.

Maddock, James (1983). *Human Sexuality and the Family.* Binghamton, NY: The Haworth Press, Inc.

Maggiore, Dolores (1992). *Lesbianism: An Annotated Bibliography and Guide to the Literature, 1976-1991.* Metuchen, NJ, London: The Scarecrow Press.

Marcia, James (1966). Development and validation of ego identity status. *Journal of Personality and Social Psychology,* 3, 551-558.

Marcia, James (1980). Identity in adolescence. In Joseph Adelson (Ed.), *Handbook of Adolescent Psychology.* New York: Wiley, 159-187.

Margolies, Liz, Becker, Martha, and Jackson-Brewer, Karla (1985). Internalized homophobia. In Boston Lesbian Psychologies Collective (Eds.), *Lesbian Psychologies.* Urbana, Chicago: University of Illinois Press, 229-241.

Marmor, Judd (1980). *Homosexual Behavior: A Modern Reappraisal.* New York: Basic Books.

Martin, A. Damien (1982). Learning to hide: The socialization of the gay adolescent. In Sherman Feinsten, A. Looney, A. Schwartzberg, and A Sarosky (Eds.), *Adolescent Psychiatry: Developmental and Clinical Studies,* Volume 10. Chicago: University of Chicago Press, 52-65.

Martin, Philip (1987). *Mad Women in Romantic Writing.* Sussex, England: Harvester.

Masters, William and Johnson, Virginia (1979). *Homosexuality in Perspective.* Boston: Little Brown.

McCarn, S.R. and Fassinger, R.E. (1991). What I am/Who we are: An inclusive model of lesbian identity development. Unpublished manuscript.

Miller, B. and Fox G. (1987). Theories of adolescent heterosexual behavior. *Adolescent Research*, 2, 269-282.

Miller, Jean Baker (1976). *Toward a New Psychology of Women.* Boston, MA: Beacon Press.

Miller, Jean Baker (1991). The development of women's sense of self. In Judith Jordan, Alexandra Kaplan, Jean B. Miller, Irene Stiver, and Janet Surrey (Eds.), *Women's Growth in Connection.* New York, London: Guilford Press, 11-26.

Millett, Kate (1978) *Sexual Politics.* New York, Toronto: Ballantine Books.

Money, John (1980). *Love and Lovesickness.* Baltimore, MD: Johns Hopkins University Press.

Monteflores de, Carmen and Schultz, Steven (1978). Coming out: Similarities and differences for lesbians and gay men. *Journal of Social Issues*, 34, 59-72.

Morin, Stephen (1977). Heterosexual bias in psychological research on lesbianism and male homosexuality. *American Psychologist*, 32, 629-637.

Moses, A. Elfin and Hawkins, Robert (1986). *Counseling Lesbian Women and Gay Men: A Life Issues Approach.* Columbus, OH: Charles Merrill.

National Health and Social Life Survey of the University of Chicago (1972). *The New York Times,* May 1, A27.

Nemiroff, Robert and Colarusso, Calvin (1990). *New Dimensions in Adult Development.* New York: Basic Books.

Nichols, Margaret and Leiblum, Sandra (1986). Lesbianism as personal identity and social role: A model. *Affilia*, 1(1) Spring, 48-59.

Nickerson, Eileen T. (1992). Low self-esteem in women: A feminist perspective. *Journal of Gender Studies*, XIV (2), Summer/Fall, 66-74.

Notman, Malkah, Klein, Rona, Jordan, Judith, and Zilbach, Joan (1990). Women's unique developmental issues across the life cycle. *Review of Psychiatry,* 10, 556-577.

Patterson, Charlotte (1995). Lesbian mothers, gay fathers and their children. In Anthony D'augelli and Charlotte Patterson (Eds.), *Lesbian, Gay and Bisexual Identities over the Lifespan: Psychological Perspectives.* New York: Oxford University Press, 262-290.

Patterson, Serena, Sochting, Ingrid, and Marcia, James (1989). The inner space and beyond: Women and identity. Presented to Canadian Psychological Association annual convention, Halifax, Nova Scotia, June.

Patton, Michael (1990). *Qualitative Evaluation and Research Methods,* Second Edition. London, New Delhi: Sage.

Peacock, N. (1982). Contraceptive decision making among adolescent girls. *Journal of Sex Education and Therapy*, 8, 31-36.

Peters, Debra and Cantrell, Peggy (1991). Factors distinguishing samples of lesbian and heterosexual women. *Journal of Homosexuality*, 21, 1-15.

Pipher, Mary (1994). *Reviving Ophelia: Saving the Selves of Adolescent Girls*. New York: Random House/Ballantine.

Plummer, K. (1975). *Sexual Stigma: An Interactional Account*. London: Routledge and Kegan Paul.

Pogrebin, Letty Cottin (1983). *Growing Up Free: Raising Your Child in the 80s*. New York: McGraw-Hill.

Ponse, B. (1978). *Identities in the Lesbian World: The Social Construction of Self*. Westport, CT: Greenwood Press.

Rand, C. Graham, D.L., and Rawlings, E.I. (1982). Psychological health and factors the court seeks to control in lesbian mother custody trials. *Journal of Homosexuality*, 8(1), 27-39.

Raphling, D. (1991). Countertransference in the treatment of sexually abused patients. *The Psychoanalytic Letter*, 1, 1-3.

Reinisch, June (1990). *The Kinsey Institute's New Report on Sex*. New York: St. Martin's Press.

Renshaw, D. (1984). Intimacy and intercourse. *Medical Aspects of Human Sexuality*, 18(2), 70-76.

Rich, Adrienne (1976). *Of Woman Born: Motherhood As Experience and Institution*. New York: W.W. Norton.

Rich, Adrienne (1980). Compulsive heterosexuality and lesbian existence. *Signs*, 5, 631-660.

Roberts, Elizabeth (Ed.) (1980). *Childhood Sexual Learning: The Unwritten Curriculum*. Cambridge, MA: Ballinger.

Roberts, Elizabeth (1983). Childhood sexual learning: The unwritten curriculum. In C. Davis (Ed.), *Challenges in Sexual Science*. Philadelphia, PA: Society for Scientific Study of Sex, 20-27.

Ross, Michael W. (1983). *The Married Homosexual Man: A Psychological Study*. London, Melbourne: Routledge and Kegan Paul.

Ross, Michael W. (1987). Normal homosexuality. In Louis Diamant (Ed.), *Male and Female Homosexuality: Psychological Approaches*. Washington, DC: Hemisphere Publishing, 237-258.

Ross, Michael W. (1996). Societal reactions and homosexuality: Culture, acculturation, life events and social supports as mediators of response to homonegative attitudes. In Esther Rothblum and Lynne Bond (Eds.), *Preventing Heterosexism and Homophobia*. Thousand Oaks, CA: Sage, 205-217.

Ross, Michael (1997). Personal communication.

Ross, Michael W. and Paul, Jay (1992). Beyond gender: The basis of sexual attraction in bisexual men and women. *Psychological Reports,* 71, 1282-1290.

Ross, Michael, Rogers, Lesley J., and McCulloch, Helen (1978). Stigma, Sex and Society: A new look at gender differentiation and sexual variation. *Journal of Homosexuality*, 3(4), Summer, 315-330.

Ross, Michael and Ryan, Lorna (1995). The little deaths: Perceptions of HIV, sexuality, and quality of life in gay men. In Michael Ross (Ed.), *HIV, AIDS, and Sexuality*. Binghamton, NY: The Haworth Press, Inc., 1-20.

Rozema, Hazel A. (1986). Defensive communication climate as a barrier to sex education in the home. *Family Relations,* 35, 531-537.

Russell, Diana (1986). *The Secret Trauma: Incest in the Lives of Girls and Women.* New York: Basic Books.

Rust, Paula (1992). The politics of sexual identity: Sexual attraction and behavior among lesbian and bisexual women. *Social Problems,* 39(4), November, 366-386.

Rust, Paula (1993). Coming out in the age of social constructionism: Sexual identity formation among lesbian and bisexual women. *Gender and Society,* 7(1), March, 50-77.

Saghir, Marcel and Robins, Eli (1973). *Male and Female Homosexuality: A Comprehensive Investigation.* Baltimore, MD: Williams and Wilkins.

Sales, Esther (1978). Women's adult development. In Irene Frieze, Jacquelynne Parsons, Paula Johnson, Diane Ruble, and Gail Zellman (Eds.), *Women and Sex Roles: A Social Psychological Perspective.* New York, London: W.W. Norton, 157-190.

Sampson, Edward (1993). Identity politics: Challenges to psychology's understanding. *American Psychoanalyst,* 48(12), 1219-1230.

Saphira, Miriam (1992). *Stopping Child Abuse.* New York, New Zealand: Penguin Books.

Showalter, Elaine (1987). *The Female Malady.* London: Virago.

Singh, Susheela (1986). Adolescent pregnancy in the U.S.A.: An interstate analysis. *Family Planning Perspectives,* 18(5), 210-220.

Sophie, Joan (1987). Internalized homophobia and lesbian identity. In Eli Coleman (Ed.), *Integrated Identity for Gay Men and Lesbians: Psychotherapeutic Approaches for Emotional Well-Being.* Binghamton, NY: The Haworth Press, Inc., pp. 53-65.

Sorenson, Robert (1972). *Adolescent Sexuality in Contemporary America.* New York: World.

Spaulding, Elaine (1991). Unconsciousness-raising: Hidden dimensions of heterosexism in theory and practice with lesbians. *Smith College Studies in Social Work Journal,* 63(3), June, 231-245.

Spencer, Colin (1995). *Homosexuality in History.* New York: Harcourt Brace.

Stern, Daniel (1985). *The Interpersonal World of the Infant.* New York: Basic Books.

Stowe, Aaron, Ross, Michael W., Wodak, Alex, Thomas, Gillian V., and Larson, Sigrid A. (1993). Significant relationships and social supports of injecting drug users and their implications for HIV/AIDS services. *AIDS Care,* 5(1), 23-33.

Strong, Bryan and DeVault, Christine (1994). *Human Sexuality.* Mountain View, CA: Mayfield Publishers.

Studer, Martena and Thornton, Arland (1987). Adolescent religiosity and contraceptive use. *Journal of Marriage and the Family,* 49, 117-128.

Thompson, Carol (1992). Lesbian grief and loss issues in the coming out process. *Women and Therapy,* 12, 175-185.

Tourney, Garfield (1980). Hormones and homosexuality. In Judd Marmor (Ed.), *Homosexual Behavior.* New York: Basic Books.

Troiden, Richard (1979). Variables related to the acquisition of a gay identity. *Journal of Homosexuality,* 5(4), 383-392.

Troiden, Richard (1988). Homosexual identity development. *Journal of Adolescent Health Care,* 9, 105-113.

Ussher, Jane (1992). *Women's Madness: Misogyny or Mental Illness?* Amherst, MA: University of Massachusetts Press.

Vaid, Urvashi (1995). *Virtual Equality.* New York, Sydney, Auckland: Anchor-Doubleday.

Vargo, Sue (1987). Effects of women's socialization. In Boston Lesbian Psychologies Collective (Ed.), *Lesbian Psychologies.* Urbana, Chicago: University of Illinois Press, 161-173.

Vida, Ginny (Ed.) (1978). *Our Right to Love: A Lesbian Resource Book.* Englewood Cliffs, NJ: Prentice Hall.

Weille, Katharine Lee (1993). Reworking developmental theory: The case of lesbian identity formation. *Clinical Social Work,* 21(2), Summer, 151-159.

Weston, Kath (1992). *Families We Choose.* New York: Columbia University Press.

Whisnant, Lynn, Brett, Elizabeth, and Zegans, Leonard (1979). Adolescent girls and menstruation. *Adolescent Psychiatry,* 7, 157-171.

Whitehead, Harriet (1981). The bow and the burden strap: A new look at institutionalized homosexuality in North America. In Sherry Ortner and Harriet Whitehead (Eds.), *Sexual Meanings.* Cambridge, MA: Cambridge University Press, 81-115.

Whitfield, Margaret (1989). Development of sexuality in female children and adolescents. *Canadian Journal of Psychiatry,* 34, December, 879-883.

Woldman, Benjamin and Money, John (Eds.) (1980). *Handbook of Human Sexuality.* Englewood Cliffs, NJ: Prentice Hall.

Wolf, Naomi (1991). *The Beauty Myth.* New York: Doubleday.

Wolff, Charlotte (1971). *Love Between Women.* New York: Harper and Row.

Yarber, William (1992). While we stood by . . . the limiting of sexual information to our youth. Reprinted with permission from *Journal of Health Education,* September/October, pp. 326-335. *Journal of Health Education* is a publication of the American Alliance for Health, Physical Education, Recreation, and Dance, 1900 Association Drive, Reston, VA 22091.

Zani, Bruna (1991). Male and female patterns in the discovery of sexuality during adolescence. *Journal of Adolescence,* 14, 163-178.

Zimmerman, Bonnie and McNaron, Toni (1996). *The New Lesbian Studies.* New York: The Feminist Press, CUNY.

Index

/